Integration in the
21st century

European
Integration in the
21st century

Unity in Diversity?

edited by
**Mary Farrell, Stefano Fella
and Michael Newman**

SAGE Publications
London • Thousand Oaks • New Delhi

First published 2002

Tables 7.1 and 7.2 adapted from National Accounts: Main Aggregates
1960/1997 1999 Edition, Volume 1. Copyright OECD, 1999.

SAGE Publications Ltd
6 Bonhill Street
London EC2A 4PU

SAGE Publications Inc
2455 Teller Road
Thousand Oaks, California 91320

SAGE Publications India Pvt Ltd
32, M-Block Market
Greater Kailash – I
New Delhi 110 048

British Library Cataloguing in Publication data
A catalogue record for this book is available
from the British Library

ISBN 0 7619 7218 8
ISBN 0 7619 7219 6 (pbk)

Library of Congress Control Number available

Typeset by Mayhew Typesetting, Rhayader, Powys
Printed and bound in Great Britain by Biddles Ltd, Guildford, Surrey

Contents

Notes on contributors

Esko Antola is a Jean Monnet Professor and the director of the Jean Monnet Centre of Excellence at the University of Turku, Finland. He is a member of the Academic Advisory Committee to the Ministry of Foreign Affairs of the Finnish government, and played a prominent part in Finland's pre-accession negotiations. He is currently engaged in a research programme on Small States and the Future of Europe. His most recent publications are *The impact of EMU on Institutions and Decision-Making in the European Union* (Turku, 1999) and *New EU?* (Helsinki, 1998).

Enrique Banús is Professor of European Literature and Director of the Centre for European Studies at the University of Navarre (Spain). He studied German and Romance Philology at the Universities of Bonn and Aachen. His main research interests lie in European Cultural Policy, Images of European Identity, History of the Ideas of European Integration, Reception and Transmission in European Literature.

Kevin Boles is a lecturer in International Business in the Business School at Manchester Metropolitan University. His research interests include the economics and strategic impact of European monetary union.

Madeleine Colvin is a legal policy consultant at JUSTICE, a legal human rights organisation in the UK. She is a qualified barrister who practised law for some ten years before becoming legal officer at the Children's Legal Centre and then Liberty. Since joining JUSTICE in 1992, she has had particular responsibility for a project involving ongoing analysis of the EU's respect for human rights standards in the particular areas of policing and criminal justice. She is the author of a number of reports, the most recent being 'The Schengen Information System: A Human Rights Audit' (JUSTICE, November 2000).

Mary Farrell is senior lecturer in European Studies at the University of North London. Her research interests include European integration, the international relations of the European Union, and international political economy. Her most recent publication is *Spain in the EU: The Road to Economic Convergence* (Palgrave, 2001).

Stefano Fella was awarded his doctorate by the University of North London (UNL) in 2001 for his thesis on the Labour Party and the 1996–97 intergovernmental conference of the EU. He is currently a Research Fellow in the Department of Political Science at the University of Genoa. He has previously lectured on European Union politics at UNL and worked as a researcher in the House of Commons and the European Parliament. He is the author of 'A Europe of the Peoples: New Labour and Democratising the EU', in Catherine Hoskyns and Michael Newman (eds) *Democratising the EU: Issues for the Twenty-first Century* (Manchester University Press, 2000).

Peter Gowan is Principal Lecturer in European Studies at the University of North London, and an editor of *New Left Review*. His recent publications include *The Question of Europe* (with Perry Anderson, Verso, 1997), and *The Global Gamble* (Verso, 1999). He is currently completing a book on pan-European transformations in the 1990s.

Nigel Healey is Dean of the Business School and Pro-Vice Chancellor at Manchester Metropolitan University. His research interests focus on the transition economies of Central Europe.

Christina Julios is a postgraduate student at the University of London, completing a thesis on English as a second language education in the UK and USA. Her interests include language policy, identity and ethnic minority issues. Her recent publications include *Social Exclusion: Current Policy and Practice* (co-authored with William Solesbury, Queen Mary University of London, 2001), 'Bilingualism and the New American Identity', in Anne J. Kershen (ed.) *A Question of Identity* (Ashgate, 1988).

Frank McDonald is Head of Department in the International Business Unit at Manchester Metropolitan University. His research interest is in the area of European business strategy.

Alan S. Milward spent several years as Professor of Contemporary History at the European University Institute in Florence. He is also Emeritus Professor of Economic History at the London School of Economics. He is Director of the research project The Expansion of the European Communities 1969–1986 at the EUI. His publications include *The European Rescue of the Nation-State*, and he is co-author of *The Frontier of National Sovereignty*. He is the Official Historian of Britain in the European Communities, and is currently Visiting Professor at the London European Research Centre in the University of North London.

Michael Newman is Jean Monnet Professor and Director of the London European Research Centre at the University of North London, and has published extensively on issues relating to democracy and citizenship in the European Union. Recent publications include *Democracy, Sovereignty and European Union* (Hurst, 1996); *Democratising the EU: Issues for the*

Twenty-first Century, with Catherine Hoskyns (Manchester University Press).

Elżbieta Stadtmüller is Professor of International Relations and Deputy Director at the Institute of International Studies, University of Wroclaw, Poland. In recent years, her research interests have focused on political relations in Europe, issues of integration and security, and she has published widely in these areas. Her recent publications include *The Border of Fear and Hope: The Poles and Germany in the 1990s* (Wroclaw), and *Political Problems of the Contemporary World* (1998).

Monica Threlfall is Senior Lecturer in Politics at Loughborough University. Her research interests include Spanish politics, new interpretations of employment trends, and gender policy. She is editor of *Consensus Politics in Spain* (Intellect Books, 2000), and *Mapping the Women's Movement* (Verso, 1996).

Alex Warleigh is Reader in European Governance and Deputy Director of the Institute of Governance, Public Policy and Social Research, Queen's University, Belfast. He previously taught at the University of Reading, and before that worked as adviser to the Chair of the European Parliament Environment Committee. His publications include (as author) *The Committee of the Regions: Institutionalising Multi-Level Governance?* (Kogan Page, 1999), (as co-editor) *Citizenship and Governance in the European Union* (Continuum, 2001), and (as sole editor), *Understanding European Union Institutions* (Routledge, 2001). He will be publishing a further monograph *Flexible Integration: Which Model for the European Union?* in 2002 (Sheffield Academic Press).

Acknowledgements

This book originated in an international conference organised by the London European Research Centre of the University of North London in May 1999, entitled 'The European Union in 2010'. We are grateful to the University Association for Contemporary European Studies (UACES) for their financial support for that event. We also want to record our thanks to all the authors for their contributions to this collective volume. Finally, we would like to thank Lucy Robinson of Sage for her help with the project.

Mary Farrell
Stefano Fella
Michael Newman
London

Abbreviations

CAP	common agricultural policy
CBI	Confederation of British Industry
CBSS	Council of Baltic Sea States
CEE	Central and Eastern Europe
CEEP	European Confederation of Public Enterprises
CEFTA	Central European Free Trade Agreement
CEI	Central European Initiative
CFSP	Common Foreign and Security Policy
CILT	Centre for Information on Language Teaching and Research
CIS	Customs Information Systems
CJIF	Combined Joint-Task Forces
CoR	Committee of the Regions
CRE	Commission for Racial Equality
DES	Department for Education and Sciences
DfEE	Department for Education and Employment
EA	Europe Agreements
EAPC	Euro-Atlantic Partnership Council
EBRD	European Bank for Reconstruction and Development
EC	European Community
ECB	European Central Bank
ECHR	European Convention on Human Rights and Fundamental Freedoms
ECJ	European Court of Justice
ECSC	European Coal and Steel Community
EEC	European Economic Community
EIB	European Investment Bank
EMU	economic and monetary union
EP	European Parliament
ESDI	European Security and Defence Identity
ETUC	European Trades Union Confederation
EU	European Union
FB	Frontier Belt
FDI	foreign direct investment
GATT	General Agreement on Trade and Tariffs
GDP	gross domestic product
GNP	gross national product
GUUAM	Georgia, Ukraine, Uzbekistan, Azerbaijan and Moldova

IBRD	International Bank for Reconstruction and Development
IDA	International Development Association
IFC	International Finance Corporation
IGC	intergovernmental conference
ILO	International Labour Organisation
IMF	International Monetary Fund
JHA	Justice and Home Affairs
MIGA	Multilateral Investment Guarantee Agency
NACC	North Atlantic Co-operation Council
NATO	North Atlantic Treaty Organisation
NCIS	National Criminal Intelligence Unit
NGO	non-governmental organisation
NIC	newly industrialised country
NMD	National Missile Defence
OSCE	Organisation of Security and Co-operation in Europe
PfP	Partnership for Peace
QMV	qualified majority voting
SDR	special drawing right
SEA	Single European Act
SEE	south east Europe
SIRENE	Supplementary Information Requests at the National Entry
SIS	Schengen Information System
SMR	single market regime
TEU	Treaty on European Union [Maastricht]
ToR	Treaty of Rome
UN	United Nations
UNECE	United Nations Economic Commission for Europe
UNESCO	United Nations Educational, Scientific and Cultural Organisation
UNICE	European Union of Industries
WEU	Western European Union
WTO	World Trade Organisation

Introduction: Unity in Diversity – the Challenge for the EU

Stefano Fella

The beginning of the twenty-first century is an obvious time to consider the future of the European Union (EU). Fifty years after the establishment of the European Coal Steel Community (ECSC), and a decade after the collapse of the Soviet bloc, what are the prospects for Europe in the new century? Are the notions of 'ever closer union' of the Treaty of Rome or 'the common European home' of Gorbachev to be regarded as empty rhetoric? Or is there a real likelihood that such ideas will be translated into practice? No one can answer such questions, but each chapter of this book contributes to the task, reviewing the trends in the light of the past and present. And while no single volume could cover all the subjects that would provide a comprehensive survey of the issues facing the EU, we have included dimensions that are often absent in more conventional texts. Nor do our contributors share a common view of the EU. While none of them expresses the bland confidence that has so often characterised official Community publications, they cover a range from moderate optimism through scepticism to pessimism, influenced by the topic in question, and their own normative perspectives. Our aspiration is to provide readers with the kind of evidence and analysis that will stimulate thought about current trends and possible futures, not to claim possession of a crystal ball.

The Treaty of Nice agreed by the EU Heads of Government in December 2000 represented yet another staging post in the moves towards 'ever closer union' embarked upon by six West European countries fifty years previously, a project that had widened to include a further nine members by the end of the twentieth century. Indeed, the limited reforms agreed at Nice, most notably the reweighting of votes in the Council of Ministers to reflect the size of the larger states more closely, the setting of a ceiling on the size of the Commission, and further modest extensions to the scope of qualified majority voting were presented as modifications to the EU's institutional framework necessary to ensure its continued smooth functioning in the light of a further enlargement to encompass twenty or more members within the first few years of the twenty-first century.

But it was clear that this institutional tinkering was not going to be enough, on its own, to prepare the EU for the challenges it faces in the coming century. Even before the Nice negotiations were concluded, an agenda had developed within the EU for a further intergovernmental conference (IGC) to consider more fundamental questions relating to the architecture of the EU treaties. The Nice deliberations resulted in agreement that another IGC would be held in 2004. The three IGCs held in the decade which followed the fall of the Berlin Wall, hailed in 1989 as signalling the end of the division of Europe, had clearly failed to provide a settled framework for this new inclusive Europe. Statements by EU leaders in 2000 mapped out a variety of contrasting routes for the twenty-first century to be addressed after the Nice summit. In May 2000, the German foreign minister, Joschka Fischer called for a federal constitution and a directly elected European executive based around a core of member states which wished to proceed with deeper integration (Fischer, 2000). This was partly endorsed a month later by the German Chancellor Gerhard Schröder who called for a further IGC to consider more fundamental reforms such as a new EU constitution (Black and Hooper, 2000). The French President, Jacques Chirac, later echoed Fischer in calling for the establishment of a 'pioneering group' of core states (Chirac, 2000). In October 2000, British Prime Minister Tony Blair mapped out an alternative vision of the EU as a 'superpower' but 'not a superstate' in which a new chamber of national parliamentarians would be responsible for ensuring the EU's adhesion to a code outlining where it should and should not act (FCO, 2000).

The European Commission had also undertaken long-term studies of the EU's possible future. These included a study by its Forward Studies Unit outlining five possible scenarios for future EU development (European Commission, 1999a) and the publication of a report by three 'wise men'[1] on the institutional implications of enlargement produced on behalf of the Commission in 1999 (European Commission, 1999b). It was notable that one of the key suggestions of the latter – splitting the treaties between one constitutional document (elucidating basic principles and outlining the institutional framework) and one concerned with specific policy instruments – did not even make the negotiating table at Nice. Following Chancellor Schröder's suggestion, it would form part of the emerging agenda for 2004.

This inability to agree a settled framework for the future shape of the EU could be attributed to the clear absence of consensus among the EU member states as to what the end-point of European integration should be, and indeed, as to what the integration process is all about. Different member states have engaged in the process of European integration for a variety of reasons and thus differ in the priority they attach to particular policy issues and in their perceptions of the institutional outcomes necessary to achieve their particular policy preferences. The difficulty of reaching consensus on the direction of European integration has been exacerbated by successive enlargements. While some consensus could be found among the original six member states of the European Communities around the objective of 'ever closer union' and the means to achieve this, the later entrants have brought with them a more diverse set of policy preoccupations and, in the case of Britain and the Nordic countries in particular, a more sceptical approach to the aspirational discourse found in the EU treaties concerning the project of political union. Moreover, institutions and policies framed with the original six in mind appear less suited to an EU with a broader and more diverse membership of fifteen and to which almost as many states again aspire to join. Successive enlargements to include island nations such as Britain and Ireland, the Nordic countries, an orthodox Balkan state (Greece) and the Iberian countries have brought a greater diversity of membership to the EU, in terms of respective historical experiences, relationships with the rest of the world, political traditions, conceptions of nationhood, ethnicity and religion, levels of socio-economic development, traditions of alignment or neutralism, trading patterns and particular policy preoccupations. Enlargement to central and eastern Europe and possibly to the south will increase this diversity.

This book therefore brings together a number of contributors with the aim of examining how a coherent model of unity can be developed which respects the EU's increasingly diverse nature and facilitates co-operation on common objectives such as political stability, security, respect for human rights, social progress and equitable and sustainable economic development. As reflected in Alan Milward's chapter, the importance of understanding historical processes is indispensable to any examination of future trends in the EU's development. Accordingly, in the chapters that follow, a number of area and policy specialists are brought together to examine the prospects for the EU's future development in the light of previous and ongoing trends.

A number of indicators of the shape that the EU would take during the early part of the twenty-first century came at the turn of the twentieth century. In 1998 and 1999, clear steps were taken towards enlarging the EU for the first time into the former Soviet bloc. In 2000, the Danish referendum result rejecting participation in the single currency (and making UK and Swedish participation in the near future similarly unlikely) provided a clear sign that, for some member states, the limits of integration had been reached for the foreseeable future, and that further flexibility in the EU's institutional arrangements would most likely be required to hold an increasingly diverse union together. Externally, the narrow and much disputed victory of George W. Bush in the US presidential elections appeared to provide confirmation of a steady drift by the world's last remaining superpower into a more isolationist path, with likely implications for European trading and security arrangements. As the US becomes more inward-looking, the likelihood of trade disputes recurring may increase while the process already launched by the EU to develop its own security identity is likely to be accelerated.

DIVERSITY IN AN ENLARGED UNION

Negotiations with five of the former Communist states in Central and Eastern Europe (CEE) – the Czech Republic, Estonia, Hungary, Poland and Slovenia – together with Cyprus began under the British EU Presidency in March 1998. At the Helsinki European Council in December 1999, EU leaders signalled their commitment to commence active negotiations with the five CEE states – Bulgaria, Latvia, Lithuania, Romania and Slovakia – previously deemed by the Commission not yet to have fulfilled the Copenhagen criteria[2] necessary for accession negotiations to commence. Helsinki also saw a commitment to launch accession negotiations with Malta, resurrecting an application which had earlier been withdrawn. Furthermore, in a compromise which followed pressure from a US administration mindful of strategic considerations, the EU also confirmed its willingness to consider Turkey as, in principle, a candidate for membership, while not yet considering it ready for the launch of accession negotiations (Wallace, 2000).

Accommodating all thirteen of these applicants would require a fundamental reorganisation of the EU's institutional framework and of various policy and budgetary mechanisms. However, the most optimistic assessment of the likely timescale for the accession of these countries is that the first five CEE states, and perhaps Cyprus (provided that some kind of solution has been found in relation to the status of the Turkish-occupied north of the island), may be granted membership by 2004. The other would-be members of the EU may still find themselves in the ante-room to membership as the second decade of the twenty-first century gets under way. But even this initial wave of enlargement looks likely to bring a shock to the EU system. Most analysts agree that radical reform of the common agricultural policy (CAP) and the structural funds will be necessary if the EU is to continue to operate within the budgetary ceiling of 1.27 per cent of member states' combined GDP. The Commission document Agenda 2000, which set out the reforms viewed as necessary to accommodate the new members, appeared optimistic that the necessary policy adjustments could be made within the financial constraints set by the existing budgetary ceiling. The Berlin summit of March 1999, at which the EU's financing for the following five years was agreed, demonstrated the unwillingness of the member states either to increase the budgetary ceiling or undertake the radical reforms necessary to ensure the sustainability of the CAP as the EU enlarges to the east. Moreover, though it seems that the opening up of markets in the CEE countries through enlargement is likely to lead to increases in unemployment and inequality in these countries, the Agenda 2000 document made clear the intention of the EU to limit the distribution of structural funds to an amount far below that which the existing structural fund regime should imply (Kaldor, 2000). Indeed, Peter Gowan suggests in Chapter 2 that in shaping its relations to the east, the EU has placed the burden of adjustment on the CEE countries, obliging them to open up their markets to the west, while EU markets remain protected from competition from the east.

EU leaders have continued to pay lip service to the need for enlargement to heal the division between east and west, while privately expressing reservations about the financial and institutional implications as well as the prospect of allowing free movement of persons from the applicant states.[3] Nevertheless, fearful of the political costs of reneging on their pledge to enlarge to the east, which might involve a possible nationalist backlash and consequent instability on the EU's borders, the EU's leaders are likely to fulfil the logic of their political rhetoric and accept a limited enlargement by the middle of the century's first decade. However, the prospects of membership being secured by the second wave of applicants looks less secure while even greater doubts surround the potential relationship between the EU and those countries which may wish to seek EU membership in the future. These include the republics of the former Yugoslavia, including the post-Milosevic Yugoslav rump, as well as Albania, Moldova, the Caucasian states and the Ukraine. Enlargement to include some, if not all, of these countries could take the number of EU member states to over thirty, requiring a fundamental assessment of the nature of the EU. As the EU begins to expand eastwards, it will also need to address the question of where the boundaries of Europe lie. Which of the states of the former Soviet Union can be considered for membership? The Baltic states of Estonia, Latvia and Lithuania, illegally annexed by Stalin in 1940, have been accepted as candidates, but what of Armenia, Azerbaijan and Georgia? The Ukraine, like Turkey, is of geo-strategic importance, but presents difficulties as a potential candidate for membership. Moreover, given its size and its dual status as a European and Asiatic power, the difficulties presented by possible Russian membership of the EU would surely be insurmountable. In the case of some of these states, a form of association falling short of membership may be more appropriate. It is essential that such arrangements foster economic and political stability and do not provoke a sense of exclusion on the part of those states that remain outside the EU. In Chapter 3, Elżbieta Stadtmüller reflects on the need for Europe to develop inclusive security structures that foster peaceful coexistence across Europe. She also emphasises that regional stability and security will come through economic prosperity in the countries of central and eastern Europe. As a powerful and relatively prosperous economic bloc, the EU has a critical role to play in ensuring that economic aid and trading policies are designed to facilitate equitable and sustainable economic development to its east. However, Peter Gowan argues that the manner in which economic relations with the CEE states have been shaped makes any narrowing in the economic gap between east and west extremely unlikely.

FLEXIBILITY TO PRESERVE UNITY

The development of a stable and secure Europe requires both a modification of the EU's external policies and adjustments to its internal workings which respect, and indeed complement, the diversity of an enlarged membership. As Alex Warleigh suggests in Chapter 6, enlargement of the EU may bring recognition of the need for greater flexibility in its institutional arrangements. The flexibility provisions introduced by the Amsterdam treaty, though themselves tightly constrained and unlikely to be much use in practice, represented a recognition that not all member states of the EU are likely to be able or willing to proceed with deeper integration at the same pace. The need for such differentiated integration had already been acknowledged by the decision of a group of states to embark on closer co-operation to remove internal frontier controls and co-operate on necessary flanking measures through the Schengen treaties, the opt-outs granted by the Treaty on European Union (TEU) to the UK on social policy (later reversed at Amsterdam) and economic monetary union (EMU) (later also extended to Denmark), and the various derogations granted to the UK, Ireland and Denmark by the new free movement chapter of the Amsterdam treaty (which partly incorporated the Schengen acquis). Though tightly circumscribed, the flexibility provisions of the Amsterdam treaty provide a generalised treaty basis for differentiated integration to take place across a broader range of policies. The Nice treaty slightly eased the constraints on the use of these provisions.[4] This approach is likely to be built upon in the future, in order for flexible integration to take place more freely within the institutional framework. The statements by Chirac and Fischer referred to above, provide strong signals of the likely movement by the EU in this direction. Enlargement to the east, where all the applicant states have levels of economic development (measured in terms of GDP per capita) considerably lower than the existing member states, is likely to increase the pressure for further differentiation.

The differentiated approach to integration is already marked in relation to membership of the single currency. The decision by three member states to remain outside the first wave of the euro for the foreseeable future formalised a form of two-tier or two-speed Europe within the treaty framework. Though this differentiation is often presented as a case of the three laggards (UK, Denmark and Sweden) proceeding at a slower pace towards the final goal of EMU, the Danish referendum of 2000 may bring a realisation that some states may have already reached their preferred destination. To talk of a Europe of different speeds may therefore be misleading. In this case, it may be preferable to loosen the constraints on those member states that wish to proceed unencumbered towards closer union. Alex Warleigh suggests that mechanisms should be designed to allow different groups of member states to engage in closer co-operation in different policy areas as they so desire. He also argues that this would enhance the legitimacy of European co-operation, as participation by particular member states would take place only where it reflected domestic political preferences.

Questions nevertheless remain over how differentiated integration can be accommodated within the existing EU institutional framework. The flexibility provisions of the Amsterdam treaty are aimed at facilitating closer co-operation on a policy-by-policy basis. The proposals by Chirac and Fischer imply that a core group will proceed on the basis of an agreed package of policies, such as economic co-ordination, defence, taxation and justice and home affairs. The Amsterdam treaty also stipulates that closer co-operation must respect the European Community (EC) institutional framework. But President Chirac's proposal for a 'pioneer group' referred to a political directorate of leading states which implied a bypassing of the European Commission. Any such moves in this direction are likely to arouse the suspicion of the smaller states who see in the executive role of the European Commission a guarantee against domination by the large states. The discussions at Nice which resulted in a reweighting of Council votes in favour of the larger states revealed a considerable degree of resentment among small states at the increased potential this provided for domination by the large states. It is important that any new institutional arrangements which seek to accommodate an enlarged and increasingly diverse EU membership respect the rights and interests of the smaller states, whether or not they are members of a future core group. Differentiated integration should not become a vehicle for domination by the larger states. Small states can play an important role in the future development of the EU, as illustrated in Chapter 4 by Esko Antola which draws on studies of small states in international relations to explore their potential role within the EU.

A SUPERPOWER NOT A SUPERSTATE

Though references to the US drift towards isolationism may be exaggerated (see Chapters 2 and 3), the victory of Bush in the presidential elections is likely to signal a tendency towards a greater unilateralism on the part of the USA. This is demonstrated by the determination of the Bush administration, despite European opposition, to pursue a National Missile Defence (NMD) system that could trigger a new arms race and leave its NATO allies in Europe exposed. Such unilateralism might also be found in the economic arena, where the USA may become less co-operative with the EU in resolving trade disputes and promoting currency stability. The Bush administration has also signalled its unwillingness to co-operate with the EU in facilitating global agreement on environmental measures seen by many climate experts as necessary to address the potentially debilitating effects of climate change.[5] Nevertheless, Peter Gowan argues in Chapter 2 that the USA continues to exert a hegemonic influence across both western and eastern Europe and will continue to do so unless the EU develops into a more coherent political bloc.

A strain of thinking has existed among proponents of European integration since the Second World War which sees in European unity the potential to develop an entity which has the strength and capacity to act as a 'third force' independently of the superpowers (given the demise of one of these superpowers, the USSR, the term 'second force' might now be more appropriate). Such a notion has traditionally aroused distrust on the part of British governments, given its prominence among French politicians who wished to steer Europe away from the Atlantic alliance with the USA. However, Prime Minister Blair appeared to give it implicit endorsement both in calling for the EU to develop into a superpower (though not a superstate) in his Warsaw speech of October 2000, and in promoting, alongside the French, the creation of a European military force which can act independently of the USA (while respecting the primacy of NATO in guaranteeing European security). This British–French initiative can be partly interpreted as a response to the evident European dependence on US military power and infrastructure during the Kosovo conflict in 1999 which brought a realisation to some EU leaders of the need to contribute more effectively to their own security and develop an autonomous and viable military structure in order to undertake actions independent of the USA. This is notwithstanding the debate over whether the NATO action was justified, which is explored by Elżbieta Stadtmüller in Chapter 3. Concerns about the future of the US military commitment to Europe have hastened the development of a European security identity, although many EU governments remain mindful of the need to ensure that the framing of future military arrangements does nothing to accelerate a loosening of ties on the part of the Americans.

In terms of the size of the European single market, representing the world's largest economic bloc, and its ability to affect patterns of world trade through its common external economic policy, the EU already acts as an economic superpower. The adoption of a single European currency (albeit by only twelve of the fifteen member states) will further strengthen the ability of the EU to shape global economic developments while also making the members of 'euroland' less vulnerable to international currency fluctuations, challenging the dominant position of the US dollar. In Chapter 7, Boles, Macdonald and Healey explore the advantages that the adoption of the euro might bring to the European economy as it develops into a major international reserve currency and the opportunities this will provide for the reorganisation of the international monetary system. Although the referendum result in Denmark, the low public confidence in the euro in several EU states and its initial weakness in the currency markets raise question marks over the future of the euro, its adoption, which will be visibly cemented by the replacement of national denominations by euro notes and coins in 2002, may transform the nature of the EU in the early twenty-first century and encourage popular perceptions of the EU as an embryonic federal state. The single currency is likely to create pressures for greater co-ordination of economic policy and, in particular, fiscal policy at the EU level, and for more coherent political governance to balance the EU's predominantly economic constitution.

The decision to establish EMU represented a significant transfer of authority by the EU states to a supranational entity in a key policy area traditionally identified with the nation-state. Yet in other key areas of policy, the EU member states (or at least some of them) appear unwilling to transfer powers to the supranational institutions of the EU. The nation-states of the EU continue to remain in control of social security systems, health, education, general levels of taxation, internal constitutional arrangements, criminal law and the definition of the rights and duties of national citizenship and the status of third-country nationals. Furthermore, the vast majority of public expenditure within the EU emanates from and is controlled by national governments (though the ability of the 'euroland' members to operate budget deficits is constrained by the terms of the 'growth and stability pact'). The member states also continue to pursue autonomous foreign policies while seeking to co-ordinate actions through the Common Foreign and Security Policy (CFSP). A future common European defence force is likely to be tightly controlled by national governments. Talk of a European super-state therefore appears to be rather off the mark. The discussions at Nice provided confirmation of the dominance of national executives in EU decision-making. The primacy of national governments in directing the EU is stressed by Alan Milward in Chapter 1. However, he questions whether a single European currency can feasibly operate without a European executive acting in place of those of the member states. Nevertheless, he also suggests that the twin effects of EMU and the action of globalised markets may lead to harmonisation of both national fiscal mechanisms and social welfare systems in the EU.

The single currency and the European defence plan appear to reflect a desire on the part of the EU states to develop an autonomous global role, pooling resources to create a powerful economic and political bloc that can act as a global superpower. Both areas of co-operation represent good examples of the principle of subsidiarity employed in practice: European nation-states delegating competences to European institutions in areas where action at the national level no longer represents a viable strategy for the delivery of policy objectives. This principle provides a useful guide for determining the nature of policy activity to be undertaken in the EU of the future. It points to the need for effective EU activity in environmental policy and combating international crime as well as defence and currency management. Indeed, while popular attitudes towards the single currency appear indifferent, opinion polls suggest that defence, environmental issues and fighting crime are areas of policy which the majority of EU citizens identify as most appropriate for European co-operation (Eurobarometer, 2000; Leonard, 1998). In relation to the latter two, the well worn cliché is that neither pollution nor crime respect national borders. While the necessary co-operation on environmental policy is well developed at the European level, the establishment of effective co-operation on the policing and judicial matters necessary to combat crime has proved difficult given the sensitivities aroused in the member states by the prospect of 'interference' by EU institutions. Co-operation in this area has tended to be ad hoc and secretive and has been characterised by a regressive approach and an absence of judicial review. In Chapter 5, Madeleine Colvin explores the development of co-operation on policing in the EU and stresses the importance of adherence to human rights norms in this sensitive area.

THE SEARCH FOR LEGITIMACY

As the EU has developed a profile in sensitive areas such as internal security and policing, the need for a parallel strengthening of the mechanisms to protect the fundamental rights of EU citizens and third-country nationals residing within the EU has become apparent. In this context, the adoption by the EU of a Charter of Fundamental Rights at the Nice summit represented a positive step. Though not legally binding, it is likely that the European Court of Justice (ECJ) will invoke its principles in future judgments, as it has done in the past in relation to other international human rights instruments. The development of a human rights dimension has the added value of enhancing the democratic character of the EU. The value of the EU as a guarantor of democracy was demonstrated in the 1980s with the accession to the then European Community (EC) of Greece, Portugal and Spain, as they emerged from periods of authoritarian rule. EC membership was viewed as integral to the maintenance of the democratic transition in these countries. A similar rationale was presented for EU enlargement to the CEE countries following the collapse of communism. But the development of a fundamental rights dimension is also viewed as a useful method of enhancing the political legitimacy of the EU. In this sense it resembles the attempts by the then EC to develop a European social dimension at the end of the 1980s, as discussed by Monica Threlfall in Chapter 8.

The need to connect the EU's policies to the concerns of its citizens and address the perceived 'democratic deficit' in decision-making has increasingly preoccupied the EU's leaders since the post-Maastricht ratification crises of the early 1990s. The inclusion in the Amsterdam treaty (1997) of provisions to extend the scope of European Parliament co-decision to a range of policy areas, increase transparency in decision-making, ensure respect for fundamental rights on the part of the EU institutions and facilitate co-operation on employment policy through a new treaty title can be viewed as an attempt to address these questions (Fella, 1999; Hoskyns and Newman, 2000). Nevertheless, the commitment of many EU leaders to transparency remains questionable and intergovernmental discussions on the fundamental rights charter revealed an unwillingness on the part of a number of member states to make these rights legally enforceable. More-over, democratic accountability in critical policy areas such as EMU, CFSP and defence, judicial and police co-operation, immigration and asylum, and agricultural spending (taking up half of the EC budget) remains minimal.

The absence of democratic accountability in relation to EMU remains a particular cause of concern to many observers (Grahl, 1997; Lintner, 2000) given the transfer of competence from the national to the EU level that has been undertaken in relation to vital levers of economic and monetary policy, such as management of exchange rates and the ability to set interest rates and operate budget deficits. The powerful economic constitution of the EU, created through successive treaties establishing the customs union, the single market and the single currency, can be contrasted with the weakness of political institutions at the EU level. This political weakness is particularly marked in relation to the European Central Bank (ECB) which, by deliberate design on the part of the central bankers and EU leaders who formulated and agreed the treaty provisions on EMU, operates independently of any political interference in the conduct of currency and interest rate policy. As Kevin Boles and colleagues suggest in Chapter 7, the operation of the euro may bring pressure for stronger political institutions at the EU level in order to ensure a more effective economic coordination which balances the influence of the ECB as regards monetary policy and its associated economic effects. Any such move to achieve a more coherent political direction of economic policy at the EU level is, however, unlikely to reach as far as creating formal lines of accountability in relation to the ECB's management of the euro, given the unwillingness of the EU's leaders to tamper with the principle of central bank independence. In any case, greater political accountability alone may not prove adequate to ensure the legitimacy of the euro should the monetarism of the ECB and the constraints of the 'growth and stability pact' exacerbate inequalities within the EU. The negative effects of EMU, particularly in an enlarged EU, may bring pressure for a larger budget and greater fiscal federalism in order to provide compensatory mechanisms for those regions less equipped to compete in the brave new world of euroland. The establishment of an economic framework which delivers wider prosperity and ameliorates inequalities may prove to be more important for the long-term legitimacy of the euro than formal lines of political accountability, though the latter may increase the likelihood of the former.

The political legitimacy of the EU requires a sense of identification with the integration project on the part of EU citizens. This appeared to be lacking at the end of the twentieth century with opinion polls indicating that the EU was continuing to suffer from low levels of public support in a number of member states. Indeed, the Eurobarometer survey cited in Alex Warleigh's chapter indicates that most citizens of the member states appeared to reject the new identity bestowed on them by the TEU as EU citizens, viewing themselves primarily as citizens of their nation-states. The EU does not, in this sense, reflect the kind of 'imagined community' on which the construction of modern nation-states was based (Anderson, 1983). It is often said that the EU lacks a 'demos' – a perceived sense of common political identity deemed as necessary to construct a democratic political system. Part of the problem is that national executives are determined to retain control of the process of European integration and have exploited the process to enhance their own authority in relation to their national legislatures. The EU treaties are based on intergovernmental bargains in which democratic considerations come second to maximising national advantage. The construction of a democratic apparatus at the EU level might therefore necessitate national executives relinquishing their control over the process. Radical reforms that might facilitate the creation of a democratic political space at the EU level, such as a separate EU constitution or a directly elected European executive have not, however, won majority support within the EU member states. Although the EU appears to be more than an intergovernmental international organisation, it still falls short of federal statehood. Alternative models of democracy might therefore be preferable, and, as Alex Warleigh argues in Chapter 6, attempts to apply traditional conceptions of liberal democracy at the EU level may be misguided.

Nevertheless, while attempts to replicate traditional models of liberal democracy may be inappropriate for the EU, public legitimacy requires further action to demonstrate the relevance of the European integration process to various individuals and social groups. In Chapter 8, Monica Threlfall examines the nature of social integration in the EU, which has proceeded on the basis of a variety of social policy instruments in the EU treaties thus leading to the partial creation of a European social space. The development of such a social space may facilitate the development of a more coherent European identity in the future. A greater appreciation of the vast number of cultural characteristics that Europeans share as a common heritage could also facilitate the development of such an identity. In Chapter 9, Enrique Banús provides a valuable examination of attempts by the EU to develop a cultural identity which respects the diversity of the member states, though he suggests that attempts to develop a single European identity as such are misguided. In terms of cultural identity, strength derives from diversity, rather than unity. Much the same could be said about the preservation of the linguistic diversity which is integral to the cultural heterogeneity of Europe. The chapter by Christina Julios reflects the need to promote respect for all European languages and encourage the spread of European multilingualism. Her chapter focuses on the EU's efforts to promote these objectives and the difficulties it faces in doing so. Greater multilingualism would also facilitate the greater social and labour mobility needed to develop the kind of European social space discussed by Monica Threlfall and also viewed by many as necessary to ensure the success of the euro. However, the increasing dominance of English, as discussed by Christina Julios in Chapter 10, could para-doxically be interpreted as part of a process of cultural homogenisation which may lead to a more coherent common identity in the EU, albeit a highly Americanised one.

In the first half century of its existence, the EU succeeded in establishing an economic community constructed around a single market. In the twenty-first century it faces the challenge of constructing a parallel political and social community, a challenge complicated by an expansion of membership taking it way beyond the original six. A failure to address the imbalance between the EU's powerful economic constitution and its underdeveloped political and social spheres could lead to an unravelling of the whole project. The construction of a political and social community which respects the diversity of an enlarged European membership and heals rather than exacerbates divisions is the critical challenge for the EU in the twenty-first century. The chapters which follow explore various dimensions of this challenge and examine possible pathways to this unity in diversity.

NOTES

I am grateful to Michael Newman and Mary Farrell for their comments and suggestions in the drafting of this introductory chapter.

1 Richard von Weizsacker, former president of Germany, Jean-Luc Dehaene, former prime minister of Belgium and David Simon, former British government minister and chairman of British Petroleum.
2 Elaborated at the Copenhagen European Council in 1993, these refer to requirements to respect human rights and operate stable liberal democratic political institutions, the existence of a functioning market economy, ability to cope with the competitive pressures of the EU single market, and ability to take on the obligations of EU membership.
3 In December 2000, German Chancellor Schröder called for a seven-year transition period following the accession of the CEE states before the full benefits of freedom of movement would apply.
4 The Nice treaty amended the Amsterdam flexibility provisions by removing the veto of non-participating states on a group of states pursuing closer co-operation.
5 An examination of the potential effects of climate change on the future of Europe and the wider world would require a scientific discussion which is beyond the scope of this book.

REFERENCES

Anderson, Benedict (1983) *Imagined Communities: Reflections on the Origin and Spread of Nationalism*. London: Verso.
Black, Ian and Hooper, John (2000) 'Showdown over Europe', *The Guardian*, 23 June.
Chirac, Jacques (2000) Speech to German Bundestag: 'Our Europe', Berlin, 27 June, www.ambafrance.org.uk

Eurobarometer (2000) *Public Opinion in the European Union*, Report No. 53, European Commission, Brussels.

European Commission (1999a) *Scenarios Europe 2010 – Five Possible Futures for Europe*, Forward Studies Unit Working Paper, Brussels.

European Commission (1999b) *The Institutional Implications of Enlargement*, Report to the European Commission, Brussels.

FCO (2000) Speech by Tony Blair to Polish Stock Exchange: 'Europe's Political Future', 6 October, Warsaw, www.fco.gov.uk

Fella, Stefano (1999) *The 1996–97 Intergovernmental Conference and the Treaty of Amsterdam: A Thwarted Reform*. London: South Bank European Paper 1/99.

Fischer, Joschka (2000) Speech to Humboldt University, 'From Confederacy to Federation – Thoughts on the Finality of European Integration', 12 May, Berlin www.german-embassy.org.uk

Grahl, John (1997) *After Maastricht*. London: Lawrence and Wishart.

Hoskyns, Catherine and Newman, Michael (eds) (2000) *Democratizing the European Union*. Manchester: Manchester University Press.

Kaldor, Mary (2000) 'Eastern Enlargement and Democracy', in C.Hoskyns and M. Newman (eds) *Democratizing the European Union*. Manchester: Manchester University Press.

Leonard, Mark (1998) *Rediscovering Europe*. London: Demos.

Lintner, Valerio (2000) 'Controlling Monetary Union', in C. Hoskyns and M. Newman (eds) *Democratizing the European Union*. Manchester: Manchester University Press.

Wallace, William (2000) 'From the Atlantic to the Bug, from the Arctic to the Tigris? The transformation of the EU and NATO', *International Affairs* 76 (3): 475–93.

1 Historical Teleologies

Alan S. Milward

The history of the European Communities has been more dominated by teleologies than any topic other than Christian histories of the early church. The assumptions of its first historians indeed can be comfortably bracketed with the working procedures of the earliest historians of the church. Both were writing the history of a goodness which by its very quality must prevail. Walter Lipgens, the Church of Europe's first great chronicler, is not now much read (Lipgens, 1977). But the assumptions which underlay his work have been widely accepted and used by historians whose research method has been much more analytical.

European integration arose, he assumed, in the depths of the national socialist night as an idea that would conquer that darkness of the soul. It arose at first in scattered, persecuted cells of political and ideological resistance. By 1948, however, the early saints had an organised church militant, the Union of European Federalist Movements, whose belief in unity and peace would inevitably triumph. The teleology of the European Communities as a triumphant will to conquer the past was established.

Leaving aside the question of how far Lipgens' assumptions were structured as a way of denying any connection between National Socialist thought and the postwar process of European integration, a denial which cannot stand up to any examination of the relationship of big business to the operations of the Nazi government (Eichholtz, 1969, 1985; Hayes, 1987), the paradigm which shaped his work has proved very influential on those who have rejected his method. The influence of the federalist movements on the historical evolutions of the European Communities has been relegated to a minor role by the post-Lipgens historiography, but the European Communities are still seen, against the background of half a century of enduring peace in western Europe, as based on the 1952 Treaty of Paris, with the newly-created German Federal Republic. That treaty, however, is now regarded as a peace treaty, regulating important economic issues, more than as a triumph of federalism. The successive major agreements which have led to present European union, by way of the Treaties of Rome, the common agricultural policy (CAP), the Single European Act (SEA), and the Treaty of Maastricht, are interpreted by most historians for the first thirty years of the story as a continuous attempt to regulate the place of Germany in Europe by controlling the scope and direction of the central and largest power's possible actions. What has made that limitation of Germany's actions possible is, nevertheless, as Lipgens implied, a continuing reaction to the two world wars of the first half of the twentieth century.

This is not always the primary interpretation. Some historians rely on primary economic or social interpretations of the evolution to the European Union, especially where they see the last twenty years as a response to globalisation of the economy, or they argue for a different primary political causation. Nevertheless, almost all seem to accept that more than half a century after Hitler's death, control of Germany, willingly accepted or cunningly exploited by successive governments of the Federal Republic, has been an essential element in the mortar which holds the walls of European integration together. Germans have been constrained or converted to being 'good' Germans and not 'bad' ones. The European construction remains a peace treaty based on a rejection of the politics of 1933–45.

The other elements of the mortar are more disputed but no less teleological in their implications. The functionalist explanations of political science live on. Until very recently all the states which have participated in the landmark agreements were functionalist states. Historians are divided over whether there is any element of functionalist 'spillover' in those agreements which exerts a constant forward traction towards cessions of areas of state sovereignty to supranational governance. But even if the agreements are seen as a series of stochastic events, each depending on a particular political conjuncture, each agreement is interpreted as being possible only between states which survive because they are functional (Milward et al., 1993). On this assumption the theory which explains the process of European integration as twentieth-century allegiance depends (Milward, 1995).

CONTEMPORARY VIEWPOINTS

The assumption of the functionality of the twentieth-century state survives, so far, the fundamental changes in the structure of some states over the last decade which have come through the process of contracting out functions to semi-privatized or wholly-privatized agencies (Foster and Plowden 1996). This process does not weaken the theory of post-1945 allegiance. It does, though, weaken the theory of spillover. Do privatised functionaries meet in international institutions to resolve problems across frontiers? And if they do, is it the states' problems which they are inherently constrained to resolve through deeper and more extensive collaboration? Were not the SEA and the Treaty of Maastricht negotiated between states whose intrinsic nature was becoming, and in the latter case had become, quite different from that of those which negotiated the Treaties of Paris and Rome?

There is little historical analysis of these changes, because historians are now purveying a different teleology: the globalisation of the economy. The SEA and the Treaty of Maastricht are seen as economic and political responses to the demands of globalisation. Having controlled Germany and kept the peace Europe can only maintain its prosperity through the larger markets and larger businesses on which economies of scale, as well as the ability to compete with the USA depend. From this logic springs the alleged necessity of economic and monetary union (EMU) and European-wide businesses and stockmarkets.

A syncretic logic is sometimes imposed on all these explanations. Together, they are alleged to represent a continuous effort to preserve a common and distinctive pattern of European culture and society, no matter what the external pressures leading to them. The emphasis on these allegedly widespread feelings of European identity and the desire that they should have a common political representation first developed strongly in the 1970s, a decade in which real political steps towards further integration came to a standstill (Stråth, 2000). With the belief in globalisation the same feelings are now urged by politicians to support further integration. The vacuous concept of the Third Way, for example, becomes part of the rhetoric of Europe's centre-left because the Third Way can be presented as a specifically European political inheritance represented by the European Union. Developments since the Treaty of Maastricht, especially the pursuit of EMU, are typically explained as inescapable if 'Europe' is to survive in a globalised economy, just as the irreversibility of the European Community treaties was earlier described as the only possible route to security against a resurgence of German power.

These teleological narratives have comfortably survived and digested historical research which has amply demonstrated that each step in the formation of the European Communities was a carefully pondered act of national choice by national governments. There were always alternatives and the choice between them was a fine one, nowhere more finely balanced, for example, than in France's decision to sign the Treaty of Rome (Lynch, 1997). They survive by exaggerating some elements of explanation and minimise or even omit others. They omit failures, like the European Defence Community and the European Political Community, killed in 1954 by the French national assembly.

While it is obviously difficult to have reliable knowledge about deeper public sentiments about Europe's cultural 'identity' or the extent of the desire that Europe should have a 'personality', it does not seem unfair to say that too much weight is placed on these sentiments as the explanation when it is so difficult to show its political influence or indeed its con-sistency. By contrast, it is possible to reconstruct the commercial and other economic foundations of the European Communities. Yet accounts which depend on such a reconstruction and which emphasise the economic purpose of the states in pursuing integration are unpopular with historians, who would prefer Europe's postwar construction to have been driven by political, or even merely diplomatic necessity, even though it is integration for commercial purposes which has generated those European institutions which have had the greatest influence in the postwar world. As a commercial negotiator the European Communities have had great power. In the world of foreign policy they have been incoherent and feeble.

The rise of globalisation as an explanatory factor for integration now brings more attention to the economic foundations of the EU. Unfortunately, there is no debate at all in such accounts about whether globalisation is genuinely an explanatory factor for present trends. The historical debate about whether economies are more globalised now than they were in 1912 is ignored, seemingly because it appears to suggest that economies were just as open to worldwide competitive pressures before the First World War as now, and so destroys the underlying teleology of the argument that advocates of further integration wish to make.

Similarly, failures on the road to integration which suggest that political will, the desire to endow Europe with a form of government which would represent its alleged unique cultural and social aspects, was weaker than teleologies proclaim are ignored. The most spectacular of these, the complete collapse in 1954 of the first attempt to give the European Communities a constitution, the European Political Community, and their own European Defence Force within NATO, the European Defence Community, is all but ignored. The only attempt at a comprehensive account was published twenty years ago (Fursdon, 1980).

Richard Mayne, whose book *The Community of Europe* stood as the first short higher education level text on the development of the EC, allocated only six pages out of 192 to the failure of this first attempt at political union, although the European Communities had only twelve years of history when he published (Mayne, 1962). The tradition which he inaugurated has been faithfully followed. McAllister's *From EC to EU: An Historical and Political Survey*, which can be taken as a good attempt at the same type of volume, gives it only one paragraph, and that in spite of the fact that the particular quality of his book is the expertise which it brings to French policies and politics (McAllister, 1997). Coffey in a rare attempt to use the history of the EC/EU to suggest policies for *The Future of Europe* does not even mention this failure (Coffey, 1995). Analyses in such books of the failure of the first attempt at a European Monetary Union, the Werner Plan, are similarly lacking.

There should be stiffer lessons to learn from failure. Was not the current decision to move to EMU before wage, welfare and fiscal harmonisation taken with the failure of the Werner Plan in mind? Waiting for acceptably safe levels of fiscal and monetary policy harmonisation before issuing a single currency made monetary union recede as a target in the 1970s, although the ultimate intention of the Werner Plan was very little different from that of the present EMU.

There seem to be two reasons for the persistence of these historical teleologies. One is that history may have a mobilisatory value. This view is particularly held by scholars who believe that 9 May 1950, the date of Schuman's proposal for a Coal and Steel Community, marks a caesura in European history. For such writers, to analyse the conjoint failure of the European Defence Community and the European Political Community or of the Werner Plan for EMU, would be to analyse vestigial traces of a historical epoch which has ended. This would not be without its own intellectual interest, but could have no explanatory value in the new, post-Schuman, historical epoch, whose different values would increasingly predominate. Secondly, there is a much sounder reason. History is not a good predictor. It cannot reduce the world to a sufficiently small number of variables to turn theory into predictive models. It can be suggestive, but only on the basis of analogies which by definition are imperfect. Historical evidence has destroyed most of the teleological functionalist theory of the growth of the European Communities over their first two decades, but one serious purpose of social science being to construct predictive theory it has good reason not to be deterred by the evidence that some predictive theory does not stand up to the historical test. The task is to replace it with something better.

PREDICTING THE FUTURE EU?

Nevertheless, as things stand, history is as good, or as bad, a predictor, if only on the basis of analogy, as social science. What does the history of the EC/EU suggest about Europe in the years to come? The value of that question is that it places the policy and attitudes of the present EU member states in a longer-term perspective, identifying what may be structural elements of the EU, those enduring historically-conditioned realities with which the EU may have to live.

While the origins of the European Communities in French security policy in the 1950s and in the struggle of the German Federal Republic towards equality of rights and a place in the comity of European nations are indisputable, the other major force in their foundation was international trade. The European Economic Community (EEC) was the political creation of a controlled and regulated market, shaped to sustain the high rates of growth of international trade which were thought to be a determining factor of the high rates of growth of national income per capita and of personal disposable income in the 1950s. The commercial advantages of the common market have remained the bedrock of the EU's foundation after the reunification of Germany altered the parameters of security policy and eliminated any German need for the EU as a ticket to political respectability. The common market is still the cement of the EU, the one institution of European integration which meets with the USA on equal terms and in whose negotiations with the outside world each member state can pursue a national advantage which otherwise would be hard to win. It remains far more important in estimating the influence of history on the EU's future than the presumption of a political will whose commitment to union has always varied very widely between member states, and within some member states has been highly volatile.

From the first attempts to expand the European Communities in 1961–3 the *acquis communautaire* which potential new entrants have been required to accept has been essentially an economic one. First and foremost has been the acceptance of the common external tariff. In entry negotiations each new entrant has been obliged to accept this powerful weapon and shield. Its impact on member states has been varied, not by minor derogations, but by accumulation of commercial and financial arrangements, in many cases more appropriately described as privileges, won by member states in negotiations for accession. The political and legal institutional framework of the EEC as set out in the Treaty of Rome has been accepted by every new applicant before making a formal application. There was no point in doing otherwise. The economic conditions of entry, on the other hand, have been in every case a matter of fierce and detailed negotiation, leading to what may be called special deals.

The economic *acquis communautaire* retained from the outset the favourable terms which France won for itself in the Treaty of Rome; open access to the common market for its overseas territories and colonies and the introduction into the Treaty of the idea of the harmonisation of wage rates, of the incidence of social security contributions on employers, and of the impact of taxation on production costs and foreign trade. While not much was done for three decades about this harmonisation of production costs where they were thought to be affected by government policy, that part of France's special deal is still central to the future of the Union and thus to all the new applicants for membership.

The Europeanisation of agricultural protection was agreed by all six signatories of the Treaty of Rome without difficulty. What policies to use, was a question left on one side. Taken up between 1958 and 1962, it emerged as the second stage of the *acquis*, the CAP, only really in operation from 1966. Although officially the process of negotiation, which began in September 1961 with the new applicants, Denmark, Ireland and the United Kingdom, included those countries in a process of mediation of what had already been decided about the CAP, in reality it was a French condition that the structure and method of financing the CAP must be decided by the six original members before the commercial terms for the new entrants could be negotiated. The methods of financing the CAP, mainly through import levies, meant that the financial terms for British entry were made significantly worse before the detailed negotiations on the British application could begin in February 1962, because the United Kingdom was a food importer on a very large scale and the bulk of its food imports came from Commonwealth countries rather than from within the common market. The application of the CAP to British agriculture and to British food imports still remained almost entirely unnegotiated when the first attempt at expansion failed. The favourable terms for France which the *acquis* represented were an important reason for the failure to expand the Community.

When Community expansion did finally come in 1973 the United Kingdom had to accept the disproportionately high financial cost of entry arising out of the full acceptance of the CAP. Dissatisfaction with that settlement led, however, to the special deal for the United Kingdom in 1984; the 'rebate' which Margaret Thatcher secured was a remission of the higher costs of financing the Community relative to GNP which fell on the United Kingdom because of its higher percentage of foodstuff imports than any other member state.

With the Iberian enlargement of the Community 'structural' funds were made available to Spain and Portugal as lower per capita income member states. The level and rate of growth of GNP per capita in Spain were such that it might have been assumed that Spain's special deal should not last long. It has been made very clear by Madrid however that expansion to include the first tiers of former Soviet bloc applicants with a much lower level of GNP per capita cannot be at the expense of Spain's initial deal. At present, because of the sums it receives in structural funds and through the CAP, rich Spain is the greatest beneficiary from the EU's financial redistributive mechanisms. The United Kingdom continues to insist that a redistribution of the burden of financing the Community to reduce the share which falls on Germany cannot be achieved by any interference with the British 'rebate'.

Although most commentators seem to believe that great changes are needed in the CAP if the financial burden on existing member states of the entry into it of Polish agriculture, as well as the agricultural sectors of some other former eastern bloc countries, is to be made acceptable, notably to German taxpayers, there is no sign that the accumulation of special economic deals, which constitutes the historical *acquis communautaire* will be modified. New entrants will be required to accept it in its totality or wait for entry until the CAP costs less.

Economic and monetary union (EMU) will now also be part of the *acquis*. There will be no more 'opt-outs', like those for Denmark and Britain. Distrust, however, of central banks in the former Soviet bloc states is such that the definition of central bank independence agreed for the establishment of the European Central Bank will be much stricter for the new applicants. They must establish before entry central banks with constitutional guarantees of independence at which west European countries would certainly have baulked, and which do not seem to have any historical precedent.

The economic aspects of the *acquis communautaire* remain therefore staunchly defended national advantages, part of the terms of entry and thus part of the supranational 'constitution' of the EU as set out in the Treaty texts and the extensions of their meaning and implications by the Court of Justice. It is the history of EC/EU with which all new entrants have to come to terms.

Those terms are harsh. The First Accession Partnership drawn up in March 1998 stipulated, for example, that Bulgaria, among other things, must restructure its industry, its financial sector and its agriculture. That is more than western European states have had to do over half a century of integration, and far more than could be done by 2006, the date for expansion, although probably not including Bulgaria, which the EU now foresees. Security policy may be a strong pressure for eastward extension. So might the admissible vision of a common European house. But the price of entry into that house mounts as the less rich seek to enter it.

As things stand it is easy for the present member states to agree that eastward expansion is desirable, for their terms must be accepted. This does not mean that it will happen, even less that it will happen on the scale envisaged, at the date now specified. First there has to be an agreement between existing members on 'institutional reform'.

There, too, the weight of history lies heavy. The existing 'constitution' cannot be changed to make it more supranational at the expense of the greater states. The Council of Ministers, in its various guises, will still exercise the authority of the nation-states at Brussels. There will, it seems now to be accepted, be some increase in the number of issues which may be decided by majority voting, but only when the number of votes for each member state has been adjusted to make room for the new members while at the same time – the essential point – maintaining a system in which the greater powers cannot be outvoted by the smaller.

Each nation will probably have a Commissioner. To make this possible the almost certain outcome is that not all Commissioners will be of equal rank. Some will be the equivalent of 'ministers'; others only of 'state-secretaries' or in the English usage 'junior ministers'. Those of less rank will not sit with the Commission when it makes decisions, except perhaps when the decision is in their field of responsibility. 'Full' Commissioners, for External Relations, for Agriculture and similar major areas of the *acquis* will be from the greater powers. For lesser Commissioners, who will come from the lesser states, new posts will have to be created, supervision of central bank independence perhaps or the standardisation of transport licensing.

It is strongly rumoured that one consequence of this may be that member states will have to form political blocs, each bloc represented at the summit by a 'full' Commissioner. At that point the concept of supranational governance may be transformed into fixed regional associations grouped around a greater state. Finland will abandon Scandinavia for Germany as Scandinavia clusters around the United Kingdom. But who will be in the French bloc? Could the EU sustain a change of this kind, in which the originator and dominator of the first European Community is left in isolation? At that point the weight of history may well limit the extent of institutional change, so that the institutional framework into which the new applicants will be obliged to insert themselves will be even more cumbersome than the present one.

In this discussion of institutional reform it seems highly unlikely that the role and powers of the European Parliament will be strengthened. The majority opinion appears to be that because only a small, and in many countries diminishing, proportion of registered voters is prepared to turn out and vote in the European elections the Parliament has no claim to greater powers. This is a useful argument for those greater member states who have never wished to see any extension of the European Parliament's role, lest it weaken their control over the Communities. Only between 1971 and 1973, when the Heath government in the United Kingdom thought that monetary union would improve its chances of re-election, has 'The Mother of Democracy' supported parliamentary democracy at the supranational level. Because any monetary union under the Werner proposals was so far away, this support was abstract. As for the originating country of Jacobin democracy, it has been throughout a resolute opponent of extending the European Parliament's powers and role, mostly on the grounds that to do so could weaken the degree of control over Germany which the original institutional framework maintained. If some historians believe in a European 'identity', it is hard to find a political scientist, and even harder to find a politician, who believes there is a true European 'demos'. It is, though, allegedly to strengthen their democracies that eastward expansion to new states is envisaged.

PROSPECTS FOR MONETARY UNION

Monetary union too has a long history which has shaped the present plan. The Werner Report envisaged it at the end of a series of stages of harmonisation of national budgetary procedures and fiscal policies. In this process, it suggested, the Community institutions could play a role by setting indicative guidelines and an indicative warning system which would show when national policies failed to stay within those guidelines. The subsequent behaviour of international currency markets in the 1970s put paid for ever to the language of indicative planning. The memory of this experience was important in the decision at Maastricht to grasp for monetary union as a way of promoting the harmonisation which had not happened.

It is, indeed, hard to believe that EMU could endure long without some degree of fiscal harmonisation. Using monetary union to force policy harmonisation and ultimately a closer political union might seem the epitome of the attempt to escape from history, were it not that history offers no analogy close enough to permit such a conclusion to be drawn. The first European Community in 1952 was, as Robert Schuman said, a leap into the dark and the intention of EMU's supporters seems to have been to conclude the voyage to integration with another one. Like the Treaty of Paris, EMU has no historical precedent. Monetary unions in Europe have a bad record, except for those between large economies and very small ones. But monetary unions in recent history between similarly sized economies do not provide any example of a union with a single currency and a single central bank. Both of these elements were seen by the founders of EMU as guarantees that it would survive.

Without a single currency and a common central bank, the Latin Monetary Union gradually disintegrated under the force of what economists most fear for EMU, asymmetric shock (Eichengreen and Frieden, 1994; Redish, 2000). In the Latin Monetary Union, formed in 1865 by Belgium, France, Italy and Switzerland, and of which Greece subsequently became a member, the asymmetry sprang from the development needs of the Italian and Greek economies. Devaluation or, in the Italian case, debasement of the coinage, was a policy response to the urgency of developmental infrastructural investment. When to this shock was added the additional asymmetric shock to the bimetallic standard of the decline in the price of silver relative to gold the monetary union was soon moribund, although it survived in treaty form almost until the First World War. The experience of the Latin Monetary Union suggests that what has been left out of the economists' discussion of monetary union is the historical evidence that even in well ordered and closely regulated states it is people as consumers and not governments who decide which currency to use. French gold coinage, the ten franc piece, continued to be widely accepted inside the Latin Monetary Union when the Union was moribund. The French silver five franc piece also had some acceptability as a convertible currency because it was minted to meet the specific silver standard of the treaty establishing the Union. Silver coinage of Italy and Belgium was not convertible, except when it was bought by the Bank of France to try to maintain the Union. The outcome was an accumulation of silver coin by the Bank of France so large as to make it unredeemable at the rates set by the treaty.

That problem kept a meaningless Union legally alive when it was in effect no more fulfilling its function (Willis, 1901). Most economists believe that the costs of exit from EMU, because interest rates are set too high for infrastructural developmental investment or too low to maintain the foreign exchange value of the euro, would, even in the short term, be a large loss and that that will preserve EMU. The history of the Latin Monetary Union confirms that prediction. But the same history also suggests that a more plausible threat is a slow erosion of EMU in which consumers lose confidence in the euro, while no government dares to bear the cost of formal exit. Against that, the EU has two defences. One is the wholly state-based concept of 'legal tender'. Three months after the euro is issued there will be no other currency in circulation. The other is the belief that there could be no plausible alternative currency. Doubts about the second defence can be seen in the way in which the steady fall of the euro against the dollar disturbed no one in the European Central Bank until it began to seem that markets would establish the euro as having parity with the US dollar. Objections to this were of course political, the purpose of the euro was to give Europe 'a personality'. Before the danger that this purpose would be thwarted appeared on the horizon a falling euro was regarded as beneficial to the faltering exports of the EU's manufacturing heartland, Germany and Italy. Historical analogy is useful at this point; it tells us that there is always another currency.

There has not been an example in modern times of a major international currency not backed by an important national government. It is far from evident that the euro is backed even by the equivalent of a national central bank. The European Central Bank is governed by a committee with many opinions. Given the obvious usefulness of the euro in the bond market there will always be pressure for it as a unit of account which can be used in monetary instruments. But the question still remains to be answered; can a currency without a government be managed through the cacophony of at least fifteen national governments, sometimes with dissimilar economic interests and a central bank which will often have no common policy on which all its Board agrees other than the price stability which it has been enjoined to maintain?

If the answer is positive, would monetary union generate some of the harmonisation which has been lacking? If it were not for the widely varying proportion of revenue raised by national governments from taxes on corporations, there would have been a convergence over the period of the EC/EU's lifetime in the shares of national tax yields derived from different forms of taxation. But it is possible that the wide variations in that proportion of the tax yields deriving from taxes on corporations has been an increasing barrier to the harmonisation of tax burdens on production to which the Treaty of Paris looked forward in 1952. Taxes on labour increase at the expense of taxes on capital because labour is immobile. Such harmonisation as there has been creates therefore another policy problem. The obvious way to resolve it is through welfare fiscal policy.

SUPRANATIONAL STATEHOOD?

The EU's inheritance of national welfare states is usually described by scholars, and seems also to be thought of in Brussels, as an intractable problem for supranational governance. Even when grouped into various typologies the welfare states still represent the very essence of national, historically-conditioned sets of policies formulated to meet the demands of national electorates in specific historical circumstances. Their harmonisation may be gradually shaped through the erosive action of globalised markets, but there appears to be little that the EU could do to help bring about such a result. The influence of these redistributory welfare systems in determining differences in the burden of national fiscal policy on particular social groups, production workers for example, has been little explored, in spite of its extreme importance for any process of fiscal harmonisation.

In the case of that particular aspect of welfare policy which gives rise to the greatest financial anxiety, the commitment of national governments to retirement and old-age pension payments to an increasing number of survivors beyond the retirement age, harmonisation is strongly opposed by member states, because for many of these commitments separate funding has not been set aside and state revenues show a declining trend.

Such public schemes vary between the two extremes of Spain, whose earnings-related pension benefits provide high returns to high earners who are also high contributors, and the United Kingdom, where over most of the period of operation of the national old-age pension provision the intention has been to provide only a uniform low-level subsistence pension benefit, which for people without other sources of income normally implies supplementary welfare benefits. In Spain public pension provision competes with private provision in benefits for lifetime high earners. In the United Kingdom it is a safety-net for those with no occupational or other form of private pension provision and few savings. It is hardly surprising that maintaining old-age pensions at their existing level does not appear as a future financial problem in the United Kingdom. But it did appear as an obstacle to social policy harmonisation in the first year of the present Labour government, when the minister charged with welfare reform was a prominent advocate of the undesirability of welfare benefit harmonisation because of his belief that British taxpayers would end up having to fund a mounting burden of future pension obligations in countries closer to the Spanish model.

Some recent research tends to show that the benefits received from most public pensions schemes correlate more with employment levels and general economic conditions during the period of active work than with contributions. Cyclical movements and background economic conditions in the member states since 1950 have shown strong similarities. It may be, therefore, that harmonisation of pension schemes may be a less daunting issue than it currently seems. If, by analogy, the same were true for other welfare benefit payments, the weight of history might well be less in this area than it is usually depicted as being. Without any research on how social welfare policy links up with national fiscal policy over the same working lives it is impossible to know what the weight of history at this point actually is, or how great the effort to harmonise. Even that conclusion, however, shows the centrality of historical knowledge in resolving a major future policy problem. That a convergence of fiscal and welfare policy might emerge is by no means implausible. But without enough of a common government to present a coherent public image of its monetary policy, will not the governance of the EU be even more lacking in these more difficult areas?

After forty years of talking about a common EC/EU foreign policy the disarray of the EU in the face of the dissolution of Yugoslavia remains blatant. After forty years of assertions of the need for a common European defence policy nothing has changed. Only France and the United Kingdom, in 2001 as in 1952, have armed forces fully capable of deterring an attack on the EU's territory by a major power. The failure of the European

Defence Community and the European Political Community in 1954 seem to have been definitive. It is easy to see why: the nations do have vitally different security interests which they must protect. The NATO campaign against Serbia showed how different they were across a spectrum from Britain and France at one end, to Italy and Germany in the middle, and to Greece at the opposite end.

CONCLUSION

While history cannot accurately predict, the evidence suggests that the situation of the member-states of the EU remains deeply embedded in its historical roots. The Union remains what it has always been, a support framework for national state policies in a period in which these have become increasingly difficult to pursue. The millenarian hope of escaping from history is not likely to be fulfilled and the future of the European Union will be like its past, a useful muddle, deceiving the hopes of prophets and sustaining the milder and more useful aspects of national governance. The EMU's durability is not guaranteed, particularly if the asymmetric shock should come from Germany, a more plausible scenario than assuming it could come from eastward expansion. The foreign policy 'pillar' of Maastricht will probably remain a broken pillar. Those are not reasons, however, to suppose that the commercial policies of the EU will not remain as common policies, or that the Union will not endure. And as the nature of the state changes it may well be that the EU will achieve a more substantial degree of fiscal and social welfare harmonisation, from which would spring a greater degree of labour mobility. Will a European demos be created, and will the institutions of the EU be democratised? On those two questions, the most serious of all, history is agnostic.

NOTE

This chapter was originally the text of a lecture commissioned in summer 2000 by Keio University. It was completed in November 2000 on the eve of the Inter-governmental Council at Nice in December. Although publication has taken place after the results of that meeting in Nice, I have left the text unchanged as a fairer test of the value of historical prediction.

REFERENCES

Coffey, P. (1995) *The Future of Europe.* Aldershot: Edward Elgar.
Eichengreen, B.J. and Frieden, J. (eds) (1994) *The Political Economy of European Monetary Unification.* Boulder, CO: Westview.

Eichholtz, D. (1969, 1985) *Geschichte der deutschen Kriegswirtschaft 1939–45.* Berlin: Akademic-Verlag.

Foster, C.D. and Plowden, F.J. (1996) *The State Under Stress: Can the Hollow State be Good Government?* Buckingham: Open University Press.

Fursdon, E. (1980) *The European Defence Community: A History.* London: Macmillan.

Hayes, P. (1987) *Industry and Ideology: IG Farben in the Nazi Era.* Cambridge: Cambridge University Press.

Lipgens, W. (1977) *Die Anfänge der europäischen Einigungspolitik 1945–1950.* Stuttgart: Klett.

Lynch, F.M.B. (1997) *France and the International Economy: From Vichy to the Treaty of Rome.* London: Routledge.

Mayne, R. (1962) *The Community of Europe.* London: Gollancz.

McAllister, R. (1997) *From EC to EU: An Historical and Political Survey.* London: Routledge.

Milward, A.S. (1995) 'Allegiance', *Journal of European Integration History*, 1 (1): 7–19.

Milward, A.S., Lynch, F.M.B., Ranieri, R., Romero, F. and Sørensen, V. (1993) *The Frontier of National Sovereignty: History and Theory 1945–1992.* London: Routledge.

Redish, A. (2000) *Bimetallism: An Economic and Historical Analysis.* Cambridge: Cambridge University Press.

Stråth, B. (ed.) (2000) *Myth and Memory in the Construction of Community: Historical Patterns in Europe and Beyond.* Brussels: Peter Lang.

Willis, H.P. (1901) *A History of the Latin Monetary Union: A Study of International Monetary Action.* Chicago: University of Chicago Press.

2   The EU and Eastern Europe: Diversity without Unity?

Peter Gowan

The aim of this chapter is to explore the challenges that are likely to confront the EU and its member states in their relations with eastern Europe over the next decade. The chapter begins with an overview of the now very different regions into which Eastern Europe has evolved, and then goes on to examine the preoccupations and capacities of the main western actors that are relevant to developments in the east. Part three will provide a sense of the key issues affecting the future development of EU–east European relations. The concluding part will look at the major choices facing the EU and its principal member states as they try to design their policies towards the region.

THE REGIONAL DIVERSIFICATION OF EASTERN EUROPE

What was once a single political and economic zone called the Soviet bloc has divided into a number of quite distinct regions during the 1990s. These different regions are identifiable on a number of different planes – economics, politics and geopolitics. These inter-regional differences have fundamental significance for the relations between countries in each region and the EU.

The following regions can be distinguished:

- The Frontier Belt (FB): those states directly bordering Germany and/or Austria: Poland, the Czech Republic, Slovakia, Hungary and Slovenia. Croatia also borders Austria, but its involvement in the wars of the western Balkans has given it a different economic, political and strategic profile from the other frontier-belt states up to now.
- South east Europe and the western Balkans: this zone includes Romania and Bulgaria, Albania and all the Yugoslav successor states and 'entities' except for Slovenia; Macedonia, the Bosnian protectorate with its two 'entities', Yugoslavia (embracing Serbia and Montenegro) and the Kosovo protectorate.
- The Baltic region: the Baltic states and Kaliningrad.

- The western CIS: Russia, Ukraine, Belarus and Moldova.
- The Caucuses: notably Armenia, Georgia and Azerbaijan.

The first three of these regions are the ones which, in principle, fall within the geographical sphere of potential EU membership, although Kaliningrad, as a province of Russia, is not, of course, eligible for EU membership separately from Russia. Although EU Commission officials have made statements, during NATO's Kosovo war, that Ukraine is a European country in EU terms and thus in principle eligible for EU membership, such statements have not been repeated by the European Council. And since the early 1990s, the EU has, in practice, drawn a sharp dividing line between the CIS republics and those states eligible for the so-called 'Europe Agreements' – the association agreements which open the way to eventual, possible accession to the EU. The Caucasian republics are a special case. Like the Western CIS, they are recognised as 'European' by the Council of Europe. But they have been treated in the same way as the western CIS as far as the EU is concerned: not eligible for EU membership for the foreseeable future. The most directly central regions for the EU are, therefore, the Frontier Belt (FB), south east Europe (SEE) and the Baltic region.

DECLINE AND REGRESSION IN SEE

The split that has opened up between the FB and SEE since 1989 is often explained by reference to deep-seated historico-cultural divisions between 'the Balkans' and western-Christian central Europe, but the actual mechanisms generating this split in the 1990s should be recognised in order to understand the current dynamics within each region. Four factors in particular may be identified as contributing to the current division: the clash between local political trends and the western campaign for shock therapy launched in 1989; the impact of German geopolitical priorities on both regions; the impact of the Yugoslav wars; the Albanian blow-out. Each one of these factors is examined briefly here.

Shock therapy and local political forces

From the Paris G7 summit in the summer of 1989, the United States led the western powers in an activist campaign for a rapid switch of the social systems of the east to a Western-oriented capitalism along broadly American lines. This drive for rapid social realignment in the east was initially broadly acceptable to the emergent social and political elites and populations in what became the frontier-belt states, but it clashed with the social and political orientations of powerful groups in what became south eastern Europe (SEE).[1]

In those parts of the east which bordered directly on Germany and Austria the first democratic elections showed communist or 'post-communist' parties as being in a small minority – the votes of such forces ranging from about 10 per cent to about 16 per cent. Such parties were also initially minoritarian in the Baltic states. But in SEE the parties of the left were much stronger. They were majoritarian in Romania, Bulgaria, Serbia and Montenegro and strong in Macedonia and Croatia (Gowan, 1997).

Following these election results, the governments of Poland, Czechoslovakia and Hungary accepted the programme for rapid social realignment (with Hungary's MDF (Hungarian Democratic Forum) government being the most reluctant) as indeed did the Yugoslav federal government, which initiated a draconian shock programme before elections. But the Romanian and Bulgarian governments elected in 1990 did not accept the programme: they prioritised economic revival over social system change. They also privileged economic links with the USSR – a pivotal economic partner for Bulgaria in particular. These policies brought hostile western pressure. Although the 1990 elections in Romania and Bulgaria were judged fair by international observers, the Western powers declared the new governments undemocratic and not eligible for western endorsement and aid (Sunley, 1990). This generated intense domestic political conflict as coalitions of assorted anti-Communist groups and parties turned for western support to overthrow the dominant parties.

This polarisation was followed by the social/political backlash in the countries that implemented shock therapy: the backlashes were produced by the extremely savage domestic depressions in the countries concerned and they were a major test of political cohesion of the states concerned. Poland and Hungary had effective political shock absorbers to manage the backlash: people turned back to the post-Communist parties in these two countries, but these parties were themselves committed to the realignment drive.

But in Czechoslovakia and Yugoslavia state cohesion could not be maintained. The split between the Czech lands and Slovakia was peaceful. But in Yugoslavia the 1990 IMF shock therapy programme interacted with the domestic socio-political configuration of forces to produce the collapse first of the IMF programme, then of the Markovic government, then of the state (Cohen, 1995; Woodward, 1995). The IMF/WB shock programme in Yugoslavia – the first in the region – was particularly draconian since it involved not only slump but also massive plant closures – a tactic not repeated elsewhere later (Chossudovsky, 1996). Although Prime Minister Markovic was far more popular than any other political leadership in the country, *and in every republic* (Hayden, 1992), his programme produced mounting popular resistance and he was prevented from turning his personal support into a democratic mandate: the first elections were instead organised on a purely republican basis. And the various anti-Markovic political parties at republican level used opposition to the IMF–Markovic programme very effectively to get elected (Woodward, 1995).

In Slovenia and Croatia, nationalist leaderships opposed this pro-gramme to gain support for their separatist goals. In the southern repub-lics, which were most severely hit by the factory closure programme, the dominant political forces – Communist ones – opposed it while seeking to maintain Yugoslav unity. Thus the Yugoslavist pro-western realignment forces were destroyed and the battle became one between Yugoslavist anti-western leftism, led by the Serbian Socialist Party, and pro-western separatists seeking the destruction of Yugoslavia and gaining strong early support from Austria and the Vatican, soon followed by Italy and then Germany.

Thus did eastern Europe begin to separate into a frontier belt, soon to include Slovenia, and an SEE made up of an excluded Romania and Bulgaria and a disintegrating Yugoslavia.

The impact of German geopolitical priorities on the region

Another important contributing factor in the differentiation was the fact that Germany from very early on was signalling a distinctive geopolitics in the region: prioritising concern for the frontier belt and showing little interest in what happened in more remote parts of the region. Chancellor Kohl indicated to the governments of Poland, Czechoslovakia and Hungary very early on that he was determined to bring them rapidly towards membership of the EU, telling Hungary's Prime Minister in 1990, for example, that he planned Hungary's admission to the EU by 1996 (Artner and Andor, 2001). These German signals applied to the Visegrad countries and from early 1991 they also applied to two Yugoslav republics: Slovenia and Croatia. But they did not apply to the rest of SEE. The importance of this German orientation should not be underestimated for the differentiation of the east into two regions. Despite the enormous strains faced by the frontier-belt region in the early 1990s, their elites were offered a clear national strategy by Germany. No such strategic perspective was offered to elites in SEE.

The impact of the Yugoslav wars

Once the tensions within Yugoslavia burst into open war in the summer of 1991, apart from Slovenia, the whole of the rest of SEE became affected by the repercussions of developments in the western Balkans. West–west suspicions and rivalries over the European post-Cold War power structure then prompted the United States to push the government of Bosnia towards a civil war there and to sabotage EU efforts to resolve the conflict with devastating results for the western Balkans (Cornish, 1997; Gordon, 1995, 1997; Gowan, 1999a, 1999b).

The Albanian blow-out and the NATO war against Yugoslavia

A western-backed but corrupt and undemocratic Albanian government provoked a popular uprising which entirely destroyed the Albanian state in 1997. This gave an opening for an ethnicist nationalist Kosovar Albanian group, the KLA, to launch a guerrilla war, challenging the moderate Kosovar Albanian leadership and threatening the stability of Macedonia. Rather than relying upon Belgrade to crush the KLA terror campaign and restabilise the region (but undermining the US demonisation of Belgrade as aggressor in the Bosnian civil war) while gaining a negotiated solution in Kosovo, the Clinton administration saw the KLA campaign as an opportunity for consolidating its new European leadership through NATO. It therefore allied with the KLA for a NATO war against Yugoslavia. This has produced a whole new set of deep political problems in the region, and beyond (Gowan, 2000a).

The key problems in the western Balkans from an EU angle may be summarised as follows. First, although the US has political control over the two NATO protectorates, the EU carries the main financial, administrative and military burdens within them and in both the EU is committed against the political identities and allegiances of the majority of the populations. In Bosnia the majority of the population have never had and do not have allegiance to a sovereign Bosnian state, despite $5 billion of western money to achieve this over five years. There is a Bosnian central bank and car number plates system, but nothing more. The 2000 elections showed Serb and Croatian rejection of the EU protectorate goals to be as strong as ever. And this is despite – or perhaps because – the NATO powers' High Representative in Bosnia is exercising dictatorial legislative and executive power riding roughshod over the rule of law and liberal rights (ESI, 2000a, 2000b, 2000c). The economy of the protectorate remains completely unviable without western aid.

In the Kosovo protectorate the situation is even worse. In the face of NATO opposition, the KLA is pursuing a guerrilla war outside the province within Serbia and has been terrorising ethnic minorities and political opponents amongst the Albanian community, with impunity. NATO seems unprepared to confront the KLA for fear, no doubt, of suffering significant military casualties but also because bringing the KLA leaders before The Hague Court could unravel the whole history of the US support for the KLA and of the nature of KLA operations before and after the war.

The EU also finds itself locked into the US political posture towards Serbia. This requires that the NATO war be vindicated. In Serbia, the majority of the population considers that NATO's war against Serbia was criminal aggression in international law.[2] It also rejects NATO's yet to be substantiated claims that there was genocide in Kosovo and considers that the KLA has always been an ethnicist terrorist organisation. And Yugoslavia's government continues to consider Kosovo an integral part of Yugoslavia. It also rejected NATO's claim that the War Crimes Tribunal in the Hague is an authentic and legitimate judicial body rather than an instrument of US power. It therefore demands that former President Milosevic should be handed over for trial for alleged crimes in Kosovo, only complying in the summer of 2001 under intense economic pressures.

The Serbian economy whose infrastructure and industrial base has been very badly damaged by NATO bombing (UNECE, 1999) now faces the strong social tensions that will be generated by a turn towards private capitalism. Meanwhile the US administration has refused aid to Serbia until it accepts the US definition of the NATO war and thus hands over Milosevic to The Hague Court established by the western powers.

While these developments have been unfolding in the western Balkans, the social situation in Bulgaria and Romania deteriorated sharply. The west's initial hostility to the left-led governments of these two countries gave way to a concern for stability while the Croatian and Bosnian wars continued. But following Dayton, the IMF adopted a new tough stance towards Bulgaria in 1996 over its failure to move fast enough towards privatisation. The IMF's suspension of lending intersected with the extreme vulnerability of Bulgaria's banking system to bring about a full-scale banking and currency collapse. This had the effect of destroying the authority of the Socialist party government, but the Bulgarian economy has not yet recovered from this catastrophe. In Romania, the Socialist party government lost the election in 1996 and was replaced by a centre-right coalition wedded to an extremely radical shock therapy and austerity programme. This plunged the economy into a depression from which it has not yet recovered, fragmented the governing coalition and led to the return of the Socialist party to government in the 2000 elections. But these elections have also produced a major challenge from an anti-western, nationalist populist party of the right.

It would thus be no exaggeration to say that the EU not only faces a series of very grave political challenges in a region whose social structures have been shattered during the 1990s, but it does so under US tutelage and without the obvious capacities to cope with these challenges.

THE 'EUROPEANISATION' OF THE FRONTIER BELT

The frontier-belt states have largely escaped the consequences of the regression in SEE. But they have had to try to cope with two social reorganisations of daunting scope during the 1990s. There was first of all the particular form of the class transformation involved in the realignment of shock therapy. Although it was legitimated as an economic efficiency drive it was more about changing the social structures of these countries in a particular way. The legitimating ideology insisted that the problems of the east European economies lay in their social institutional systems of planning rather than in such areas as debt, exclusion from world product markets or political and cultural systems. It was thus insisted that a radical destruction of central planning systems and the introduction of free markets for all factors of production would lead to a reallocation of production factors through market signals and a consequent leap forward to far greater allocative efficiency and far more rapid growth than was ever possible under central planning (Schmieding, 1993).

This turned out to be a cruel illusion. The shock realignment produced no such result: instead, the region plunged into a deep slump, without precedent in peace-time history, in 1990–92. The IMF combined a drive to generate such a slump with an effort to turn these economies towards export-oriented growth, very much on the lines of the Latin American structural adjustment programmes of the 1980s. But in the Latin American case the powerful US banking sector had ensured an opening of US product markets to Latin American goods: it wanted its Latin American debts repaid. But the European situation was different. In the midst of this slump, the EU revealed itself to have very different preoccupations from those of the United States vis-à-vis Latin America in the 1980s. It was driven by what may be called industrial and agricultural mercantilism: using political leverage to maximise its exports to the east and minimising competition from eastern producers in its own domestic product markets. Thus an American-inspired shock therapy programme turned the east European economies towards an export drive which the EU was not prepared to accept.

This was revealed in the EU's Europe Agreements (EA), which revealed that the task of the east was, in effect, to service the needs of existing EU capital. This meant a massive restructuring of the productive apparatus of the east to fit in with the distinctive needs of west European capitalism. This EU programme was unveiled early in 1991 just at the point of maximum economic dependence of these states on the EC market, since they were in the depths of slump. The draft EA came as a big shock to the governments of the region, placing even the states most enthusiastic for realignment in an acute dilemma.

The EAs included the following: the blocking of significant agricultural exports to the EU while allowing the EU to engage in dumping agricultural products in the region; tough non-tariff barriers against the main regional export industries' products coming into the EU in significant quantities namely, steel, chemicals, textiles, clothing and so on; the systematic use of western export subsidies for industrial products to enter the region's product markets, tight national controls on migration into the EU making it impossible for the region's economic operators to establish undertakings in the EU while opening up the region to EU economic operators; a mass of complex rules of origin to block inward investment by capital from centres other than the EU for the purpose of exporting into the EU market; a battery of trade protection instruments in the hands of the EU, violating the spirit and often also the letter of the GATT, and a refusal to designate these economies as 'market economies' thus enabling the EU to take protectionist measures against them regardless of GATT rules.

The shock therapy tactics had, in principle, won the support of many new elites in what became the frontier-belt states because it gave strong international backing for their domestic drive to construct new capitalist societies. But they were shocked by the EU when it revealed its hand in 1991. The governments of the frontier-belt states seriously considered breaking off the negotiations with the EU and denouncing the whole EC package as a mercantilist outrage. In April 1991 Commissioner Andriessen, in charge of implementing the EC's policy towards the east, reported to the Council of Ministers that the negotiations were deadlocked and on the point of collapse (Merritt, 1993). But in exchange for very minor EU concessions, the frontier-belt states decided to accept the terms of their integration path.

They had, in reality, little choice but to accept whatever the EU offered because they had justified the turn to capitalism and their new property rights as a turn to 'Europe'. To then denounce 'Europe' was not a serious domestic option. And there was also a second argument for acceptance: the strong, clear evidence that Germany had a strong vital national political interest in drawing the frontier belt into close political relations that would include eventual membership of the EU. This did not in the least mean that Germany was a force for watering down the political-economic terms in the EA. On the contrary, the German government was as tough as the French government on the economic terms. But the political side of German policy was a powerful argument for accepting the terms in the EAs. And the final argument against rejection was that this was a risky option for economies desperately dependent on maintaining access to the EU market.

The economic evolution of the frontier belt

In quantitative terms, the frontier-belt economies, with the exception of Poland, have diverged further from west European GDP per capita levels since 1989. The expected catch-up benefits of turning to the capitalist market have not yet materialised. The statistical patterns of divergence are a reflection not only of the systemic transformation slump of 1990–93, but continue in the 1993–99 period (see Table 2.1; UNECE, 2000).

As to whether the frontier belt can escape this pattern of economic peripheralisation over the next decade and experience sustained growth higher than the EU average depends upon whether they can escape the structural blockages and vulnerabilities they are currently facing. On present trends the prospects of their doing so are not encouraging because many of these blockages derive precisely from the EU regime to which they are being forced to adapt. This generates processes of agricultural decline in the east[3] (Landesmann, 2000), and de-industrialisation, while severely constraining legally the policy options available to frontier-belt governments to combat these trends (see Table 2.2).

TABLE 2.1   *The pattern of divergence in frontier-belt economies from west European GDP per capita levels*

Country	Per capita GDP as percentage of EU	
	1989	2000[1]
Czech Republic	64.9	56.3
Hungary	56.7	52.9
Poland	38.0	39.9
Slovakia	56.7	56.3

[1] Projected figures.

Sources: UNECE (2000), Berend (2000).

TABLE 2.2   *Economic indicators for frontier-belt states, 1999*

Country	GDP 1990 = 100	GDP 1995 = 100	Industrial production 1990 = 100	Trade deficit 1999 ($bn)	Gross external debt 1999 ($bn)
Czech Republic	96.3	101.1	81.3	2.6	22.5
Hungary	102.4	115.6	126.5	3.3	28.3
Poland	137.7	123.5	163.3	20.5	57.4
Slovakia	104.3	120.9	83.7	0.8	10.4
Slovenia	113.3	116.6	84.0	1.2	4.9
Bulgaria	74.9	88.7	50.4	0.7	9.7
Romania	79.0	88.0	52.1	1.9	8.1
Croatia	82.2	113.4	63.1	3.6	8.5
Macedonia	92.5	108.5	51.4	–	1.4
Yugoslavia	45.1	94.1	39.9	–	11.5[1]
Estonia	85.8	118.9	–	–	–
Latvia	56.8	114.7	–	–	–
Lithuania	65.0	112.2	–	–	–
Russia	58.7	94.6	49.7	27[2]	145.0[1]
Ukraine	40.8	85.4	50.3	0.5	11.5[1]

[1] Figures for 1998.
[2] Surplus.

Source: WIIW Database.

The growth potential of the frontier-belt economies seems to be constrained by a number of factors which prevent them from achieving catch-up growth rates vis-à-vis the EU. In the first place, they seem to be trade-dependent economies whose growth depends upon growth within the EU (Poeschl et al., 2000). Secondly, they tend to suffer from chronic and often dangerously acute trade deficits with the EU. They are generated in large part by the EU's trade restrictions, imports of consumption goods and of inputs for western-owned plants operating in the east as well as by the trade policies of the EU, both blocking exports in key sectors of the eastern economies and also subsidising and promoting exports from EU states into the region. When we add debt-servicing obligations, which are heavy for many of these states, their current accounts as a whole are chronically under strain. A third source of vulnerability lies in the fragile banking systems of the region. This has been largely the result of governments (rightly) seeking to preserve industrial assets during the slump of the early 1990s by transferring their economic problems into the banking system in the form of non-performing loans. But the consequence of this has been difficulties for industrial companies to find cheap sources of domestic banking finance for their efforts to restructure and raise productivity. The tendency for governments to put their banking systems in foreign ownership may guard against future bank collapses but may not result in such foreign-owned banks helping important industrial companies through recessionary difficulties. A final source of vulnerability derives from the extremely volatile international financial and monetary relations to which these economies are prey thanks to the EU requirement that they end capital controls. This tends to produce surges of hot money into their financial markets, pushing up their exchange rates, generating domestic inflation and thus tending to generate higher trade deficits in the future. Such surges of hot money, benefiting from high interest rates within these economies (rates which are nominal for domestic consumers but real for western financial operators) and from rising exchange rates of local currencies can then be suddenly reversed with devastating local consequences.

The frontier-belt states have not, of course, been equally affected by these economic dependencies/vulnerabilities and the extent to which they have had to accept pressures from the EU states depended upon their domestic capacities. By vigorous and effective domestic restructuring, which at the same time maintained elite cohesion and domestic mass control, they could enlarge their international room for manoeuvre. Luck and policy tactics could also be extremely important.

Broadly speaking the most sustainable economy amongst the frontier-belt states is that of Slovenia. Paradoxically, it is also the least 'globalised' or 'Europeanised' of the frontier belt economies.[4] The reasons for this lie above all in two unique features of Slovenia: first, as part of Yugoslavia, it was able to spend a quarter of a century adapting to the tasks of exporting to the EU zone since Yugoslavia gained market access to the EU in the late 1960s; secondly, Slovenia escaped Yugoslavia's debt trap by seceding, with western support, from Yugoslavia. It thus lacked this economic burden and the western political leverage which accompanies such burdens. The quantitatively most successful frontier-belt economy of the 1990s, Poland, in fact faces very severe structural problems, with an ultimately unsustainable trade deficit, a very high debt burden (despite its unique ability, thanks to its geopolitical links with the United States, to get almost half of its debt burden cancelled in the early 1990s) and a very dangerous dependence on short-term financial inflows from the west. The Czech Republic's efforts to retain a largely nationally owned productive system were defeated by a

TABLE 2.3   *The share of the foreign-owned sector in frontier-belt states*

Country	Foreign-owned share of GDP, 1999	Foreign-owned share of sales, 1997	Foreign-owned share of exports 1997
Bulgaria	15.5	–	–
Czech Repbulic	32	26.3	42
Hungary	40	66.7	75.4
Poland	18	30.3	33.8
Romania	16	–	–
Slovenia	15.5	21.6	–
Slovakia	10.5	19.6	25.8
Russia	9.8	–	–

Source: Landesmann (2000).

devastating currency and financial crisis in the spring of 1997. This was of the kind which is very familiar within the current international monetary and financial order for countries with weak financial systems that succumb to western pressure to end their capital controls too early – the Czech Republic dismantled its capital controls earlier than any other frontier-belt state. Hungary has been the paradigm of an economy which has been 'globalised/Europeanised': most of its industrial system has gone into foreign ownership. This has resulted in some high-tech export sectors, but a balance sheet of the foreign-owned sector which takes account of indirect as well as direct imports and which also takes account of repatriated profits seems to suggest that the 'globalisation' of the Hungarian economy is overall value-subtracting from a national point of view. It is also generating symptoms of a dual economy (see Table 2.3).

But the frontier-belt economies do have some advantages. Their geographical location near the heart of the EU market makes them a prime location for maquilladora types of foreign direct investment (FDI).[5] In the Czech Republic and Slovakia, unit labour costs were only 20–25 per cent of Austria's in 1997. In Hungary, wage levels are strikingly low at 10–15 per cent of those in Austria. In Slovenia, wage levels are about 30 per cent of Austrian levels (Landesmann, 2000). Secondly, in their industrial sectors, productivity has recovered and risen in the second half of the 1990s. In 1998, productivity across manufacturing as a whole in these countries taken together amounted to 50 per cent of Austrian levels, with Hungarian industry leading on 65 per cent (Landesmann, 2000). And these states remain much less dependent on labour-intensive exports than are Turkey, Portugal and Greece.

Political system integration in the frontier-belt states

Considering the enormous strains which the populations of this region have undergone, the political systems of these states have proved remarkably stable and robust. From an EU point of view, the main risks within them come from nationalist backlashes against perceived west European mercantilism or imperialism. If these states are denied short-term entry into the EU, such currents will strengthen, perhaps even dramatically. And if entry is set on terms that produce further economic dislocation such trends will also gain openings.

While some of these nationalist currents could be described as centre-right or centre-left, others are on the extreme right. This is most evidently a problem in Hungary, linked, no doubt, to perceptions that the country's assets have been sold cheap to westerners, but it could also arise in Poland where anti-western nationalist traditions remain significant.

As in western Europe, and for the same basic reasons, related to the social consequences of contemporary forms of European capitalism, xenophobia is a problem in the frontier-belt states, particularly in relation to the Roma and travellers. This is a serious problem for the EU states because they do not want to have the Roma coming towards them for their own xenophobic reasons.

THE BALTIC REGION AND KALININGRAD

Although the three Baltic states have experienced very grave economic decline over the last decade, there are good reasons for expecting that their economic prospects are favourable. Not only has their economic performance improved over the last five years, despite the impact of the rouble collapse of 1998, but they are becoming less dependent upon the Russian market and are being drawn more strongly into linkages with the Scandinavian economies. These trends should continue.

The main longer-term problems confronting the Baltic states concern the stability of their political systems and strategic situation. Domestic political stability could be jeopardised in Estonia and Latvia if they fail to integrate their large ethnically Russian populations effectively. Partially linked to this issue is the question of their political relations with Russia. If this relationship deteriorates dramatically, the Baltic states could become a flash-point between NATO and the Russian Federation.

This is partly, but by no means only, a matter for the governments of the Baltic states themselves. Attempts by right-wing nationalists in these states to brand Russian citizens as war criminals for their role in the annexation of the Baltic republics by the USSR during and after the Second World War, while seeking to rehabilitate citizens who collaborated with the Nazis, have caused tensions with Russia and could do so again. The issue of citizens' rights for ethnic Russians in Latvia and Estonia could also become a tense inter-state issue with the Russian Federation.

But a more likely threat to the region would lie in it becoming a pawn in a wider conflict between Russia and the NATO powers. One source of such a conflict could be Kaliningrad. This triangle of territory lacks a direct border with the rest of the Russian Federation. Moscow has raised a demand for a secure land route for military and other supplies crossing Lithuania. At the same time, Lithuania is campaigning to become a member of NATO, a goal supported by Poland and by influential voices in Germany. This would mean that Kaliningrad was territorially surrounded by NATO forces. Russia is strongly against any of the Baltic states becoming NATO members. The enlargement of the EU into Poland and Lithuania would also tend to isolate Kaliningrad economically.

The United States, NATO and the Scandinavian countries have been advancing the idea of a Baltic Charter Treaty to resolve all such issues in the region via conference diplomacy involving Russia. A co-operative approach with Russia to all the major security and economic issues in the region is obviously highly desirable. But events have already demonstrated that such an approach is hostage to the more general relationship between Russia and the United States. The struggle for influence between Russia and the United States in the Caucuses and Caspian and in Ukraine could easily derail the whole effort to find lasting political solutions in the Baltic.

RUSSIA AND THE WESTERN CIS

The changes in the FB, SEE and the Baltic have taken place during an extraordinary collapse eastwards of Soviet then Russian power. During the Russian collapse, the United States has vigorously projected its power eastwards both in the northern zone through Poland and along a southern axis, seeking to reshape political allegiances in these areas. In the north, the main American step has been a particular form of NATO enlargement into Poland, one which gives the US the right to deploy nuclear weapons and construct US bases in eastern Poland. The US has also prioritised Poland as a key US ally in more general political and economic matters. And the US's military link with Poland must also be seen in the context of NATO's new doctrine giving it the right to strike militarily out of area eastwards.

On the southern axis, the US has launched a major push towards the Caspian, declaring its goal of acquiring control over the oil resources of that region to be a vital US national interest. The key state here for the United States is Azerbaijan, but Georgia is also extremely important. Turkey has been America's main partner in this campaign and American bases in Turkey are supplemented by a strong US naval presence in the Black Sea.

The pivotal state linking together the United States' northern and southern advances is Ukraine. Ukraine offers the US the prospect of a thick Polish–Ukrainian corridor between Russia and Germany from the Baltic to the Black Sea, a formidable barrier not only to some future German–Russian rapprochement but also to a strong return of Russian influence into east central and south east Europe (Garnett, 1997). But Ukraine also links in with the American drive for the Caspian. Under Washington's tutelage, the Ukrainian government has built an alliance stretching from

Moldova through the Caucuses and Caspian into Central Asia: GUUAM – Georgia, Ukraine, Uzbekistan, Azerbaijan and Moldova. Although this alliance is weak, it blocks Russia from asserting its leadership over the CIS. And despite the fact that Russia maintains its naval base in Sevastopol, a Ukraine linked with the United States could, in the future, transform the Black Sea into a zone as fully dominated by the US as the Mediterranean is. And although Romania and Bulgaria are often viewed in Western Europe as principally oriented westward towards the EU, they are, in fact, deeply affected by the new, American-centred military-political operation in the Black Sea.

The spectacular high point of the US demonstration of its dominance over Russia was the NATO war against Yugoslavia through which the Clinton administration indicated that US commitments in the NATO–Russia Founding Act of 1997 concerning respect for the UN Security Council's authority and other such principles were not to be taken seriously.

But since the 1998 rouble collapse and the simultaneous collapse of the US–Chubais clan economic policy for Russia (Wedel, 2001), the Russian productive economy has begun to revive strongly, albeit from an extremely low base.[6] And under Putin, there are signs of a determination both to rebuild Russian state authority domestically and to begin to rebuild Russian political influence abroad. This latter effort will certainly involve an attempt to halt the US advances around Russia's borders – notably the US drive in the Caspian and in Ukraine – and to assert Russian interests in the Baltic. The second Chechnya war was a clear indication of this Russian determination to reassert itself in the Caucuses. The NATO war against Yugoslavia has unleashed a growing, if still covert, struggle between Russia and the United States in Ukraine. And Russia could equally exert pressure in the Baltic region and seek to rebuild its support in south east Europe.

The problem for the United States is that although its military capacity reach and its power in the international financial institutions can play a large role in shaping political relationships with state executives it lacks the resources to build solid foundations for its new zones of influence in the political economies of these states. Russian capital and economic statecraft seem far more able to extend Moscow's influence at this level, at least in a country like Ukraine.

The EU and its member states, with the partial exception of Germany, are not serious players in this US–Russian great game, but they and their relations with various East European zones described above will, of course, be profoundly and probably fundamentally influenced by its outcomes. A destabilisation and collapse of the Ukrainian state, for example, could make the Bosnian war seem trivial from the angle of its impact on the EU. Once the Baltic states are incorporated into the EU, the latter will be more directly dependent upon the US–Russian relationship. And given the chaotic political situation in the western Balkans, a revived Russia, could, at small resource costs, make life considerably more difficult for the EU states in that region if it was minded to.

The crucial EU state in the future evolution of EU–Russian relations is Germany. It has the capacity to alter the economic incentive framework of the Russian government in the fields of debt relations, investment and trade deals. Much will therefore depend upon whether future German governments seek to buttress the US drive to the east or to attenuate or undermine US attempts to consolidate Europe's repolarised international political system between a US-led NATO pole and a Russian security zone.

THE STRATEGIC CHOICES FACING THE EU

The analysis in this chapter suggests that the EU and its member states face four major challenges in their relations with the east over the next ten years. These comprise an economic challenge vis-à-vis the frontier belt states; a set of multiple political, military and economic challenges in SEE; a diplomatic challenge in the Baltic; and a strategic challenge vis-à-vis Russia and the western CIS. Only the first of these challenges is firmly in the hands of the EU and its member states. All the other three depend upon the relationship between the EU states and the United States.

The first challenge is briefly reviewed here, while the other three are considered in the context of an assessment of West European–American relations.

The economic challenge vis-à-vis the frontier-belt states

The EU states have to decide whether they want the FB to remain in general in the condition of a dependent periphery, with isolated success stories (such as Slovenia) or whether they want a full integration of these societies into the west European core. Up to now the basic EU choice has been to opt for the former. Continuation along this line will almost certainly generate potentially serious political conflicts both between the EU and some FB states and also within some FB states, conflicts which would have a stronger impact on the existing EU region once the FB states are inside the EU. The most acute focus of these choices for the EU is Poland, by far the biggest FB state.

A social integration strategy could take a number of different forms. One possible option could comprise a single market regime (SMR), a tough agricultural regime, a blockage on free movement of labour plus large financial transfers. The latter could ease the current account and budgetary strains on these states, offering them better growth prospects. A second option that could be considered might be derogations for the FB from the SMR for a substantial period, the granting of free movement of labour, a generous agricultural regime and large financial transfers. All in all, this second option seems extremely unlikely but even the first one is not yet on the EU's agenda and, even if adopted, it may not be sufficiently resourced in the next EU budget plan to structurally transform the FB states' macro-economic environment. The EU member states would, on current trends, probably adopt the most restrictive terms for accession and seek to rely on negative incentives to maintain political disciplines on FB states – especially human rights statecraft: the threat to suspend countries from membership if they acquire governments judged hostile to the human rights values of the EU.

A set of multiple political, military and economic challenges in SEE

If the EU persists in the NATO line of maintaining the political fragmentation of the Serbian and Albanian nations and trying to impose a US version of history on Serbia while leaving the western Balkans as fragmented and in many cases scarcely viable states, it must maintain military forces and aid funding for decades to ensure minimal stability.

It might be thought that a free market economic programme along with regional economic integration may provide the instrument for eventual political stability, but this seems extremely unlikely. The EU's Stability Pact does not seem to be a serious economic programme. It is a mixture of symbolic conferences and funding for various non-governmental organisations (NGOs). And there are serious problems with trying to lead with economies in the region. First, regional economic integration will not be acceptable to Croatia which is looking for ways of 'joining Europe'. That would tend to make any regional economy Serbia-centred – hardly attractive to an EU committed to US leadership in the region. Secondly, the free market nostrums presuppose strong state institutions above private interests and these cannot be built without a new political settlement corresponding to real political identities and regional security pacts based upon co-operation between these identities. Thirdly, the role of the present EU market regime is one that generates competition amongst similar external economies for the niches in the EU market. So a strong insertion of a western Balkan economy in the EU would require real planning of what that insertion could consist of – something that goes against the grain of free market ideology and could have wider implications for the EU trade regime for the east as a whole.

An alternative approach would be to lead with a new political programme geared to producing a genuine political settlement. But this would require the EU both to gain autonomy from US policy and to be able to impose its political will in the region, if necessary against the line of the US government. It may be that the EU's projected Rapid Reaction Force may be put to such use. But the EU has already learnt bitter lessons on the dangers of trying to act autonomously from the US in this area.

Thus the most likely variant will be paralysis for very many years in the western Balkans and in EU policy towards the region. In such circumstances, the main thrust of EU policy will be 'containment': keeping the populations of the region in the region.

EU relations with Russia and the EU–US relationship

The challenges facing the EU vis-à-vis the Baltic region and the western CIS hinge on EU relations with the United States. So far this chapter has ignored the most important determinant of EU–eastern relations over the next ten years: the role and aims of the United States in Europe. Over the last decade, the most important political goal of the United States in Europe has been to securely re-anchor its political hegemony over the region, after its old Cold War anchorage was shattered by the collapse of the Soviet bloc (Garten, 1992). It has pursued this goal through reorganising NATO so that it can strike militarily out of area outside UN legality, through a drive to enlarge NATO eastwards while excluding Russia from European affairs, and through vigorously seeking to prevent the EU states from building a unified political-military centre in western Europe, acting as a caucus in NATO, and acquiring rights to autonomous military action outside the NATO area (Cornish, 1997; Gowan, 1999b). Much of the current political chaos in the western Balkans is a direct by-product of this US drive: notably the long Bosnian war and its outcome and the NATO war against Yugoslavia (Gowan, 1999a, 1999b, 2000c). So too, is the determination of Russian elites to gain a new settlement in Europe that will end Russia's exclusion.

There is not the slightest reason to suppose that the new Bush administration or its successor will abandon this drive to re-establish its political dominance over Europe (Waltz, 2000). On the contrary, its NMD plans must be seen in large part (though not exclusively) in that political context. The main ways in which the US has and will use its military assets to achieve and maintain its political dominance over Europe are threefold: first, establishing a new military stand-off with Russia which will make western Europe security-dependent on the US–Russian relationship; secondly, through retaining US military control over the EU's geographical periphery in the Mediterranean, SEE and the Black Sea, as well as, possibly in the future, Poland and Ukraine; and thirdly, through controlling energy sources and supply routes, including, if possible, the new sources around the Caspian and routes from there previously under Soviet control. At the same time, the US has been seeking to insist upon its monopolistic control over the deployment of west European armed forces in the pan-European theatre and preventing a new west European political-military centre.

The programmatic vision offered by the US to Europe is one of expanding NATO into the Baltic states, the whole of the frontier belt and SEE and ideally eventually into Ukraine and perhaps even the Trans-Caucasian republics. This NATO expansion can be far more rapid, of course, than EU enlargement. This vision therefore offers the prospect of an EU entirely encased within a US-led security zone. There is, of course, a utopian element to this vision. It would entail a very large commitment of US resources, it would be fiercely resisted by Russia and it would also be resisted by some members of the EU. At the same time, it would be enthusiastically endorsed by many governments in the East seeing their inclusion as giving themselves a protector – and advocate with regard to the EU – in the form of the US. Such governments, which gain next to nothing – or indeed less than nothing except demands for economic reorganisation – from their relationship with the EU, would be happy to support US demands for the EU to stop trying to assert its political-military independence: the Polish government already openly opposes the Nice Plan for a Rapid Reaction Force out of loyalty to the US.

Against this background, possible options for the EU and its main member states in policy towards the east over the next ten years can be very schematically mapped out:

1 More of the same: This implies a continued acceptance of EU political subordination to the US and its policy towards Russia, the Caspian, SEE etc., qualified by an insistence on protecting the EU's main western members' economic interests. This implies a tough stance against FB economies, a basic stance of 'insulationism' towards SEE and the western Balkans and the Rapid Reaction Force as a bluff which is European only in name but firmly under US control. Structures like the 'Stability Pact' in the Balkans would continue, largely to persuade EU opinion that the EU was being constructive.

2 The EU as an expansionist military bloc: This implies seeking to consolidate an autonomous sphere of influence not only in the frontier belt but also in SEE with an at least partially autonomous and distinctive orientation towards Russia. This would imply a determination on the part of the EU to consolidate a security zone under its own control not only in the frontier belt but also in SEE and to achieve this it would also have to take priority, to a considerable degree, over the hitherto treasured EU economic regime for the east, for it would imply radical new approaches to gain rapid economic growth in the frontier belt and real development in SEE. Concomitantly, the EU would have to attempt to solve the problems of the western Balkans, bringing the region under its exclusive sway on a development path. The European Rapid Reaction Force would have to be a strong, cohesive instrument, with effective, autonomous command and most fundamentally the EU would have to be united on a common political-military security concept and strategy. This would, of course, risk heavy American hostility. The obvious trade-off with the United States would come in the field of global military action: the EU could engage in a massive military build up and offer the US a readiness to turn NATO into a global strike force under US leadership provided only that the US gave the main EU states joint regional hegemony in Europe.

3 The EU as a federation with a distinctive set of values and norms on global governance from those of the US and without global militarism: This implies the EU becoming a genuine federal-style state uniting in the external and defence policy field and ending its existing basis for unity, namely as a mercantilist bloc externally and as a vehicle for neo-liberal restructuring internally. This would imply a dramatic shift of the political base of the EU from one in which strong commitment is largely confined to big capital to one gaining strong commitment on the part of the broad population of western Europe and the consequent capacity to mobilise internal political support for strategic action for political and economic development in the east (and elsewhere). The EU could develop a Rapid Reaction Force strictly for European operations or for action under UN mandate. The EU would have to buttress itself by a principled insistence that NATO should be banned from military action without a United Nations Security Council mandate and unless its action was under the rules of the UN Charter. This would at least give Russia a veto on US military action in Europe. At the same time, the EU should support the restructuring of NATO to allow Russian membership and should insist upon Russia being a security partner of the EU as much as the US is such a security partner. EU involvement in global imperial militarism should be rejected.

4 Political gridlock and internal regionalisation within the EU combined with a stronger direct US role: A final variant would imply an actual decline of EU external political capacity as a result of increasing gridlock within EU institutions and a tendency towards initiatives by west European states towards the East to bypass the EU institutional framework altogether. There could be the growth of regional operations and unilateral moves as well as a shift towards an expanded range of NATO initiatives under US direction. The EU would be reduced to the (still not completed) single market and perhaps the euro zone as a purely 'domestic' currency.

Each of these options is really a description of different 'finalities' of the EU project as the challenges of the east, in reality, demand an answer to what the telos of the EU actually is. Option 1 is that the EU is a business concert of states under US political control on an international level; option 2 is that the EU is a military/currency bloc acting as a junior imperial partner of the US on a global scale; option 3 is that the EU is a federation which is a civilian power on a global scale and offers distinctive civilian-political values for international governance as a counterweight to US attempts to consolidate the 'global leadership' of a single state; option 4 is that EU-Europe is internally fragmented and is a variable resource for Europe's dominant power, the United States. Option 3 would seem the most favourable variant, but is surely the least likely.

NOTES

1   Discussion of the motives for the Bush administration's shock therapy drive are beyond the scope of this chapter. But they were heavily influenced by geopolitical concerns. For a fuller discussion see Gowan (2000c). On the origins of the drive, see Beschloss and Talbott (1993) and Merritt (1993). For an intellectual rationale for the strategy, see Sachs (1990).
2   The view that the action was in breach of international law was shared by the British government's own legal specialists (Rubin, 2000).
3   The Bulgarian exception results from the enormous scale of deindustrialisation in Bulgaria.
4   By 'globalisation' I mean an economic configuration dominated by a western-owned industrial sector and a financial sector both highly sensitive to and vulnerable to Western financial markets and operators. In the east European context 'globalisation' and 'Europeanisation' are largely synonymous concepts.
5   FDI to exploit cheap labour on one side of a border for export to large markets on the other side of the border.
6   The reorganisation of the Russian economy during the Yeltsin period was managed, to a very great extent, by a small team of Russians and Americans led by Anatoli Chubais on the Russian side and steered on the American side by Larry Summers, the US Deputy Secretary at the Treasury in the Clinton Administration. Chubais carried out this work while occupying various formal posts within the Russian government. Wedel (2001) covers the administrative processes and funding aspects in great detail. The macroeconomic side of the programme involved a priority for a high, stable rouble, free movement of funds, a liberalised import regime and the funding of the budget deficit through issuing government debt at very high rates of interest. These policies had a very damaging effect on Russian production and on the Russian state's fiscal position, but proved unsustainable and collapsed with the fall of the rouble in autumn 1998.

REFERENCES

Artner, A. and Andor, L (2001) 'Hungary and the Enlargement of the EU', paper to Conference 'Europe After Nice, Copenhagen. 21–23 January.

Berend, I. (2000) 'The Transition from Central Planning to the Market Economy as a Process of Systemic or Régime Change', paper for UN Economic Commission for Europe Seminar: From Plan to Market: The Transition Process after Ten Years', UNECE, Geneva. 6–8 April.

Beschloss, M.R. and Talbott, S. (1993) *At the Highest Levels: The Inside Story of the End of the Cold War*. New York: Warner Books.

Chossudovsky, Michel (1996) *Dismantling the Former Yugoslavia*. Research Paper, University of Ottawa.

Cohen, L. (1995) *Broken Bonds: Yugoslavia's Disintegration and Balkan Politics in Transition*. Boulder, CO: Westview.

Cornish, Paul (1997) *Partnership in Crisis: The US, Europe and the Fall and Rise of NATO*. Chatham House Papers. London: Royal Institute of International Affairs.

ESI (2000a) European Stability Initiative, Reshaping International Priorities in Bosnia and Hercegovina.

ESI (2000b) European Stability Initiative, Background Paper 6, Elections in 2000. Risks for the Bosnian Peace Process

ESI (2000c) European Stability Initiative Background Paper 7, for Stockholm Seminar on Bosnia and Herzegovina

Garnett, Sherman (1997) *Keystone in the Arch: Ukraine in the Emerging Security Environment of Central and Eastern Europe*. Washington, DC: Carnegie Endowment for International Peace.

Garten, Jeffrey E. (1992) *A Cold Peace: America, Japan, Germany and the Struggle for Supremacy*. New York: Times Books.

Gordon, P.H. (1995) *France, Germany and the Western Alliance*. Boulder, CO: Westview.

Gordon, Philip H. (ed.) (1997) *NATO's Transformation: The Changing Shape of the Atlantic Alliance*. Lanham, MD: Rowman and Littlefield.

Gowan, P. (1997) 'The Post-Communist Parties in the East', in Donald Sassoon (ed.) *Looking Left*. London: I.B. Tauris.

Gowan, P. (1999a) 'The NATO Powers and the Balkan Tragedy', *New Left Review*, March–April: 83–105.

Gowan, P. (1999b) *The Twisted Road to Kosovo*. London: Labour Focus on Eastern Europe.

Gowan, P. (2000a) 'The War and Its Aftermath', in P. Hammand and E.S. Herrman (eds) *Degraded Capability. The Media and the Kosovo Crisis*. London: Pluto.

Gowan, P. (2000b) 'Making Sense of NATO's war in Yugoslavia', in L. Panitch and C. Leys (eds) *Necessary and Unnecessary Utopias, Socialist Register 2000*. Rendlesham: Merlin Press.

Gowan, P. (2000c) 'The EU and the Unsettled Future of the East', *Labour Focus on Eastern Europe*, Autumn: 65–108.

Hayden, Robert (1992) *The Beginning of the End of Federal Yugoslavia: The Slovenian Amendment Crisis of 1989*. The Carl Becker Papers, No.1001, University of Pittsburgh.

Landesmann, M. (2000) 'Structural Change in the Transition Economies since 1989', paper for UN Economic Commission for Europe Seminar, 'From Plan to Market: The Transition Process after Ten Years', UNECE, Geneva. 6–8 April.

Merritt, G. *(1993) Eastern Europe and the USSR: The Challenge of Freedom*. London: Kogan Page.

Poeschl, Jozef et al. (2000) *Transition Countries Clamber Aboard the Business Boom in Western Europe*. Research Reports, No. 264, The Vienna Institute for International Economic Studies.

Rubin, J. (2000) 'Count Down to a Very Personal War', *Financial Times*, 20 September.

Sachs, J. (1990) 'What is to be done?', *The Economist*, 3rd January.

Schmieding, H. (1993) 'From Plan to Market', *Weltwirtschaftliches Archiv*, 2.

Sunley, J. (1990) 'Bulgaria: the Election', *East European Reporter*, Autumn/Winter.

UNECE (1999) *Economic Survey of Europe*. Geneva: United Nations Economic Commission for Europe.

UNECE (2000) 'Catching up and Falling Behind: Economic Convergence in Europe', *Economic Survey of Europe*, 2000, No. 1.

Waltz, Kenneth N. (2000) 'Globalization and American Power', *The National Interest*, 59 (Spring).

Wedel, Janine (2001) *Collision and Collusion: The Strange Case of Western Aid to Eastern Europe*. New York: Palgrave.

Woodward, S. (1995) *The Balkan Tragedy*. Washington, DC: The Brookings Institution.

3 Future Paths to European Security

Elżbieta Stadtmüller

At the beginning of the 1990s, following the end of the Cold War, the hope
was expressed that the twentieth century would end in a climate of peace
and that the European continent which, in the course of the century had
endured a series of bloody wars, would become an example of international cooperation and mutual understanding. However, by the end of
the 1990s, these hopes were shown to be illusory. Instead, Europeans were
living in an atmosphere of growing insecurity: a dramatic conflict had
erupted in the Balkans. It was this dowry that Europeans would take into
the twenty-first century.

Across the continent, individuals, organisations, societies and governments are confronted with the fundamental question of whether they have
the ability to shape the Europe of the twenty-first century. Can the required
decisions be taken in order to stabilise and develop the European continent? Can a European order and an effective security system be built? It
could be argued that there is a need simply to accept that events will
always outflank us and the only solution is to adapt to them, accepting all
consequences. However, the Balkan catastrophe compels us to search for
paths to European security even if finding this path is a long-term process.

Debate on the question of European security must take into account a
few obvious and fundamental factors. First, there is a need to decide to
which geographical area the term 'Europe' applies and subsequently to
determine the most important separate interests both among states and
between different groups within states. Secondly, there is a need to take
into account all dimensions of security, not just the military ones, and
consider them in the light of the above. Thirdly, there must be a recognition that European security cannot be isolated from global processes and
events that affect world order. The fourth element concerns the shape of
the institutions which will have the role of responding to the expectations
of states in the region and seeking solutions to military and non-military
problems. Finally, it must be recognised that security is a state of mind as
well as a state of being. In this sense, even where fears and anxieties have
no foundation in reality they still have the potential to create stability or
instability. This chapter explores these five fundamental factors which are
crucial to the shaping of a stable and secure European continent.

BORDERS OF EUROPE

Europeans discovered again at the start of the 1990s that defining the identity of the European area was not such a clear-cut process. In 1989, eastern Europe celebrated its 'return to Europe' and was given a fraternal welcome by the west. However, very quickly the question re-emerged of who belonged to the European family. Defining these borders is one of the fundamental tasks of European integration and the Atlantic partnership. But in families – domestic or international – peace and quiet are sometimes valued more than affection for distant relatives. Decisions in 1997 taken at the NATO summit in Madrid, and by the EU in Luxembourg to proceed with limited enlargement, and the NATO–Russia agreement, also in 1997, seemed to draw the dividing lines. Some former socialist countries began to be more 'western' than others in the opinion of their societies, particularly in the field of national security. Even the position of Russia was seen as privileged in comparison with for example, the Baltic states and Romania. These divisions cannot be permanent if European security is to be taken seriously. This problem pertains not only to those countries which are knocking at the door of NATO and of the EU (such as Slovakia, Bulgaria, Romania and the Baltic states) which present themselves as democratic but which are not yet fully developed in this sense or which have had the bad luck to be too far to the east or south. It also pertains to the Balkan states, Belarus, Ukraine and Russia. Unfortunately for the west, Europe is not a piece of Swiss cheese in which the more holes there are the better it is to eat. Undoubtedly there is much force in the argument that Russia cannot be treated in the same way as other European countries, both because of its size and its Asian if not global interests. On the other hand, any solution based on leaving Russia outside Europe or building a security system against her must be rejected. Triumphalist comments in the context of the attack on Kosovo – that it revealed Russian helplessness and its 'final defeat' as a superpower – were premature. In the contemporary world there is no possibility of marginalising a state of such size and ambition. One condition for European security is a stable Russia – albeit one that has abandoned its imperial ambitions. In this context a key role might be played by Ukraine which is, according to Brzezinski (1998a), a significant element in the process of European reconciliation which began with France and Germany, continued with Germany and Poland and whose next stage will be Poland and Ukraine. Not only Brzezinski but also almost all Polish politicians and many of their Ukrainian partners stress the importance of an independent and stronger Ukraine. Russia without this part of its previous domain cannot seriously think about being an imperial state able to intervene in central Europe. So Ukraine is a bulwark against the rebirth of Great Russia but possibly also a bridge to Moscow. Its mainly pro-western policy so far, including the naming of Poland as its strategic partner, together with its continuing close relations with Russia, can aid the development of links between Russia and central Europe (the specific question of the Balkans is considered later).

The problem of defining the European area does not apply only to the east. The position of the US in Europe is a recurring question. Should it remain an intrinsic element or a friend across the ocean only occasionally asked for its advice or support? A close look at the Europe–Atlantic community also raises the question of Turkey's position, not only because of its location and Islamic roots, but because of its domestic problems and its geopolitical utility to the west.

Given the complexity of the whole region it is difficult to imagine a unified security system especially if we employ a broad concept of security. However, we need to think in terms of a network of different structures, that does not exclude any state or region. This would have to be based on existing organisations which are responsible for different dimensions of security – military, political, economic, for example, NATO, OSCE, the Council of Europe, the EU (with its possible defence structure) – but also various subregional institutions of co-operation. These different combinations of interests and links would seem a simpler way to bind the countries of Europe through strong ties of common goals, rather than the very difficult task of searching for a new institutional solution which could be both effective and acceptable for all states. This network must inevitably accept (but not be overwhelmed by) the fact that Europe and its security are perceived differently by the USA, Russia, the Balkans, small and big states, rich and poor countries, and of course the island of Britain. But divisions within European states must not be overlooked either. Europe is not one homogeneous area. Within European states, there coexist not only different cultures and historical experiences – which need not automatically lead to fundamental conflicts (Huntington, 1996) – but also different stages of socio-economic development, from pre-industrial to post-industrial. It is these differences that can divide most deeply.

EUROPEAN SECURITY: CHALLENGES AND DIMENSIONS

The concept of a European security extends beyond military criteria and comprises economic, political, ecological, social and cultural elements. Examination of these broad dimensions of security reveals the vast catalogue of challenges that Europe faces in developing a security system. Europe was affected most profoundly by the consequences of the end of the bipolar world order, which provoked positive but also dramatic events. The processes of disintegration and integration collided. Relationships between states were reshaped, and, all the while, Europe sought to find its place in the new world order. The fact that an exceptionally large range of decentralising tendencies emerged even in regions considered to be stable was a cause of disappointment. The process of transition in Eastern Europe provoked political, economic and ethnic crises. Problems that had diminished but had not been resolved in the preceding period, particularly the question of ethnic and religious identities, re-emerged and combined with new issues. The search for independence led to an explosion of nationalism because, in a region which has been for many centuries under the power of the Ottoman, Habsburg and Russian empires nations and ethnic groups had become so comprehensively intermingled that the creation of pure national states was impossible. This led in turn to the next set of divisions: involving clashes between minorities and majorities and resulting in open conflicts and wars.

Significant decentralising tendencies could also be observed in western Europe. The characteristics of this were restrictions towards immigrants, xenophobia, slogans about defending national identity and even violence towards other ethnic groups. Western Europe as a whole has begun to retreat from ideas of multiculturalism and openness. This is illustrated by its tendency to separate itself from eastern European problems, and by its growing anxiety at creeping Americanisation, the cultural and political expansion of Islam and the economic power of Asia. Such fears, tendencies and attitudes were generally not expressed by the mainstream of western European politicians, although the case of the success of Jorg Haider in Austria showed that individuals on the margin can take centre stage. Public opinion polls also indicated that support in western societies for closer relations with eastern Europe, for example in the framework of enlargements (NATO, the EU) was and is low.[1] Nevertheless, since the end of the 1980s the process of European integration has become more dynamic. The EC has been reshaped in the form of the EU and undergone fundamental change. Regional structures of close cooperation have also emerged in this period, for example the Visegrad Group and CEFTA, the Central European Initiative, the Council of Baltic Sea States, the Economic Cooperation of the Black Sea and the CIS.[2] Despite the different roots, nature, level of advance and perspectives of these structures, they reflect the need for common solutions to regional problems.

In comparing the two conflicting processes of disintegration and integration, a huge range of consequences of the former can be identified while the latter is still in its initial phase. Aside from this, it is unclear whether the process of integration is stable. This was illustrated by the ratification crisis following the adoption of the Treaty of European Union (TEU), problems arising from poverty, inequality and social exclusion in Europe, and the possible collapse of international markets as closer regional links bring greater protectionism in relation to the outside world. In this sense a process of integration which develops on a smaller scale can mean disintegration in a broader area.

The effects of the technological revolution also accompany these processes. This has enormous positive and negative influences both economically and politically and also a psychological impact. As with the earlier industrial revolution (the effects of which are still present), the information revolution has for many brought a violation of fundamental elements of their stable lifestyle. These changes require constant activity and readiness amongst individuals to adapt to new forms of employment. Not all are able to cope successfully with this. Consequently, some societies prefer not to adapt to a dynamically evolving reality but to defend old positions. This reaction is demonstrated in the growing number of electors who demonstrate their lack of confidence in their governments, who show their indifference to oppression or support parties which stress traditionalism, nationalism, defence of poorer groups and populism (e.g. supporters of Le Pen in France and Haider in Austria).

Europeans have to overcome many problems: the need to achieve a more dynamic development in order to allay fears of Eurosclerosis; the consequent need to make radical decisions in the sphere of integration; the need to address inequalities and strengthen the process of stabilisation; the need for further democratisation and more effective protection of human rights; and the need to compete effectively with other regions with high economic growth. These political, economic, social and ecological problems exist alongside fundamental questions concerning the perspective of cultural development, the values, ideas and myths of the new epoch, and the shape of interpersonal relations, individual and group identity in the age of the internet, new technologies, genetic engineering and globalisation. These questions emerge not only in the context of typical fears connected with the fin-de-siècle mentality but stem from mass-media influences, possible marginalisation of specific local cultures in the face of globalised homogenised popular culture, drugs and alcohol overwhelming the younger generation, and from the emphasis on extreme individualism in achieving successes, leading to social atomisation and possible alienation. However, these same revolutionary changes in technologies and lifestyles can also lead people to better and wider education and participation in culture, to diminishing inequalities, to material improvements and improved quality of life and could consequently lead to a more open society.

In the present circumstances, it is difficult to see beyond an 'à la carte' Europe in the twenty-first century based on a number of different scenarios and variants. It might be a multicultural Europe closer to universalist ideas, which also removes the borders between states. Although there are several possible political and institutional versions of this solution – further development of European integration, federalism, a Europe of the regions, a Europe of the states – the final outcome is likely to be some form of unification, though with due regard to differences. But Europe might also become a contemporary version of Babel's tower where all are talking more and more, maybe wisely, but where real communication does not exist. Alternatively, Europe could proceed in the direction of separatism, ethnic or religious conflicts, the multiplication of barriers against the poor, both within the continent and elsewhere. It might conversely be a Europe of economic integration and sustainable development, seeking solutions which permit a reduction of inequalities, capable of self-control and self-limitation in order to maintain balanced development, or a Europe of increasing, economic and structural crises, social tensions and individual tragedy.

Any solution must be intimately connected with acceptance of a broad notion of security. Here it is worth observing that a strong measure of consensus was reached towards the end of the twentieth century in the acceptance of the economic and social dimensions of security, viewed as basic for national and international security (Perczynski, 1990; Sperling and Kirchner, 1997). This was not the first time such a view had appeared. Often in the past economic developments led to security being treated in this way. But two world wars followed by the Cold War involved an emphasis on military power which pushed such views into the background.

Stronger and more complicated economic ties and the globalisation of problems in this field since the 1960s led to changes in the interpretation of the role which economic factors play in security. By the 1990s these trends had become more visible, with security and the power of states, regional stability, international order and a peaceful future depending more on economic solutions. This process has been accentuated by the increasing interdependence of economies, reflecting the obvious benefits to be derived from co-operation rather than autarky and the acceptance of integration processes which imply partial surrenders of sovereignty to transnational and international institutions and therefore a wider range of acceptance and respect for the norms of common law. And despite all the possible dangers mentioned above, the 1990s brought to the European landscape many positive signals for a more optimistic approach. After 1989 the decline of ideological hostility made possible the participation of the countries of CEE in integration processes. The absence of military threats in Europe, except perhaps in local conflicts, the aspiration of most post-communist states to membership of western structures and the awareness in western Europe of the necessity of supporting the processes of trans-formation, have promoted a growth of trust in international relations. We can assume that the more friendship replaces hostility, the greater the tendency will be for lasting co-operation because of the expectation of absolute gains deriving from it (Powell, 1991). In addition, the more widespread application of liberal democratic principles has led to a greater acceptance than in the past that the rights of individuals are to be con-sidered a condition of stable security.

EUROPE IN THE BROADER CONTEXT

It must be remembered that Europe cannot be viewed in isolation. It is only an element of a contemporary world dominated by an increasing interdependence in all dimensions. This is typified by a pace of change which requires exceptional flexibility and adaptation if events and pro-cesses are to be controlled, even to a limited degree. Theorists and politicians considering various prognoses predict an increasing number of dangers at the beginning of the new century. These are scenarios in which conflict dominates (Peters, 1997).

Popular among these scenarios are the theses involving 'world ethnic war', international organised crime plaguing states (the spread of narcotics, the weapons trade, corruption, perhaps the results of controversial genetic discoveries) and the increasing criminalisation of economies. Samuel Huntington has warned against war between civilisations. He predicts fundamental differences emerging in this respect following the end of ideological conflict (1996). Brzezinski considers that the world of politics suffers from a lack of ideas and values required to contribute to the building of a stable world order. Extreme consumerism and primitive egocentrism prevail in place of these values. His thinking emphasises the crucial role of the USA but he also stresses the situation of CEE as a key area for stabilisation (1993, 1998b). Similarly, Benjamin Barber views the main problem as the domination of cultural laziness and lack of values, reflected in the preference for popular culture and primitive, greedy consumerism as a dominant lifestyle (2000). Some stress the need for the 13 per cent of white people in the world to confront the expectations and demands of the non-white majority. Alvin Toffler expects increasing numbers of rebellions of poor people both within states and between them; but also rebellions of rich people fighting to keep separate from the poverty which exists in their own country or neighbourhoods. He also argues that the economy of 'the third wave' represents a tendency to put the nation-state in the shade because it develops across states' borders and serves the interests of transnational corporations (Toffler, 1998; Toffler and Toffler, 1996, 1997).

The prognosis of economists very often indicate the Pacific area as the winner in the economic competition of the twenty-first century. More optimistic views, for example those presented by Francis Fukuyama, which anticipate the final triumph of liberal and democratic values, are rare (1996). In the broader context, the question emerges as to which of the above versions of Europe can be competitive with the economic superpowers, so that Europe does not become a Skansen museum but rather remains a centre for ideas and culture and a partner for America and Asia, and which, thanks to its accumulation of painful experiences of ethnic conflicts, can become an important contributor to security and mediation.

THE ROLE OF INSTITUTIONS AND POWER IN THE CONTEMPORARY WORLD

These general conceptions must be reflected in legal formulations and in a network of institutions. Hence the need to examine the role of institutions in the development of a stable security system. In the literature, security is most often described dynamically as a situation in which the state creates such conditions as will eventually lead to its greater safety. This security can be attained through a number of elements, such as sovereignty, territorial integrity and freedom from any kind of foreign influences.

However, more specifically security can be viewed as a condition in which there is no threat of military invasion or non-military pressure or where there is a capacity to provide effective defence against such threats (Bobrow et al., 1997; Buzan, 1991; Clarke, 1993).

Observance of the law becomes increasingly important when relations between states become more complex and when various kinds of threats grow in number. This is the reason for the constant search for optimal models of international security – or rather an architecture of security. The term 'architecture' is used with good reason – it indicates the need for a multidimensional construction which can organise the whole international reality. This architecture has to be built on institutional foundations, or else it will be built on sinking sand.

One direction of current debate is the search for security based on regional solutions. This idea stems from the fact that universal organisations are unable as yet to create a system that can be both really effective in the preservation and ending of current conflicts and acceptable to the whole international community. In this situation a regional organisation could provide an intermediate stage between state and global interests. The advocates of this regional conception assume that political, economic and cultural ties are much stronger than merely territorial ones and therefore that these institutional links could reinforce peace and order in particular regions of the world. In such conditions it would be much easier for the members of universal organisations to negotiate global interests and to resolve problems that are common for the whole international community. The most obvious precondition for this is the motivation to eliminate divisions and conflicts between particular states in the region. Of course these motivations differ for various regions, but are often based on the existence of commonly acknowledged threats of a supreme state which has the power to integrate all the lesser states. However, only the unity of interests which derives from the equality of states and the voluntary character of membership in this regionalisation process, together with open access for all, can assure the stability of a regional order.

This is a prerequisite for the creation of a pan-European security community – an idea which took more practical shape just after 1989. In the literature the requirements are vividly set out. They include: compatibility of fundamental values, democratisation of the member states, communication and mobility, economic growth, the existence of an organised core-area of this community, the expectation of mutual benefits, political efficacy, constructive management of ethnic and nationalist conflicts, successful arms control and the existence of common dangers or common concerns in relation to the rest of the world (Reychler, 1992).

Europeans look for a guarantee of political and military security mainly from the long-established organisations – NATO, OSCE and WEU – but not without such modifications as an increase in the privileges, military power and territorial range of these organisations. At the global level, opportunities also arise from the United Nations. The EU and regional forms of integration have become an ideal in the fields of economic and ecological security to which most of the post-communist countries aspire. Different security options which originate from these possibilities could be competitive as well as complementary. Ole Waever presents a compact system in the shape of an isosceles triangle, whose three sides are NATO, the EU and the OSCE,[3] responsible respectively for military questions, the politico-economic order, and drawing up rules and supervising their observance. Other institutions would exist among them: WEU between NATO and the EU; PfP, the NATO–Russia agreement and the North Atlantic Co-operation Council between NATO and OSCE; the Stability Pact in Europe and the EBRD between the EU and OSCE (Waever, 1994).[4] It is also possible to include here the Council of Europe. However in the political life of the 1990s there prevailed a rather competitive vision of the role of these organisations: an Atlantic model (NATO) was set against a Pan-European one (OSCE), while a European model with WEU, ESDI and the CFSP of the EU was interpreted as diminishing the role of NATO (Hyde-Price, 1991).[5] On the one hand it was attractive for Europeans to keep close links with the USA. But on the other hand, the perception of the EU as an economic giant but a political dwarf (as Josef Strauss once referred to West Germany) is not flattering for Europeans. The role of the USA in European structures is therefore widely discussed by politicians with variable responses. However, most Americans, despite some misgivings, want to retain their influence in Europe – as Henry Kissinger or Zbigniew Brzezinski express clearly – while within Europe, the opposite view appears mainly among French politicians (Brzezinski, 1998c; Juppe, 1998; Kissinger, 1997). President Clinton's administration undoubtedly led the USA closer to Europe. Notwithstanding some apprehensions about George W. Bush's understanding of international politics, he has also emphasised his continuing commitment to Europe. However, Europeans should take into account that the Bush administration appears more committed to the National Missile Defence system, and might also be more impatient with Europeans over burden sharing in European defence and security costs. There may also be a tougher stance on CFSP and the Rapid Reaction Force and less American tolerance over any temptation by the Europeans to flirt with Russia over missile defence. However, a nationalist or unilateralist presidency will not have very much room to manoeuvre given the composition of both houses of Congress, where the Democrats will play an important role.

The preservation of international peace and security is closely connected with the methods and measures leading to it. Consequently, questions concerning the right to use violence in resolving disagreements and conflicts must be considered. In the past sheer military force was an attribute of authority. The right to wage war could, depending on the particular historical period, be regulated by conditions and rules in many ways. However, the right to use military force in certain circumstances was never contested, the only exception to this being in the works of moralists.

The twentieth century, beginning with the First World War, brought great changes to international law. The use of force was rejected as an appropriate method of realising interests or resolving conflicts. In the practice of international relations the problem of using force remains real and controversial. There are many reasons for this but the principal one is the continuing violation of commonly accepted rules. Other issues connected with the difficulty of defining the notion of force in modern times are also evident: the complex forms of its use; its importance and effectiveness in the matter of national and regional security; and the right of the international community to invoke force in the case of emergencies – for example in the prevention of conflicts.

In the past the notion of power was mainly or even exclusively connected with the military field. Today the belief in the supreme position of military power remains strong. This is mainly based on the fact that our world still experiences many wars and states invest huge sums of money to enlarge or improve their armies. So the fact that many states even now resort to violence while dealing with external or internal threats is not surprising. Improvements in armaments continue to be major governmental priorities and consume enormous quantities of financial, scientific and technical resources, while nuclear and chemical weaponry act as determinants of state power. States still look for guarantees for their security in military alliances and until the 1990s the balance of power was the main safeguard of global stability. The importance of military factors is also emphasised by the fact that détente was connected with debates and decisions about disarmament. In addition, the issue of the non-proliferation of nuclear arms remains one of the key problems in the field of security.

Despite this continuing significance of military force, it nonetheless appears that its role in the modern world is decreasing and also that it is useless in building stable security on a global and state level. There are numerous arguments to suggest that the military factor can reduce conflict but cannot resolve it: the use or threat of force brings a great deal of tension and strife in international relations; the growth of armaments makes the world less stable and also has a negative influence on the economy of even the wealthiest countries. The creation and development of nuclear force could lead to genocide and has proven to be unusable on the battlefield.

The fact that legal limitations are not enough to stop the process of nuclear proliferation was evident in the last years of the twentieth century. Despite the agreement in 1995 by 178 states to prolong the non-proliferation Treaty of 1968 unconditionally and without limited duration, India and Pakistan decided in 1998 to develop their arsenal. In addition, the question remains as to whether countries like both Koreas, Libya, Iraq, Iran, Israel and South Africa are ready definitely to give up production of such weapons. A change in this situation could be positively accelerated by the introduction of mechanisms that would ensure that the decisions of international organisations which safeguard the peace, such as the UN, are respected and obeyed by all. The suggestion that such effective mechanisms could be met at the global level is met with understandable scepticism. First, the political philosophy of many states stems from realist principles, which preclude the value and sense of strengthening the role of international institutions at the expense of state autonomy. Secondly, there appear to be too many obstacles to the establishment of an effective UN armed intervention force for it to be a realistic possibility.[6] So it seems that effective global mechanisms to enforce adherence to international institutions, containing (like national legal systems) not only norms but also sanctions, can only be built from 'the bottom' up. The elimination of force would be the natural consequence of several developments: the liquidation of the origins of tension and conflicts; a constant decrease in the level of arms, the creation of such a world order as could guarantee multidimensional security for all members of international society.

Promoting wider acceptance of the view that the use of force is both immoral and inefficient could play a big role here. Despite the lengthy nature of such a process and its dubious potential from the realist political point of view some changes have begun to appear: military doctrines stress more generally than ever before their defensive character and states have also tried to exclude from school courses any content that might contradict the rules of coexistence. This latter stems from declarations of the UN, and UNESCO (it was first a recommendation of the XVIII conference of this organisation in 1974), and from European law created by the Council of Europe, implemented by the EU members, and other democratic countries.[7] Even where governments resort to actions which contain some degree of violence, they simultaneously try to achieve some kind of international consent. This applies to superpowers as well.

The attempts indicated earlier to find effective ways to prevent conflicts and to ensure peace also bring new challenges. The creation of international forces which could solve conflicts through military intervention (working under the UN, or existing alliances or powers) is one of them. On the one hand, the imposition of peace by external powers in unstable regions could aid the well-being of the whole international community, protect civilians from heavy casualties or extermination, and/or force warring parties to solve their conflicts in a peaceful way. On the other hand, such methods, regardless of intention, stand contrary to the norms of international law and bring new problems, for example, interference in the sovereignty of particular states, and the possibility that the 'pacifiers' will abuse their privileges. This suggests the necessity of creating an effective system of international control concerning the use of such force. In the light of recent experiences, this will not be too easy.

In considering the importance of the use of force in the modern world, one must also consider other forms of power. States and alliances can also utilise economic, technological or cultural power as well. These factors determine the real role of the state in international relations more often than previously, contributing to the power status of states and allowing them to exert a large influence over weaker partners. Of course states which combine all these attributes of power are in a much stronger position but the predominance of non-military factors is clearly visible in the modern world. Possession of large military forces is not a guarantee of full security for a state and is not enough on its own to determine the security situation in a region or the whole world. Possession of such forces can indeed bring instability, for example, as in some countries in Africa and Asia. On the other hand, economic and technological might is enough for Japan (which has limited military power) to be one of most important states in the world. Similarly, Germany built its position after the Second World War without military force.

This constantly broadening meaning of the notion of power causes many problems. The use of non-military power could support the peaceful development of co-operation and also serve the interests of weaker states. Ties created in this way can have a durable character and facilitate stability. However, economic, cultural or political pressure can also mean submission to a stronger state or group of states and therefore bring negative results (though not as visible as those resulting from war). Additionally this form of aggression is difficult to define in international norms and hard to combat.

It is worth remembering the new elements caused by the technological revolution and now built into the notion of power. One of the most valuable factors at states' disposal, is the knowledge which allows us to create new technologies, convert data, fully and quickly access information and control its transmission. It is not unlikely that in the coming century this factor will decide who, at the global level, will be the rulers and who the ruled. On the other hand this kind of ownership is extremely difficult to keep to oneself eternally. In addition to these developments, achievements in the military field will also change the use of force itself. The wide utilisation of new technologies which supposedly bring new power could also paradoxically bring weakness in highly developed states which could be rendered defenceless if an enemy paralysed or dominated their electronic systems.

The emergence of analyses concerning not only defence against existing and potential threats but also the prevention of emerging threats is a consequence of accepting a broad interpretation of security. Such 'prevention' leads to a consideration of the positive conditions for the development of groups and individuals, and the protection of their rights. So security is both a goal and a medium. Against this background it seems that a prerequisite for the creation of an effective European security structure is the development of institutional solutions containing military, political and economic dimensions. Such solutions could most effectively influence the stable development of CEE and regulate relations between the highly developed countries – not as a forum of discussion but as a force which can implement the preferences of states (Buzan et al., 1993: 69). The stability and effectiveness of institutions are also affected by their geographical range and criteria of membership; decisions regarding the acceptance or non-acceptance of new candidates; their clarity of competence; their simultaneous ability to co-ordinate activities which concern intersecting fields; and the capacity of these institutions to project an image of the whole order. Finally, they depend on the nature, form and degree of support for their creation or development.

PERCEPTIONS AND NORMS OF SECURITY

The human factor in security is no less important. An effective European system can be created only as a result of consensus among all (or almost all) states. It cannot work efficiently unless the rules and conditions of this system are accepted by all, or at least the majority, of societies. A sense of security – even if it is partly irrational – is pivotal. Whether dangers really exist or not is not always relevant to these perceptions. Though crucial, the existence of such dangers is secondary to how people perceive particular situations.

It is appropriate to relate this discussion to a real example – the problem of Kosovo – which shows the scale of difficulty in building European security, and simultaneously raises a fundamental question about security developments in the near future. The beginning of the 1990s saw the eruption of conflict in the Balkans. At this time the weakness of all the European structures, and the clashes of interests among the allied states were already evident. The Dayton agreement only outwardly solved this problem. The goal of the agreement – the integration of the society of Bosnia within a federal framework – met with resistance and a settlement based on the presence of military forces from abroad. NATO's decision to bomb Serbia in defence of the rights of the Albanian population of Kosovo is still highly controversial. The Kosovo conflict highlighted almost all the above-mentioned dilemmas: What is more crucial in international relations – the integrity and sovereignty of states or the right of self-determination of nations? What measures can be used by international society in defence of people who are the victims of domestic war? Is it right to break treaties and international law for the sake of humanitarian ideas? Is the exercise of force, against the opinion of some European states, including Russia, and against the opinion of part (sometimes a majority) of their own societies, pertinent from the perspective of longer-term processes of peace and the construction of a stable security system? Are double standards of morality a good foundation for a European security system? For example, the Kurds have been the victims of terror in Turkey for years, while we could also add the question of Cyprus or non-European conflicts with a similar background (such as the Tamils in Sri Lanka). Finally a fundamental question is raised – whether the use of military force, especially in the specific form of bombing, brought a real opportunity for peace in the Balkans region?

Answering these questions provides an opportunity to draw up a balance of the costs and gains of the NATO action. A positive element, first and foremost, was the fact that the international community reacted for the first time against a brutal violation of human rights, and that a network of solidarity and humanitarian aid for the victims of the conflict could be observed throughout Europe. The action could perhaps be viewed as the first step towards a permanent and universal rejection of ethnic cleansing, providing a warning to dictators that their impunity is limited. Perhaps we were witnessing the emergence of an effective power which could safeguard security in the broader sense. The action may have signalled a new NATO doctrine following the Washington summit of April 1999 based on a preparedness to act 'out of area'. These circumstances undoubtedly provoked a degree of activity amongst the EU member states which began to consider fundamental changes in security issues, leading to a reassessment of the CFSP and the decision at the end of 1999 to construct a common European defence force. However, the effectiveness of this and its implications for the controversial issue of the US–EU relationship remain unclear.

Among the negative consequences of the NATO action were that decisions were taken in violation of international law, that it led to a complete loss of face on the part of the UN, and that the NATO alliance placed itself in an ambiguous position. The action also led to an upsurge in support for anti-western, anti-NATO groups in Russia, Belarus, Ukraine and the Balkans and reignited a long-running argument concerning the underlying aggressiveness of NATO – an aggressiveness which might also be used against other countries with internal conflicts. These inevitable problems could, however, prove to be acceptable costs if the attack could be shown to have brought positive benefits, such as protecting Albanians and contributing to peace in the region. But there are serious doubts about this. If the NATO leaders had calculated that a few air raids would force Milosevic to talks, this showed total ignorance of eastern European matters as a whole, and the Balkans region in particular. For ordinary people from this area it was clear that in such matters one fights to the end, and political differences can even disappear in the face of an attack on one's country; even more so in the context of Kosovo as it was not a clear-cut issue. Not only could the bombing not stop the ethnic cleansing, it even provided an opportunity and pretext to do it with impunity and on a massive scale. Hence the enormous problem of the refugees was created. NATO leaders were not prepared to risk military casualties on their own side 'for Kosovo' and therefore embarked on only a partial action. Once the conflict was over, it appeared that hatred divided Balkan societies even more than before, and that though the expelled people returned, they lived under a military shield. Furthermore, a series of violent and bloody actions against Serbian inhabitants ensued. On the other hand, the events of autumn 2000, when a large majority of Serbs voted against Milosevic in the presidential election, and the defence of this result in mass-protests, also stemmed from the international isolation of Serbia caused by

Milosevic's policies. Without this pressure Vojislav Kosztunica would not have had a chance to mobilise so many supporters. But, scenarios for the future unfortunately seem to be highly unclear. The new president emphasised his readiness for co-operation with European countries but also for keeping the integrity of his state, and seemed far from accepting any kind of intervention in the internal policy of Yugoslavia. And other possible areas of conflicts have emerged: local elections in Kosovo in 2000 brought success for the moderate politician, Ibrahim Rugova but also showed the clear desire of Kosovans for their independence. The same ideas of separatism emerged in Montenegro which, in a less radical form, could lead to a loose confederation with Serbia. Yet the 'international community' did not appear to have clear ideas on the future of the Balkan conflict. In October 2000, a report of an independent commission led by Swedish Prime Minister Goran Persson, was produced on behalf of the UN. This suggested 'conditional independence' for Kosovo but clearly this opinion was not accepted widely. A few days later the mass media indicated that the USA was ready to support a free Kosovo but the reaction of its allies in NATO was very cold. Europeans feared that the USA might leave them with continuing problems in the Balkans, after creating a new order around Serbia. The EU countries reacted positively to the results of the election in Yugoslavia, ending economic sanctions, and even promising, in the case of the French president, Jacques Chirac, a fast track to EU membership. This aroused fears among Albanians and strengthened radical groups in this society.

CONCLUSION

The example of Kosovo provides a rather clear direction for the future: a European security system cannot mean only that the international community will charge NATO or European defence forces with a task of military action. An opportunity existed for economic solutions to the Balkans problems: for example a new Marshall plan for the Balkans where really large sums could be linked to restrictive conditions, for example demands for multidimensional co-operation. Had a leader of Yugoslavia or another country rejected participation in it, echoing the decision of the Soviet Union in the aftermath of the Second World War, this would have provoked strong opposition, both domestically and in the surrounding countries that hoped to derive benefits from such a development. The expense of providing such aid would in the long-term perspective be profitable (as Marshall Aid was for USA), and would offer the best chance for stabilising the region. On the one side, the victims of air raids, expulsion and a ruined country would benefit, while on the other, the enormous costs of battle borne by NATO would not be lost irreversibly (although NATO may have already benefited from the profits of weapons production and trade, and through the strategic points it has scored vis-à-vis Russia). It seems that EU countries are now definitely closer to searching for solutions in the economic area rather than the military sphere.

Economic growth and stable development are not the only possible response to the question of European security but they are at least a necessary substructure without which one cannot imagine peaceful relationships. Europe has already built quite a strong and well-rooted system of democracy and shows a broad consensus in acceptance of human rights. Various institutions of multidimensional cooperation also exist and the necessity of maintaining dialogue between states is not questioned. Such a background of regimes, institutions and values, and a relatively high level of economic development leads to the hope that the optimistic scenario for Europe is also realistic.

The above argument has emphasised the idea of a network of organisations, and states which can be completed by ad hoc initiatives. This seems the most realistic and fruitful path towards stabilising Europe and preparing it to deal with global processes. However, it is also a stage towards an eventual reduction in the number of institutions to the one or two most effective ones. National interests are now becoming increasingly convergent in the whole region, and this tendency permits states (from a realistic, not only a liberal perspective) to accept close regional cooperation, and an institutional framework: provided that they can shift from seeing their relations as a zero sum game.

In summary, there are small paths that can take us towards European security. These are numerous and lead across a variety of fields – the economy, democratisation, human rights, the political stabilisation of states, sustainable development, the protection of the environment and cultural freedom. They run across the areas of law, institutions and military structures but also of social activity and the perceptions of groups and individuals, and do not exclude people from any European country. A stable security system can only be built if all these elements are taken into consideration. However, putting in place a realistic timeframe for the emergence of such an effective European security system is difficult and may take a decade or more. All prognosis in the field of social sciences is a hazardous activity. This is evident to those who tried to build scenarios about the 1980s and 1990s when communism and the system based on it, including the Soviet Union, suddenly collapsed, when Germany unified so quickly, and all these developments together created a new Europe. On the other hand, the diversity of challenges in our epoch obliges us to have scenarios for every eventuality, however unlikely.

NOTES

1   According to the Eurobarometer (1999: 57–8) welcoming new member states is seen as a priority by 28 per cent and as not a priority by 59 per cent of those

polled within the EU. Among existing EU member states, support for the accession of new members does not exceed 50 per cent in respect of any of the central and eastern European applicants. And 79 per cent see (quite naturally though not realistically) an absence of cost for the existing member states as an important criterion for supporting enlargement.

2   The Visegrad Group was created by Czechoslovakia, Hungary and Poland in February 1991 as a forum for consultation. Since the split of Czechoslovakia it has had four members. CEFTA – the Central European Free Trade Agreement – was signed following an initiative by the Visegrad Group in December 1992, and embraced other countries – Slovenia, Romania and Bulgaria. The Central European Initiative (CEI) developed from November 1989, first as Quadragonale (Austria, Italy, Yugoslavia and Hungary), then as Pentagonale (Czechoslovakia 1990), then Hexagonale (Poland 1991), and at last in its present form, embracing in addition to the above states: Albania, Belarus, Bulgaria, Romania, Ukraine and Moldova. The Council of Baltic Sea States (CBSS) was created in March 1992 in Copenhagen, and all countries of this region became CBSS members – Denmark, Estonia, Finland, Germany, Iceland, Latvia, Lithuania, Norway, Poland, Russia, Sweden, and additionally the European Commission. The Economic Cooperation of the Black Sea was established in June 1992 by Albania, Armenia, Azerbaijan, Bulgaria, Georgia, Greece, Moldova, Romania, Russia, Turkey and Ukraine. The Commonwealth of Independent States (CIS) emerged in December 1991 from an initiative of Russia, Ukraine and Belarus and contains all former republics of the Soviet Union apart from the three Baltic states.

3   The Organisation of Security and Co-operation in Europe (OSCE) is a new form of the CSCE (the irregular west–east conference which began in 1975), existing from 1 January 1995. It is a regional organisation including all European states, as well as the USA and Canada, and non-European former republics of the Soviet Union, totalling 55 members. According to Russia the OSCE could be the main European security organisation replacing NATO in this role. As others have rejected this idea, the OSCE has been given the residual roles of monitoring conflicts and ethnic problems, mediation, and acting as a forum of political debate and initiatives, particularly connected with human rights, and democracy (the so-called 'human dimension') and consultations in the politico-military field to foster mutual trust.

4   The North Atlantic Co-operation Council (NACC) was established in December 1991 at a meeting of NATO members and former socialist countries. Following the collapse and split of the Soviet Union and Yugoslavia it comprised 44 members. In May 1997 it became the Euro-Atlantic Partnership Council (EAPC). Its first aim was to build a forum of consultation and later a network of cooperation between former enemies in the area of multidimensional security. It was also a first step to the Partnership for Peace (PfP). This latter was created as a programme of co-operation between NATO and eastern European countries in the military sphere in anticipation of NATO enlargement on the part of former socialist countries. The decision was taken in 1994 when NATO formulated invitations to these states together with documents containing conditions of partnership. These were signed by all countries as individual programmes of co-operation. The NATO–Russia agreement was signed in May 1997 as a condition and a result of the decision on enlarging NATO to the east. This special relationship in the area of security was demanded by Russia, given that it had, in principle, objected to Czech, Hungarian and Polish membership of NATO. According to this agreement, Russia can expect to be consulted in the actions and policy of NATO, and has received the promise that nuclear weapons will not be positioned at its western borders. The Stability Pact in Europe was an idea put forward by the then French Prime Minister

Edouard Balladur and accepted by the EU in June 1993. A preparatory conference was called in May 1994 in Paris where 57 participating states declared their readiness for negotiations on ethnic and border questions. The Stability Pact was signed within the framework of the OSCE by the Conference of Foreign Ministers in Paris, in March 1995. The European Bank for Reconstruction and Development (EBRD) was established in 1990 by 51 countries (51 per cent of shares belonged to the EU members, and the European Investment Bank (EIB). The EBRD provides credit to former socialist states for development.

5   The 1994 Declaration of NATO expressed support for the construction of a European Security and Defence Identity (ESDI). An agreement of June 1996 provided for the possible creation of the Combined Joint-Task Forces (CJTF). The Amsterdam Treaty (Article 17:2) indicated humanitarian aid, peacekeeping and peacemaking as elements of EU security policy, and also strengthening the role of the WEU as an element of the EU defence structure in the realisation of the Petersberg missions. The European Council in Cologne (June 1999) designated Javier Solana to head the CFSP, emphasising in the declaration the necessity of the EU having autonomy in managing conflicts. In Helsinki (December 1999) the European Council took the decision to create the Rapid Reaction Force in three years. The future of the Common Foreign, Security and Defence Policy (as the CFSP is more often being described) is still dependent on discussions within the EU on its precise relationship to NATO (though the Nice summit of December 2000 confirmed the creation of a Rapid Reaction Force compatible with the primacy of NATO in European security) but also on the US position in the negotiations between the EU and NATO.

6   Problems include: When would decisions about using this force be legal? Who is ready to cover the costs of such actions? Which principles of international law should be put at the top of the list as a priority during such actions?

7   The rule of building education on the principle of international co-operation and elimination of national hatred is also implemented by neighbouring states with a history of conflicts, where special commissions have developed the contents of schoolbooks, for example, in Germany and Poland.

REFERENCES

Barber, B.R. (2000) *Dzihad kontra MC Swiat* (originally published as: *Jihad contra MC World*), Warsaw: Muza.

Bobrow, D.B., Halizak, E. and Zieba, R. (eds) (1997) *Bezpieczenstwo narodowe i miedzynarodowe u schylku XX wieku.* Warsaw: Fundacja Studiow Miedzynarodowych.

Booth, K. (ed.) (1991) *New Thinking About Strategy and International Security.* London: HarperCollins.

Brzezinski, Z. (1993) *Bezlad, Polityka swiatowa u progu XXI w* (originally published as: *Out of Control: Global Turmoil on the Eve of the Twenty-First Century*), Warsaw: Editions Spotkania.

Brzezinski, Z. (1998a) 'Karty ma Ameryka', *Gazeta Wyborcza*, 28 February.

Brzezinski, Z. (1998b) *Wielka szachownica – Glowne cele polityki amerykanskiej* (originally published as: *The Grand Chessboard – American Primacy and its Geostrategic Imperatives*). Warsaw: Barlesbman Media.

Brzezinski, Z. (1998c) 'Klopoty dobrego hegemona', *Gazeta Wyborcza*, 4–5 July.

Buzan, B. (1991) *Peoples, States and Fear: An Agenda for International Security Studies in the Post Cold War Era.* New York: Harvester Wheatsheaf.

Buzan, B., Jones, C. and Little, R. (1993) *The Logic of Anarchy: Neorealism to Structural Realism*. New York: Columbia University Press.

Clarke, M. (ed.) (1993) *New Perspective on Security*. London: Brassey's for The Centre for Defence Studies, University of London.

Eurobarometer (1999) *Public Opinion in the European Union*, Report No. 52. Brussels: European Commission.

Fukuyama, F. (1996) *Koniec historii* (originally published as: *The End of History and the Last Man*). Poznan: Zysk i Spolka.

Huntington, S. (1996) *The Clash of Civilizations and the Remaking of World Order*. New York: Simon & Schuster.

Hyde-Price, A. (1991) *European Security beyond the Cold War: Four Scenarios for the Year 2010*. London: Sage Publications.

Juppe, A. (1998) 'Wasal czy partner?' (Interview with A. Michnik), *Gazeta Wyborcza*, 12–13 December.

Kissinger, H. (1997) 'Radzcie sobie sami', *Polityka*, 19 July.

Perczynski, M. (1990) *Globalne uwarunkowania bezpieczenstwa ekonomicznego*, Warsaw: Polski Instytut spraw Miedzynarodowych.

Peters, R. (1997) 'The Perspective From 2021', *A Quarter Century's National Defense, Strategic Review*, 25 (2; Spring): 24–47.

Powell, R. (1991) 'Absolute and Relative Gains in International Relations Theory', *American Political Science Review*, 85 (4): 1303–20.

Reychler, L. (1992) 'A Pan-European Security Community: Utopia or Realistic Perspective?', in L. Rychler (ed.) *Vredesonderzoek en Internationale Conflictbeheersing*. Leueven: Centrum voor Vredesonderzoek.

Sperling, J. and Kirchner, E. (1997) *Recasting the European Order: Security Architectures and Economic Cooperation*. Manchester: Manchester University Press.

Toffler, A. (1998) 'Fala za fala' (Interview by Jakowski), *Gazeta Wyborcza*, 24–27 December.

Toffler, A. and Toffler, H. (1996) *Budowa nowej cywilizacji. Polityka trzeciej fali* (originally published as: *The Third Wave*). Poznan: Zysk i Spolka.

Toffler, A. and Toffler, H. (1997) *Wojna i antywojna, jak przetrwac na progu XXI w* (originally published as: *War and Anti-war: How to Survive at the Beginning of the 21st Century*). Warsaw: Muza.

Waever, O. (1994) *The European Security Triangle*, Working Papers No. 8. Copenhagen: Centre for Peace and Conflict Research.

4 The Future of Small States in the EU

Esko Antola

Small states do not constitute a coherent group of members in the European Union. Size as such is not the decisive factor in the member states' coalitions in decision-making situations. Other cleavages like the north–south divide, intergovernmental–federal split or political divisions between the ruling governments are of much greater importance. A divide between Euro-sceptical governments and more pro-integrationist governments is also more prominent than the one between large and small members.

Yet the tension between small and large member states has emerged as one of the main issues on the agenda of last three intergovernmental conferences. The Maastricht process revealed the issue. The enlargement of 1995 and the Amsterdam process further emphasised its relevance. The European Council meeting in Nice, and negotiations prior to it, finally brought the tension into the limelight as a major topic. The agenda of Nice, consisting of so-called 'leftovers' of the Amsterdam negotiations, appeared technical in nature, containing the reform of the weighting of votes and the composition and size of the Commission. These areas of reforms related directly to the relative size of the Member States. The 'leftover' question actually dated back to the Ioannina Compromise of 1994 and to the accession of Austria, Finland and Sweden. The compromise was achieved over the claims of Spain and the United Kingdom concerning the blocking minority threshold. The roots of the 'problem' are in the evolution of EU membership, which has disproportionately increased the number of small states.

Paradoxically, the large member states, not the small states, brought the tension to the agenda of the IGC 2000. Smaller member states, on the contrary, have avoided raising these institutional questions, anticipating that this might provoke the bigger member states. The tension surfaced in the unofficial European Council meeting in Biarritz in October 2000. News reports and statements by the negotiators highlighted the disagreements (*Agence Europe*, 14 October 2000). Because of the style of management of the Council by the French Presidency, the dispute gradually developed into the major issue in the European Council meeting in Nice in December 2000.

The issue is not merely the balance of powers in terms of voting strength. It goes beyond matters of arithmetic and touches the fundamental principles of the union and its institutions and indeed, the future shape of the EU. The initial power balance between the small and large members has remained unchanged although the number of small states has increased. Future enlargements will affect the initial balance even further and constitute a major controversy in the institutional restructuring of the union. The anticipation of the future enlargement may have provided the spark for its emergence but it is rooted in the early history of European integration.

The relationship between the small and large member states in the institutional design of the EU was set in the initial establishment of the European Community. The founding treaties of the Union linked territorial representation to proportional representation based on population. This is reflected in national quotas of representatives in the European Parliament and in the weighting of votes in the Council. Quotas are also applied in the composition of the Commission and advisory bodies, the Committee of the Regions and the Economic and Social Committee.

The existing system is increasingly seen by larger member states as containing an over-representation of small member states. This 'over-representation' was brought to the agenda of Maastricht negotiations by large member states. The Benelux countries then defended the prevailing arrangement. In their joint memorandum to the Lisbon Council meeting in June 1992 the Benelux group argued that the larger countries should accept 'some over-representation of smaller member states' (quoted in Pijpers and Vanhoonacker, 1997: 139). In the Amsterdam negotiations this was an element in a 'triangle' of sensitive institutional issues together with the extension of qualified majority voting and the composition of the Commission (McDonagh, 1999: 156). Larger member states voiced their views that the existing voting weights were not in balance but favoured smaller member states. These issues were not solved in the Amsterdam negotiations and constituted the core of the Amsterdam 'leftovers' for Nice.

The weight of small states in the EU decision-making process rests on their great number. Out of fifteen member states ten are usually classified as small member states. Their number could double as a consequence of future enlargement. The number of small states is a significant factor, particularly in decisions requiring unanimity. All member states, large and small, have an equal opportunity to use their right of veto. Thus the small states have an opportunity to prevent large states from using the EU for pursuing their national interest or interests common only to the large states. Equal treatment and equal rights are fundamental principles, which culminate in representation, even if such representation is relative. Representation in institutions and decision-making is a combination of the principles of territorial representation and the relative size of populations.

The power structure of the EU today has a strong historical background. When the European Coal and Steel Community was instituted, the small states (that is, Benelux) were allowed over-representation in voting in order to balance the power of larger member states. The controversy of over-representation did not arise until the EU enlarged to include new small member states whose integrationist tradition differs from that of the original founder states. The number of small states has increased, but corresponding changes in the rules concerning the institutions have not been introduced.

SMALL STATES IN INTERNATIONAL RELATIONS

The question of small states in European politics goes far beyond the context of EU decision-making. In the study of international relations the size of a state has been approached from the structural and resource perspectives. The structural approach emphasises the international system as a hierarchical entity. Hierarchy has been regarded as a central factor in the anarchistic international system of sovereign states. Hierarchy, that is classifying states according to their size in different levels, is a principle that creates order (Clark, 1989: 197–8).

The structure of hierarchy is not predestined – in reality states change their status in the course of time. Even the greatest of powers is able to enjoy that status only as long as the small powers give it recognition (Wight, 1978: 50). Prestige, rather than power, is an essential element of hierarchy. From a resource perspective the difference between large and small states can be measured by analysing the distribution of resources and wealth. States have a different critical mass as measured in physical terms. States do not only differ by their military power and economic capacity but also by their ability to utilise their existing resources.

Small states differ from large ones in that their fewer resources limit the scope and intensity of their activities in foreign policy. On the other hand, they enjoy the privilege of being able to focus on foreign policy actions that reflect their national needs since their aspirations are not regarded as threatening from the point of view of the power-holders of the inter-national system. Large states place more emphasis on the advancement of general interests while, due to their lesser resources, small states have narrower and more limited interests.

As actors in international relations small states do not fundamentally differ from the great powers. Small nations, like the bigger powers, pursue their own national interests and articulate their national goals inde-pendently from other states, small or large. Leaders of small states arrive at their decisions in a similar way to stronger states. National interests are essential to both, as are the patterns of conduct and ways of doing business. According to Knudsen, small states are countries which 'have to deal with the potential threat of being swallowed up or integrated into an adjunct and significantly more powerful neighbour' (Knudsen, 1997:

3–10). This reflects the idea that smallness is independent of the size of the country as such but depends on the relationship with other countries.

Smallness is associated with vulnerability. Vulnerability is not just a concept of external threat in a world of powers but is associated with economic vulnerability. Small states often prefer open economic relations and thus make themselves vulnerable to international pressures and competition (Commonwealth Secretariat, 1999). Changes and pressures in the international atmosphere tend to be more important for the small than for the large states, because the small states have less capacity to influence their surroundings (Elman, 1995: 176). For small states success in foreign policy is essential and they must therefore have the ability to focus on relevant issues.

Smallness is a comparative rather than an absolute idea (Hanf and Soetendorp, 1998: 4). It is difficult to draw a line to indicate where smallness begins or ends. It is particularly difficult to distinguish precisely between a small power and a middle power. This is also a relevant question in the EU. In fact the category of small states covers a group of ten countries which, in population terms, range from The Netherlands (population 15 million) to Luxembourg (population 350,000). They include middle powers with a colonial history (Belgium and Denmark) and some of them can be regarded as former great powers (Austria, The Netherlands, Portugal and Sweden). Others (Finland and Ireland) have gained their national independence during the twentieth century. The category of small member states thus contains countries with a variety of different historical backgrounds.

Small member states of the EU also differ in many ways from small states globally. Small states are generally seen not only as weak states in the world hierarchy of power, but also as having weak state apparatuses and weak institutions. But as Olav Knudsen, points out: 'West European small states represent ideal cases or archetypes of small states, highly developed economically, strong administratively, legitimate wielders of power within their borders, weak only in their lack of military power' (1997: xvi).

In post-Cold War Europe, globalism has made the distinction between small and large states less relevant. All European countries are becoming small since their influence in world affairs is decreasing and autonomy diminishing, as a result of the advance of globalism. Countries are increasingly dependent on each other as well as on external influences. Small countries may no longer be described as the poorer and exploited, since the wealth of the nation no longer relies so much on natural resources as on creative capacities. The liberalisation of international trade has also been extremely beneficial to small states in spite of the increasing risks associated with vulnerability. Despite these changes, in order to survive and even gain from global political and economic development, small states are still forced to adapt and adjust (Svetlicic, 1997: 4–5, 20).

The study of the position and role of small states has gradually moved from a perspective of pure power–political configuration towards a perspective of influence. The shift is associated with profound changes in the structure of the international system. The first period of change was seen in the 1960s when the rapid increase of the number of small states as a result of decolonisation made them a recognisable force in world politics. Their impact was recognised in particular in global issues and in the framework of the United Nations.

Another, and even more profound, change in the position of small states took place in the 1990s as a consequence of the collapse of the postwar power structure. The number of small states in Europe increased and existing sovereign states changed their political orientation dramatically. The fall of the Cold War power–political configuration and the growth in the importance of international institutions have shifted the perspectives and roles of small states in many ways.

SMALL STATES AS A BLOC: A MISTAKEN ASSUMPTION?

The very nature of decision-making in the EU does not encourage the establishment of permanent coalitions. Stable or frequent coalitions are possible only in a few issues like agriculture, social policy, foreign commercial policy, structural policy and the Community budget. But even in these sectors the coalitions are not based on the size-factor. They are always composed of both small and larger member states (Zbinden, 1998: 226).

Every country has been forced to change its policies following accession in the multi-level and multiple arenas of the EU and studies of small states in the EU show no substantial differences in adaptation (governmental, political and strategic). After joining (with the exception of Belgium) no major institutional or organisational changes were made at central government level. Adaptation has occurred on an ad hoc and piecemeal basis.

Small states have made arrangements with other member states to interact at the European level, and all have adopted some system of co-ordination to structure their national input into European decision-making (Hanf and Soetendorp, 1998: 188). Further, in order for the small states in Europe to act effectively, they need to develop coherent, justified national positions and to be able to present these views in negotiations. Most of the countries have formed successful co-operation procedures to enforce their interests, even though there have been differences between them in terms of being proactive or reactive. In this sense the small member states have some advantages in comparison with large political units. Smallness provides the advantage of effective national policy co-ordination. This helps small member states to concentrate their efforts on the issues that are of real relevance to them.

Hanf and Soetendorp suggest that despite the difficulties and limits the smaller member states encounter in influencing decision-making in the EU, they can still gain from membership. Within the EU they can exert more influence and achieve more than they would outside it (Hanf and Soetendorp, 1998: 193). Traditional coalitions, such as that between the Benelux countries, have maintained much of their appeal. Common experiences, traditions and views enable them to behave as a cohesive group. Although the Benelux countries do not constitute a stable bloc in day-to-day policy-making, they are nevertheless able to produce common statements and views when necessary. For example, they have produced common policy documents on the issues arising at the intergovernmental conferences leading to the Treaties of Maastricht, Amsterdam and Nice (Memorandum, 1996; Benelux Memorandum, 2000).

The Nordic countries are somewhat different. The three Nordic EU members have a long tradition of co-operation and integration in the Nordic context but as members of the EU they have drifted apart. Finland has opted into the core of the union and is a member of the euro zone, while Denmark and Sweden have chosen to remain outside. Issues on the European agenda and geographical reasons have drawn them into different positions despite a long common history as small states. In fact, Finland is changing from a Nordic identity towards the kind of small state identity in the traditional core of the EU. Yet the Nordic caucus has still functioned on specific issues. Finland and Sweden have co-operated successfully on matters on which they have common interests. Two outstanding examples are their joint proposal at Amsterdam concerning crisis management provisions and their support for the inclusion of the employment provisions in the Treaty. In relation to crisis management they share a common interest as militarily non-aligned countries with a strong background in peace keeping. The employment question is another typical regional issue derived from the Nordic welfare model.

PRIORITIES: POWER OR PARTICIPATION

Small states' strategies are often characterised by a preference for strong institutions in order to defend their interests in the framework of more powerful and often dominant powers (Wallace, 1999: 13). If they want to enjoy the benefits that strong institutions provide they have to be ready to accept the power of such institutions even if this means surrendering aspects of their own sovereignty. In most cases they have accepted the latter in order to achieve the support of strong institutions against the dominance, perceived or real, of large member states.

Small states are supportive of the power of institutions in the hope that enforced rules and procedures will help them defend their vital interests and promote their national aspirations. Institutions are useful because they channel information flows and provide an opportunity for negotiation. Within the framework of an institution, governments have an opportunity to oversee each other's commitment to common rules and regulations and to pursue their own interests. They can thus commit themselves in a framework of reliability. Furthermore, inherent in institutions is the pre-supposition that international treaties will be respected (Keohane, 1989: 166–7).

For small states in particular, institutions offer a reliable forum in which they can gain information on the actions and preferences of other states – large and small. Institutions also give small countries an opportunity to influence the compliance of powerful states to joint decisions and rules while emphasising their own input in common projects. They believe that states will adhere to international treaties monitored and executed by institutions more effectively than in cases when there are treaties without institutions. In this latter case relative differences in size and power assume greater importance.

The traditional way of viewing the relationships between the member states is to focus on the balance of power within the EU. The most sensitive issue is the distribution of votes in the Council of Ministers. The debate concerning the definition of the qualified majority and the different methods of establishing thresholds for calculating it are focal points in the power relationship. Similarly, the distribution of seats in the European Parliament is an element of power distribution. The composition and status of the Commission are also regarded as vital questions for small states, which tend to overestimate its importance because they view it as a 'neutral' partner in balancing the power disparities.

The debate on the weighting of votes in the Council is important and sensitive because it also contains a great deal of symbolic value. Changes in the weighting of votes involve elements of prestige as well as dimensions of influence and power, as was demonstrated at the Nice summit in December 2000 when the reweighting issue was dominated by the overriding interest of France in maintaining parity with Germany. In fact, voting in the Council of Ministers is rare and coalition formation is not stable. Voting blocs vary according to different issue areas and are dependent on the interests and bargaining behaviour of the member states. According to Hayes-Renshaw and Wallace (1997: 295) there is no systematic cleavage between smaller and larger members within the Council.

The larger powers normally justify the reweighting of votes as an important element in reforming the union on the grounds of legitimacy and efficiency. As the main contributors to the EU's budget, they aim at securing their positions against the increasing number of small states. Their argument is that the over-representation of small members alienates both the governments and citizens of the larger members from the work of the EU. The situation has been described as a Gulliver's dilemma in which the big countries share a fear that small member states will have the power to block decisions by forming coalitions (Hayes-Renshaw and Wallace, 1997: 295).

The efficiency argument must be measured against the composition of the winning majorities and blocking minorities. As the negotiating strategies at Nice revealed, the majority-building issue marked the most important divide between large and small countries. Large member states advocated the dual majority system with two thresholds: a minimum number of member states and a minimum percentage of the total population of the EU. Smaller members again advocated the model of two simple majorities: population majority and the majority of votes.

The weighting of votes dominated the Nice summit where three models were offered. The basic model was based on the existing weighting or a weak reweighting coupled with a population 'safety net' of 58 per cent of the total population of the EU. A modest reweighting consisted of doubling the existing votes by two and giving five extra votes for big states to compensate for their loss of a second Commissioner. Two other models included the 'Swedish' variation, or moderated reweighting based on a square root calculation of population figures, and a third model of 'substantial reweighting' proposed by Italy which reflected the interests of the large member states (CONFER 4801/00).

Theoretically the double simple majority, supported by the small states, would have guaranteed both efficiency and legitimacy. Had the threshold been set at 50 per cent, it would clearly have been superior in terms of efficiency. The double majority requirement would also have ensured legitimacy and prevented conflict between the big and small member states. The principle of one vote to each member, regardless of population, would have given the small member states an opportunity to make or break coalitions. (Baldwin et al., 2000: 6–25).

The final solution in Nice, after a complex process of negotiations, marked a shift of the balance in favour of the large member states. This has several elements. In the first place, the new weighing of votes clearly favours large member states. The numbers adopted are a compromise of the three models offered but reflect the content of the Italian proposal. The final agreement increases the number of votes for the big four threefold (from 10 to 29) but the votes of smaller states are on the average only doubled (see Table 4.1). A new threshold for a qualified majority of 74.8 per cent of the votes, thus upgrading the long-standing threshold of 71.3 per cent, accompanied the reweighting of votes. A step in the same direction is the rule that a qualified majority must also embrace 62 per cent of the population if verification is demanded.

The issue of representation of the small states in the institutions is reflected in all its complexity in the extension of qualified majority voting to new areas and the increased application of co-decision has fortified its position. The role of the Parliament has been strengthened in successive intergovernmental conferences. The reweighting of votes, leading to a decrease in the relative power of small member states in the Council, has been matched by a parallel reduction in the number of MEPs from small states thereby weakening their voice in the Parliament (see Table 4.1). This produced a triple negative effect for the small members: more powers to the Parliament where small member states have less weight and simul-

TABLE 4.1 *The Nice Treaty 2000 – the new distribution of weighted votes in Council and seats in European Parliament (to be implemented in January 2005)*

Members	Council votes		EP Seats	
	Pre-Nice	Post-Nice	Pre-Nice	Post-Nice
Germany	10	29	99	99
France	10	29	87	72
UK	10	29	87	72
Italy	10	29	87	72
Spain	8	27	64	50
Netherlands	5	13	31	25
Portugal	5	12	25	22
Belgium	5	12	25	22
Greece	5	12	25	22
Sweden	4	10	22	18
Austria	4	10	21	17
Denmark	3	7	16	13
Finland	3	7	16	13
Ireland	3	7	15	12
Luxembourg	2	4	6	6
TOTAL	87[1]	237	626	535
Applicant states				
Poland		27		50
Romania		14		33
Czech Republic		12		20
Hungary		12		20
Bulgaria		10		17
Slovakia		7		13
Lithuania		7		12
Latvia		4		8
Slovenia		4		7
Estonia		4		6
Cyprus		4		6
Malta		3		5
TOTAL		345[2]		732

[1] Qualified Majority requires 62 votes out of the 87 total (71.3% of total).

[2] Should all 12 applicants join the EU, a qualified majority will require 258 votes out of the 345 total (74.8% of total votes). In addition, as from January 2005, any member state can request verification that the states constituting a qualified majority represent at least 62% of the total EU population. Should this not be the case, the decision will not be adopted.

Source: Intergovernmental Conference on Institutional Reform. Brussels, 12 December 2000.

taneously a diminution in their weight in the Council. In the end the small states will find themselves in a situation where they have less influence over a wider range of issues. This disadvantageous situation is worsened by the fact that large groups from the bigger member states also dominate the decision-making process in the political groups of the European Parliament.

The end result of the Treaty of Nice can thus be seen as the first move to meet the demands of the larger member states since the initial solution of the Treaty of Rome. However, there was no coalition of small states to prevent the shift. Only three of them – Portugal, Belgium and Finland – resisted the change in the end. Yet the need for a deep institutional reform in the EU will continue to be a key issue in the years ahead. The necessary reforms are much wider in scope than those concerning the relations between small and large member states.

The doctrine of equal participation is a fundamental element in the equality between the member states. The key issues are the rotating presidency, the definition of official languages and the composition of the institutions. These topics will remain on the agenda.

The rotating presidency is of a high value for small states. Holding the presidency helps them to maintain a visible and high profile not only in the everyday practise of the work of the EU but also internationally as well as domestically. In running the presidency small member states may perform functions that are associated with the role of small powers in international relations in general. They perform functions of 'honest-broker' and pro-cedural leadership. Their policies are often issue-specific and mission-oriented, crossing ideological, regional and development boundaries. These countries are free from hegemony baggage and therefore less limited in their actions and more able to seek creative solutions (Higgott, 1997: 37, 41).

Middle range and smaller countries can also be successful in their diplomatic actions because of their societal and technical capabilities. Cooper, Higgot and Nossal specify these capabilities 'as [a] mixture of entrepreneurship, diplomatic knowledge and ability to manage knowledge of sectoral issues that are the object of international co-operation' (cited in Bélanger and Mace, 1997: 166). Multinational institutions, such as the EU, also provide particular opportunities for the international role of such states. The rotating presidency offers a convenient opportunity for small member states to perform these functions and capabilities, to perform 'niche diplomacy'.

Niche diplomacy emphasises coalition building and co-operation. Small members could be seen as 'catalysts and facilitators'. This catalyst role includes the ability to focus political energy on particular issues and that of facilitator involves the organising and housing of meetings as well as planning rhetorical manifestos (Cooper, 1997: 8–9). The rotating presi-dency is a high priority for small members and is considered an important aspect of equality between the member states. But there are strong pressures, in the interest of efficiency, that automatic rotation should be abolished (Prodi, 2001). Yet small members have shown a readiness to accept considerable economic and administrative burdens in order to hold the Presidency. Their performance is often at least as good as that of larger member states. Small states may have smaller resources but they also have smaller national aspirations and interests.

All member states also have the right to nominate their citizens to the Commission and the Courts. Small member states have therefore tried to resist proposals to decrease the number of Commissioners and the ending of the system of automatic membership. For them the Commission has been seen as a crucially important institution in view of its supranational character and pledges, at least in theory, to treat all member states on equal terms. Yet in reality the Commission performs several functions, which are often in conflict with the interests of particular states. It is therefore not quite the honest broker that small states tend to assume (Nugent, 2001: 10–15).

From the perspective of a small state the equal opportunity of its citizens to be recruited to the personnel of the EU is of vital importance. The multinational staffing policy is an established principle although this has not prevented the weighting of the staff by nationality benefiting the large member states. The French share of A-grade posts in October 1999 was 15 per cent while the figure for The Netherlands, another founding member state, was 5 per cent. Among the small members, Belgium, the host country of the main EU institutions, had 11 per cent of such posts. At the bottom of the list are Finland (2 per cent) and Luxembourg (1 per cent). A similar pattern exists in the highest A1 category of civil servants where France, Germany and the United Kingdom together occupy almost half of the top 52 positions (Nugent, 2001: 174–75).

The question of national languages is a further aspect of equal participation. The language regime is of special importance for small states whose domestic regime consists of a less-spoken tongue. The existing language regime of the EU is two-dimensional. On the one hand the Treaty of Amsterdam establishes the rule that every citizen of the union shall have the right to write to EU institutions and bodies in one of twelve languages named in Article 314 and have an answer in the same language (Article 21). The basic rules take into consideration equally the interests of all member states.

The other dimension of the language regime is the system of working languages. Smaller languages suffer from a lack of adequate services in interpretation. The full interpretation of twelve official languages is not provided for all meetings of the institutions. The working language regime has no formal rules and practice varies in institutions. In the day-to-day work of the institutions French and English predominate. The bottom line, from the viewpoint of the small members, is to maintain the regime that gives each citizen the right to approach any of the EU institutions or bodies in any one of the Treaty languages and to ensure that official documents continue to be provided in official languages. The ongoing enlargement process will further complicate the language regime. In particular, the interpretation services will be under heavy pressure. The possibility of creating a hierarchy of languages or a reduced number of official languages poses clear challenges to small member states with national languages.

The principle of equal participation is associated with fundamental issues related to the future of the EU. It is linked to democratic legitimacy and the equal rights of EU citizens. In particular, if people in the small countries perceive any continuing reduction in the status of their states within the union, they are likely to become more alienated from the European institutions.

INTERGOVERNMENTAL INTEGRATION AND THE CONTINUING CHALLENGES FOR SMALL STATES

The Common Foreign and Security Policy (CFSP) regime is dominated by a tension between intergovernmental and communitarian structures. External economic and trade relations are communitarised and decision-making takes place within the institutional framework of the European Community. The position of small states in decision-making is confirmed by the Community rules and norms. In political co-operation and security matters intergovernmental rules and procedures predominate. The key institution in the CFSP is the Council of Ministers and increasingly also the European Council. Both of these institutions reflect member states' interests and thus also their powers. The question of size has retained much of its relevance in the intergovernmental components of the EU.

Small states face special challenges in intergovernmental co-operation. The emerging defence dimension will sharpen the situation. A particular concern is the fear of the emergence of *directoires*: formal or informal groups of larger and more powerful member states that share common interests and wield power together in the name of the EU and/or steer it in the direction of their preferences. The emergence of *directoires* is evident although not on a permanent basis. The Franco-German tandem is often seen as the motor for the overall dynamics of the integration process. Similar, if not as extensive, bilateral contacts also take place between other larger member states (Werts, 1992: 97). In particular, the emergence of a common defence policy has largely been based on bilateral negotiations between France and Great Britain. The St Malo declaration of 1998 as well as the London declaration of 1999 serve as good examples of bilateral interests and initiatives by large member states in the intergovernmental dimensions of integration. The emergence of a permanent political directorate is, however, as unlikely to emerge as is a permanent coalition of small states.

The establishment of the office of a High Representative has marked a shift towards more intergovernmentalism. The power of external representation and planning has changed the balance in favour of the Council Secretariat at the expense of the Commission. From a small state perspective this is a problematic trend. A power change from the Commission to the High Representative implies that intergovernmental rules and procedures dominate the CFSP and thus the element of size becomes more relevant. The role and composition of the defence policy institutions present further challenges, with the weight of the Political and Security Committee and the Military Committee requiring particular attention. The emerging relationship between the EU and NATO/US is also crucial in this respect for this will define the role of small states with limited interests in the emerging security structure. A solution must also be found to the accommodation of their national security needs within the common defence policy. This presents particular problems for countries with a neutral past.

Flexibility in the CFSP may further complicate the situation. The Nice process brought to the surface the option of predefined flexibility that might create a kind of a *directoire* or a coalition of the willing. Flexibility in defence matters could develop into a club of nations whose interests and assets bind the EU into actions that may contradict the interests of members that are outside the core.

This again is a particular problem for small states with a neutral past. They see the European Union as a community of solidarity. This implies for them, first that the member states have a duty to consult and inform each other in the framework of the Council; and secondly, that the member states have a duty to ensure that the union's influence is exerted as effectively as possible by means of concerted action. This could be seen as an obligation to provide a security guarantee of a kind without a collective defence commitment.

Furthermore, in a community of solidarity the member states would ensure that their national policies conformed to the common positions adopted and smaller states could expect wide and unconditional support should they need it. They would expect their interests to be taken into consideration in policy-making in a spirit of loyalty and mutual solidarity. In reality, however, there is a danger that new institutions, including the Political and Security Committee and Military Committee, will increase the weight of the larger member states, whose contribution to defence is much greater than that of the smaller member states. Small members therefore face the danger of marginalisation with this added power dimension in the common defence policy. The danger of marginalisation is considerably enhanced should flexibility be adopted in the common defence policy.

THE FUTURE: FROM ADAPTATION TO INFLUENCE?

After joining the European institutions the small member states were forced to reconsider their tactics and roles. They have worked largely through adaptation. They have adapted themselves to European institutions with a sense of purpose. For example, small members are at the forefront in transposing internal market legislation. In an institutionalised international subsystem such as the European Union the line between external relations and domestic policy is fluid. European policies are rapidly domesticated.

Small states have been able to adapt to this process more easily than larger member states.

Adaptation has called for a domestic consensus. The building of national unity is easier to achieve in a small state than in larger ones. But small states are effective at the international level only if they have prepared and organised their position by being united and adaptive at domestic level. A notable exception is Denmark where the domestic consensus has been difficult to attain in referenda but where, on the other hand, the Parliament is closely involved in the Government's policy-making.

The capacity to adapt is crucial for a small member state to be able to focus its attention on the key issues. Governmental adaptation focuses on the central government's institutional capacity to meet the new demands, especially in external relations. Political adaptation reflects the policy-makers' willingness to change their behaviour to meet new challenges and strategic adaptation marks the policy-makers' capability to develop a bargaining strategy and ally with other states (Hanf and Soetendorp, 1998: 8–11). Small states are unable to act effectively on their own but they may have a major impact in a small group or through international institutions.

The EU offers a favourable platform for co-operative strategies. European integration has produced a remarkable regional system of rule, conceptualised by the notion of 'governance' (Sandholtz and Sweet, 1998). The EU appears as a unique attempt to regain the action potential of the state, which has been lost in the course of globalisation. When theorising about the European polity, claims made by several independent lines of thought in the social sciences about the role and nature of the state should be taken seriously. Because the EU lacks government we need leadership for successful governance.

In this context a leader often performs the function of a 'broker'. Co-operation does not happen automatically but needs to be created and nurtured. The leader has to bridge the various distributional concerns associated with co-operation and forge consensus among potential co-operators. A broker is neither hegemonic nor completely dominant. Leadership is necessary to establish institutions for successful co-operation and these institutions become fragile when leadership declines. However, the foundations for leadership differ. Hegemonies possess a significant advantage in various resources but a leadership role can be based on other resources than those of sheer power.

The post-Nice agenda provides a major challenge for small states. As demonstrated above, the Treaty itself has led to an apparent decrease in the relative power of such states in the EU as a whole. On the other hand, the *number* of small states within the union has increased with recent enlargements and this trend will be reinforced in future. The question therefore remains as to whether these states will be able to exploit the potential that they have through niche diplomacy so as to overcome the apparent disadvantages in the redistribution of power that took place at Nice.

The 'post-Nice' agenda for the EU consists of four challenges. The core of the process is the preparatory work for a new intergovernmental conference in 2004. The Declaration attached to the Nice Conclusions consists in itself of four items, which point to the central challenges the EU shall face (Treaty of Nice, 2000: Annex IV). The four items – simplification of the treaties, the future status of the Charter of Fundamental Rights, the division of powers between the EU institutions and the member states, and the role of national parliaments in the decision-making structure – are fundamentally different from the power-related agenda of the Nice process. Even the preparatory process of the agenda differs from traditional methods of intergovernmental negotiations. It is open to inputs from national parliaments, the European Parliament and different sections of the civil society. This provides a framework where arguments rather than prestige or voting power will be of pivotal importance.

Parallel with the IGC 2004 process the union must work to meet the challenge of the Helsinki Headline Goals in developing its defence policy capacity. This debate is probably going to be dominated by larger members and will put the smaller members on a defensive stance. The nature of defence policy integration favours power-related arguments and also involves a strong element of prestige. The debate is likely to be dominated by larger member states whose contribution to the common defence policy is bound to be more extensive than that of smaller members.

The management of the euro and EMU also poses challenges to small member states. Arguments that bigger economies should have more say in the management of the European Central Bank system have been heard. The main argument is that of effectiveness. In particular, the composition of the Governing Council, now including Central Bank directors from all EMU countries, is seen as a possible obstacle to effective decision-making (Baldwin et al., 2000: 40–1). The debate on economic policy management of the EU again opens new avenues for the influence of small member states. The e-Europe concept and the outlines for economic policy co-ordination highlight the strengths of many smaller nations. Scandinavian countries in particular are forerunners in such key sectors of e-Europe as internet connections and mobile technology thus providing benchmarks for the rest of the EU and for bigger members as well. Many of the small member states may assume a leadership role in these key sectors. An obvious 'niche' role is open for smaller member states.

Improving the governance of the EU is a further issue on which the smaller member states are potentially key contributors in the reform process. Many of them emphasise the improvement of the institutional effectiveness of the Union as their main aim. Prestige and power, on the other hand, are less visible in governance than in sectors where power relations are directly involved.

The post-Nice agenda will therefore show whether the small states are able to move from adaptation to greater influence, and whether they are able to use their diplomatic and bargaining skills in an atmosphere where power configurations are less dominant. The nature of the EU in years to come may depend upon the degree of their success. If they fail, it would suggest that traditional power politics still operate, but if they succeed it would imply that the EU could move towards a community of solidarity.

REFERENCES

Agence Europe, 14 October 2000. Lugano.

Baldwin, Richard, Berglöf, Erik, Giavazzi, Francesco and Widgrén, Mika (2000) 'EU reforms for tomorrow's Europe', Discussion Paper Series No. 2623. Centre for Economic Research, November.

Bélanger, Louis and Mace, Gordon (1997) 'Middle Powers and Regionalism in the Americas: The Cases of Argentina and Mexico', in Andrew F. Cooper (ed.) *Niche Diplomacy: Middle Powers after the Cold War*. Ipswich: Ipswich Book Company.

Benelux Memorandum on the IGC and the future of the European Union, The Hague, 29 September 2000.

Brown, Jennifer (2000) 'Small States in the European Institutions', Jean Monnet Unit, University of Turku, Working Papers, No. 8.

Clark, Ian (1989) *The Hierarchy of States: Reform and Resistance in the International Order*. Cambridge: Cambridge University Press.

CONFER 4801/00: Presidency, IGC 2000 – weighting of votes in the Council. Brussels, 16 November 2000.

Cooper, Andrew F. (ed.) (1997) *Niche Diplomacy: Middle Powers after the Cold War*. Ipswich: Ipswich Book Company.

Elman, Miriam Fendus (1995) 'The Foreign Policies of Small States: Challenging Neorealism in its Own Backyard', *British Journal of Political Science*, 25: 171–217.

Hanf, Kenneth and Soetendorp, Ben (1998) *Adaptating to European Integration: Small States and the European Union*. New York: Addison Wesley Longman.

Hayes-Renshaw, Fiona and Wallace, Helen (1997) *The Council of Ministers*. London: Macmillan.

Higgott, Richard (1997) 'Issues, Institutions and Middle-Power Diplomacy: Action and Agendas in the Post-Cold War Era', in Andrew F. Cooper (ed.) *Niche Diplomacy: Middle Powers after the Cold War*. Ipswich: Ipswich Book Company.

Hocking, Brian (1997) 'Finding Your Niche: Australia and the Trials of Middle-Powerdom', in Andrew F. Cooper (ed.) *Niche Diplomacy: Middle Powers after the Cold War*. Ipswich: Ipswich Book Company.

Keohane, Robert (1989) *International Institutions and State Power*. Boulder, CO: Westview.

Knudsen, Olav F. (1997) 'Analysing Small-State Security: The Role of External Factors', in B. Werner, A. Clesse and Olav F. Knudsen (eds) *Small States and the Security Challenge in the New Europe*. Exeter: BPC Wheaton.

McDonagh, Bobby (1999) *Original Sin in a Brave World: An Account of the Negotiation of the Treaty of Amsterdam*. Dublin: Institute for European Affairs.

Memorandum on the IGC from the Governments of Belgium, Luxembourg and the Netherlands 7 March 1996.

Nossal, Kim Richard and Stubbs, Richard (1997) 'Mahathir's Malaysia: An Emerging Middle Power?', in Andrew F. Cooper (ed.) *Niche Diplomacy: Middle Powers after the Cold War.* Ipswich, Ipswich Book Company.

Nugent, Neill (2001) *The European Commission.* London: Macmillan.

Pijpers, Alfred and Vanhoonacker, S. (1997) 'The Position of the Benelux Countries', in Geoffrey Edwards and Alfred Pijpers (eds), *The Politics of European Treaty Reform: The 1996 Intergovernmental Conference and Beyond.* London: Pinter.

Prodi, Romano (2001) press conference, Stockholm, 9 January.

Sandholtz, Wayne and Sweet, Alec Stone (eds) (1998) *European Integration and Supranational Governance.* Oxford: Oxford University Press.

Commonwealth Secretariat/World Bank (1999) *Small States: Meeting Challenges in the Global Economy.* Interim Report of the Commonwealth Secretariat/World Bank Joint Task Force on Small States. The Commonwealth Secretariat and World Bank, Washington.

Svetlicic, Marjan (1997) 'Small Countries in a Globalized World: Their Honey Moon or Twilight', paper prepared for presentation at the ECPR Workshop on Small States in Transforming the European System. Bern, 27 February–4 March.

Treaty of Nice (2000) Provisional text approved by the Intergovernmental Conference on institutional reform. *Conference of the Representatives of the Governments of the Member States, 12 December, SN533/00.*

Wallace, William (1999) 'Small European States and European Policy-Making. Strategies, Roles, Possibilities', in *Between Autonomy and Influence. Small States and the European Union.* Proceedings from ARENA Annual Conference 1988. Arena Report no. 1/1999: 11–26.

Werts, Jan (1992) *The European Council.* Amsterdam.

Wight, Martin, (1978) *Power Politics* Leicester: Leicester University Press.

Zbinden, Martin (1998) 'Implications of the Intergovernmental Conference and the Treaty of Amsterdam for Smaller EU Member States', in Laurent Goetschek (ed.) *Small States Inside and Outside the European Union.* London/Boston/Bordrecht: Kluwer.

5   Emerging Integration in Policing and Criminal Justice

Madeleine Colvin

Prior to the Amsterdam Treaty there was a relatively fragmented approach to justice and home affairs matters, including policing and judicial co-operation at European Union level. By setting some clearer objectives, including the creation of an 'area of freedom, security and justice', the Treaty has become the impetus for more comprehensive measures to integrate law enforcement efforts at the pan-European level.

Cross-border joint policing operations backed by EU police and judicial bodies is one part of the programme to tackle the increasing level of organised crime. The other is to create a European legal area where the decisions of one member state are directly enforceable in another. Both are aimed at countering the increased sophistication of criminals to operate across borders and to exploit the differences between the legal systems of member states.

This chapter therefore looks at these developments under three main headings: police co-operation, the creation of EU databases and the agenda for mutual assistance over criminal matters. With different policing traditions and criminal justice systems being deeply rooted in the idea of national sovereignty, there are significant obstacles to this ambitious programme. However, as the chapter points out, the risks posed to human rights standards by these far-reaching moves also raise critical questions – from the need for greater judicial and democratic control of EU policing bodies to the need to guarantee the individual rights of privacy and fair trial. European integration requires a structure that can both facilitate greater police cooperation and at the same time question the legitimacy of it in individual cases. At present insufficient attention is being paid to the latter.

POLICE CO-OPERATION

There is nothing new about police co-operation across state borders. Over the years a multiplicity of international contact and co-operation has developed between various law enforcement agencies, including customs and immigration officers. This ranges from formal arrangements, underpinned by bilateral or multilateral treaty agreements, to less formal arrangements based on memorandums of understanding. There is also an array of informal links based on personal contacts.

An example of co-operation developing through different stages is the arrangements in the English Channel region. This started with informal contact between senior police officers in the 1960s, and it led to the more formal establishment of the Cross Channel Intelligence Conference set up in 1971 which continued for the next fifteen years. This was the principal forum for chief police officers to exchange ideas and information on criminal intelligence and cross-border policing generally. As the Channel Tunnel project got under way in the 1980s this local network became more formalised until in 1991 the European Liaison Unit was established, based at the Channel Tunnel site in Folkestone. This links Kent police in the UK with their counterparts in France, Belgium and Holland and is now the vehicle through which criminal intelligence is routinely exchanged. It is also underpinned by legal protocols which allow French and British police to operate on each others' territory for the purpose of policing the Tunnel.

Transnational policing is now a feature of day-to-day activities in many border regions of the EU, particularly along its external borders. In the initial stages, this was largely driven by the police themselves. It was not until the arrival of the TREVI group in 1975 when the process of turning policing into a political issue at the European level really began. This was an intergovernmental group led by the interior ministers of member states with representatives of police forces. It was set up specifically to examine the mechanics of police co-operation across a range of international and organised crimes: from drug trafficking, terrorism and money laundering to football hooliganism.

For many years thereafter the issue of policing, along with immigration, was dealt with in closed, unofficial and non-accountable ad hoc groups such as TREVI. They were outside the EU's system of consultation and accountability. It was not until the Maastricht Treaty in 1991 that a more formal – although not significantly more accountable – structure was introduced for dealing with justice and home affairs matters at the EU level under what is known as the intergovernmental 'third pillar'.

The present shift towards creating a formal, high-level layer of police co-operation in the EU, which started after Maastricht, was given practical effect by several key developments, most particularly the implementation of the previously agreed Schengen Convention,[1] the EU Action Plans of 1997 and 1998 and the recent Convention on Mutual Assistance in Criminal Matters (2000).

These developments, which are examined in detail below, are based on a new and radical approach to policing serious crime. Increasingly, at both national and international levels, the police, customs and other law enforcement agencies are turning to proactive, intelligence-led methods. Essentially this means using covert investigative methods to target known or suspected criminals rather than waiting to investigate a crime after it has happened. Informers and undercover officers, together with sophisticated surveillance devices, provide the intelligence on potential crimes. A more proactive, intelligence-led approach has been viewed as necessary to detect and interrupt organised criminal activities, apprehend the offenders, demolish the criminal networks, and seize and confiscate the proceeds of crime.

This phenomenon of modern policing raises serious questions of control and accountability largely because its very success is predicated on the operations being secret and covert. It is within this context that the key developments in police co-operation within the EU need to be viewed.

THE SCHENGEN CONVENTION

In 1985 five countries – France, West Germany and the Benelux countries of Belgium, Luxembourg and the Netherlands – signed a formal agreement at Schengen in Luxembourg to abolish their internal border controls ahead of the rest of the EU. This did not come into effect until after a more detailed Convention of Application of the Schengen Agreement (called the Schengen Convention) was signed in June 1990 but only finally implemented in March 1995. It is this that sets out the 'compensating measures' on policing and immigration flowing from abolishing internal borders. Most of the remaining EU countries signed up to this Convention in the intervening years, together with the non-EU Nordic countries.[2] Only the UK and Ireland remained non-signatories by the time that the Convention and its *acquis* were incorporated into the EU legal framework on 29 May 1999 under the Treaty of Amsterdam (see below).

The provisions of the Schengen Convention were always viewed as the probable model for how internal controls and border policies were likely to develop in the EU as a whole. Some of the key features include:

- Increased policing at external borders to check on those entering from outside the Schengen area, particularly non-EU citizens. These are backed by, for example, a common list of 'unwanted aliens', visa requirements and limitations on periods of stay.
- A 'one chance only' rule for asylum seekers setting out a complex set of rules as to which Schengen country is responsible for processing an application.[3]
- Cross-border surveillance and 'hot pursuit' by the police (see below).
- A computerised database called the Schengen Information System (see below).
- Mutual assistance, extradition and harmonisation of legislation and policy (see below).

Article 39 of the Convention is the cornerstone of police co-operation. It provides that the police authorities of the various states shall provide assistance to each other not only in relation to specific crimes but in preventing crime generally. The term 'assistance' is not defined and therefore can (and has) covered many forms, particularly exchanging information. The other provisions (Articles 40–3) are more operational in nature covering cross-border observation, pursuit and controlled delivery operations. Most controversially, 'hot pursuit' allows a foreign police officer to follow a suspected criminal across a border, although the arrest of the person must be left to the local police.

These provisions on police co-operation have been of immense significance, both in practice and as a matter of principle. Up to this point, the regulation of co-operation between national police authorities had not featured in international agreements. Although co-operation had undoubtedly been taking place, its legal basis had been questionable at the best. In practice, therefore, these provisions have provided a legal basis (together with bilateral agreements) which led to 370 cross-border surveillance operations and 39 cross-border pursuits in the Schengen states in 1998 (Schengen, 1998).

Although limited in nature, the provisions are nevertheless radical moves challenging the underlying principle of sovereignty in relation to greater law enforcement cooperation. As Malcolm Anderson in his history of Interpol remarked:

> [T]he doctrine of sovereignty is still almost universally accepted in the field of criminal justice and criminal law enforcement. Liberals and socialists, democrats and authoritarians hold the view that the authoritative source of criminal law is the state and the means of its enforcement should be exclusively controlled by the state. . . . Integrated police operations are not possible until the theory and practice of state sovereignty changes. (1989: 30)

Subsequent negotiations to build on and improve the Schengen provisions have again shown the degree of sensitivity with which member states treat this whole area (see below). It was also the reason why policing and judicial co-operation in criminal matters continues to remain intergovernmental (and subject to unanimity) under the 'third pillar' rather than being incorporated under the Amsterdam Treaty into the EU legal framework along with border controls, immigration and asylum. This institutional arrangement has often been given as the reason – together with political unwillingness – why progress in the area of police co-operation has been slow and patchy.

EU ACTION PLANS

The EU's most comprehensive plan to tackle organised crime was agreed in 1997. The High Level Group's Action Plan, adopted by the Amsterdam European Council in June 1997, had some thirty recommendations with the aim of providing an integrated approach to police co-operation at each stage: from the prevention of crime at one end to its successful prosecution at the other. However, it has been the Amsterdam Treaty that has provided the added impetus to this programme. The new Treaty objective is:

> To maintain and develop the Union as an area of freedom, security and justice, in which the free movement of persons is assured in conjunction with appropriate measures with respect to external border controls, asylum, immigration and the prevention and combating of crime.

Its strength is seen in setting precise policy objectives that can be used as the basis of a work programme. This led to a further Action Plan being agreed at the Justice and Home Affairs (JHA) Council meeting in Vienna in December 1998. Building on the previous plan, it sets out a detailed list of measures to be adopted within the next five years, including the development and expansion of operational co-operation between law enforcement agencies and greater mutual recognition of decisions in criminal matters (Council/Commission 1999).

This large and highly ambitious programme which will extend well into the twenty-first century was given further impetus at the European Council meeting held at Tampere in October 1999. It sent a strong political message to reaffirm the importance of establishing the 'area of freedom, security and justice'. In particular, it set the milestones in three main areas: for a union-wide fight against crime, for greater mutual recognition of judicial systems and for a common European asylum system. At the same time, the Tampere Presidency Conclusions note that:

> From its very beginning European integration has been firmly rooted in a shared commitment to freedom based on human rights, democratic institutions and rule of law. (European Council, 1999)

In March 2000 the European Commission produced a detailed scoreboard 'to facilitate the internal monitoring by the EU institutions of their progress' in achieving the Tampere objectives (see below).

CONVENTION ON MUTUAL ASSISTANCE 2000

Running alongside the Schengen Convention, the EU member states as a whole have agreed several policing co-operation measures. This includes a handbook for police co-operation in connection with international football matches and other major public order events. There has also been the development of an annual report on organised crime in order to assist in defining common strategies.

However, the most significant agreement reached in recent years is the Convention on Mutual Assistance in Criminal Matters signed by member states on 29 May 2000. Its purpose is to 'supplement the provisions and facilitate the application' of existing international instruments on mutual assistance, particularly the 1959 Council of Europe Convention of the same name. Its difficult and complex topics were negotiated over four years, going through a proliferation of amended texts. Although the initial aim was to improve judicial co-operation (see below), its scope was later extended to cover surveillance policing. At the same time, similar provisions were being included in the 'Naples II' Convention on Mutual Assistance and Co-operation between Customs Administrations adopted earlier in December 1997 but not yet in force. Both instruments represent a major shift in existing arrangements with important implications for human rights.

Seen as key instruments in the fight against organised crime, the surveillance provisions of these new Conventions are justified with reference to the major changes in the nature of organised crime and the policing methods used to tackle it. Some of their provisions are modelled on, and intend to update, the Schengen *acquis*; while others are new, especially in relation to joint investigative teams and interception of telecommunications. The key features on the policing side furthering cross-border investigations in the Mutual Assistance Convention are:

- Controlled deliveries (Article 12): This provision is based on Article 73 of the Schengen Convention but no longer limits such action to drug trafficking offences. It allows the transportation of illegal goods into the jurisdiction of one or more other countries for surveillance reasons and is justified by the potential to thereby cause greater damage to the criminal network. Each member state is obliged to adopt the legal means to ensure that, when requested, it can permit a controlled delivery to take place on its territory as part of a criminal investigation of an extraditable offence.[4] The operation must comply with the procedures of the requested state.
- Joint investigation teams (Article 13): The importance of operational co-operation among law enforcement agencies has been a consistent theme in EU instruments but one of the obstacles has been the lack of a specific legal framework within which such teams could be established and operate. This Article sets out the details: membership of the team, its purpose, the applicable law covering the investigation and use of the information obtained. Unlike other police operations, it is not limited to serious crime. Officials from Europol or other international organisations may take part in these joint teams.
- Covert investigations (Article 14): This is concerned with investigations by undercover officers or agents who wish to operate in another member state in the investigation of a crime. There has to be agreement on a number of matters, including the duration of the investigation, how it is to be pursued and the legal status of the officers involved.
- Interception of telecommunications (Articles 17–22): This is the first time that a multilateral convention has attempted to deal with this issue internationally. Its provisions are highly complex, covering one of the more sensitive areas and where technology has created new situations

which are difficult to regulate. The provisions cover both interceptions on national territory with the assistance of service providers and those where the technical assistance of another member state is not required. The UK's House of Lords European Union Committee expressed particular misgivings as to whether the 'right balance has been struck between the interests of member states in improving mutual assistance and the rights of the individual' in relation particularly to these provisions on interceptions (House of Lords, 2000).

The difficulties posed to law enforcement agencies by new communications technology has been the subject of agreements going back a number of years. On the technical side, there have been (and continue to be) moves to harmonise the various international requirements on service providers to provide built-in facilities for intervention. At the EU level, a 1995 Council Resolution on this was agreed followed by a similarly worded Memorandum of Understanding between the fifteen EU member states and Norway, Australia, Canada and the USA (Council, 1995).

These agreements commit the signatories to facilitating surveillance by law enforcement agencies (including the security services) through a detailed list of minimum requirements. Service providers must arrange for real-time access by authorised agencies, to cover actual communications and all call-associated data. If a mobile phone is used, information on its geographical location must be supplied.[5] Recent new laws in member states, including the Regulation of Investigatory Powers Act 2000 in the UK, closely follow these requirements.

When it comes to joint investigation teams, member states are reluctant to wait until the Convention has been fully ratified before applying this provision, particularly as they may already create such teams on a bilateral or multilateral basis. There is therefore a draft framework decision to allow joint teams to become operational before then, although agreement is still awaited on the exact role to be played by Europol officers.[6] A proposal by the French EU Council Presidency in 2000 stated that Europol should facilitate the co-ordination of operations within a joint team and advise on appropriate techniques and analysis of offences.

Members of the Eurojust unit (as proposed by the Tampere meeting) are also to become members of joint investigative teams. This is to be a unit of national prosecutors, magistrates or police officers drawn from each member state. To be accommodated in The Hague alongside Europol, its task will be to facilitate the co-ordination of national investigating and prosecuting authorities in serious crime cases affecting two or more member states.[7] A decision to set up a provisional unit in the meantime was taken in July 2000.

One of the key issues surrounding Eurojust is the nature of its eventual powers. The decision is between whether it is an administrative body or a quasi-judicial unit with powers to affect the course of an investigation or prosecution. A consensus among member states is that it should have 'teeth' in making decisions on key aspects of the investigation and prosecution of cross-border crime. In these circumstances the question of the unit's accountability becomes a critical question. One obvious risk is that it will become the vehicle for 'forum shopping' whereby investigations and trials are steered towards those countries where a conviction is more likely – either because of lower controls over surveillance policing or the trial process itself. This is also relevant to the proposed mutual assistance programme (see below).

Closely related to the proposal for Eurojust is the continuing debate over the *corpus juris* proposal. This is the establishment of an EU prosecutor (and an autonomous criminal code) to prosecute crimes of fraud against the EU's finances. There is a core group of member states, notably led by Germany, that would like to see the European Prosecutor's office proposed by *corpus juris* being expanded to a network of such offices in each member state. It would also have a broader remit to prosecute all serious cross-border crime. These states view Eurojust as merely a first step in achieving this kind of supranational prosecuting authority.

Other support systems to greater police co-operation include an operational taskforce of European police chiefs to exchange experience and best practices on current trends in cross-border crime. These will be supported by the European Judicial Network which was inaugurated in September 1998 to provide legal and practical information on mutual legal assistance to practitioners in their own countries, particularly through the internet.

EU DATABASES

Increased international co-operation by law enforcement agencies is dependent on the development of large databases that can be speedily accessed through thousands of computer terminals across national borders. This is because such co-operation is heavily reliant on the exchange of large quantities of data, particularly 'soft' criminal intelligence data. This is particularly so within the EU that now has three such databases: the Schengen Information System (SIS), Europol and the Customs Information System (CIS) on the policing side, with a proposed fingerprint and DNA database to be developed. Often holding highly sensitive data, such databases have the potential seriously to affect the lives of those who are the subject of an entry. The need for proper controls and safeguards are therefore critical for compliance with human rights standards.

There has been little strategic thinking about the establishment of these databases and, in particular, the sharing of data between themselves and with other systems such as Interpol. Each has been negotiated on an ad hoc basis without proper research as to their need, what they are intended to achieve and the arrangements for sharing with other databases. Some clearly overlap in the categories of information held. Increasingly they will also be required to operate on a level that is wider than the EU. For example, in 1999 Europol started planning individual seminars to discuss its relationship with twenty-three third states and three non-EU bodies. The negotiations around the regulations on sharing with non-EU states confirmed that it will be permissible for information which has been obtained in violation of a human right in a third country to be held and used by Europol.

There is also a lack of consistency in the data protection provisions of the various databases, a matter that is now the subject of examination by a Council working group (see below). The SIS and Europol systems illustrate this and some of the other problems of regulating large databases.

The SIS

The SIS, which came into operation in 1995, is at the heart of the Schengen security system that compensates for the abolition of internal borders. Its structure is a network of national databases (N.SIS) connected to a central system (C.SIS). It is supplemented by the little-known SIRENE[8] system which provides the infrastructure for exchanging additional information to that held on the SIS, as well as facilitating the 'free standing' exchange of police information.[9] Together these systems represent the first experiment in large-scale sharing of sensitive data at an international level; they are also likely to develop into being the long-proposed European Information System.[10]

As the centrepiece of Schengen co-operation, the data held on the SIS is used for the dual purposes of immigration and policing. It currently holds around 9.7 million files: of these around 1.3 million relate to individuals who are either 'unwanted aliens', wanted for extradition, missing persons or suspected criminals under surveillance. The rest – some 8.4 million – relate to objects such as stolen vehicles and documents. The system can be consulted from over 50,000 computer terminals by thousands of police and immigration officials, including embassy staff of member states responsible for issuing visas.

A recent report which places the database under scrutiny for compliance with human rights standards for the first time raises serious concerns about the accuracy, supervision and monitoring of the system (JUSTICE, 2000a). Its overall conclusion is that there are significant flaws in the highly complex data protection regime governing the system. These range from a lack of criteria for making entries in the first place to the major obstacles faced by individuals seeking redress. The report also reveals serious weaknesses in the independent supervision of the system, both at national and supranational levels.

Europol

Although the Europol Convention came into force on 1 October 1998, the unit only became fully operational on 1 July 1999. Its role is to collect, analyse and share intelligence on organised crime including drug trafficking, illegal immigrant smuggling and terrorist activities. For example, it is required to provide services on offender and offence profiling and provide a risk assessment so as to enable the better targeting of resources. It operates via national units, such as the National Criminal Intelligence Unit (NCIS) in the UK and liaison officers posted at its headquarters.

The European Parliament, which was not consulted during the negotiations to establish Europol, highlighted some twenty issues of concern (European Parliament, 1996), many of which were to do with exercising proper control and data protection. In addition, a recent House of Lords report concerned with exchanging data with non-EU states and bodies stated:

> Information which is incorrect or misused can seriously undermine individuals' rights and freedoms. The exchange of data between Europol and Third States or bodies may aggravate the risk of error or misuse as, in such cases, it may not always be clear which data protection rules apply and which, if any, body is responsible for supervising the data flows. (House of Lords, 1998)

The focus in the EU Action Plans mentioned above has been on the strengthening of Europol's role on the operational side of cross-border investigations, in accordance with Article 30 of the Amsterdam Treaty. This was confirmed at Tampere when it concluded that Europol should receive operational data from member states and be authorised to initiate, conduct or co-ordinate investigations or to create joint investigative teams. Although how this is to be achieved is still under negotiation, it would seem that requests from Europol for a joint investigation are to be non-binding and that Europol staff will work in a support capacity without having any independent, executive powers on foreign territory.

However, the long-term development of Europol and its relationship with other EU bodies such as Eurojust is still open to debate. Again, there are several member states that would like to see the establishment of a supranational EU police unit with full operational powers. Even the European Parliament, for example, believes that Europol's powers should include being able to issue directives to national police authorities.

The need for proper judicial and democratic oversight of EU bodies like Europol whose activities may impinge directly on the criminal judicial system in any one or more member states is generally acknowledged. Although under the Amsterdam Treaty the European Court of Justice's jurisdiction has been extended to include third pillar bodies, it may not review police operations or a member state's exercise of its law and order responsibilities, including national security (TEU, Article 33). It is far from clear what this means but there is a danger that the Court's role may be limited in those very areas which call for vigilant oversight in order to protect individual rights. At the same time, the UK government is continuing to refuse to sign-up to the Court's jurisdiction to give preliminary rulings over a third pillar matter. The judicial supervision of the databases is therefore somewhat of a lottery.

The regulation of data protection is another fundamental human rights issue relevant to these databases. Unfortunately, the developments currently taking place at the EU level over data protection will mean that the differences in treatment between the first and third pillar bodies will deepen. For instance, the 1995 EC Directive on data protection only applies to the first pillar, as will the proposed European Data Protection Supervisor whose powers are to be significantly greater than those exercised by any of the equivalent third pillar bodies. Although the Information Systems and Data Protection Working Party has recently made proposals for a joint secretariat for the various supervisory authorities and a common set of data protection rules for the third pillar instruments, these have been described by the European Parliament as a 'timid step forward that will do nothing whatsoever to resolve the basic problem' (European Parliament, 2000).

It is therefore increasingly anachronistic that only first pillar bodies are to be governed by a harmonised and up-to-date data protection regime, while the others are not. It is arguable that having different standards of data protection – especially when the lesser standard under the third pillar covers areas involving extremely sensitive data – may itself raise questions of compliance with the privacy rights guaranteed by Article 8 of the European Convention on Human Rights (ECHR).

MUTUAL ASSISTANCE

Like police co-operation, judicial co-operation and assistance between member states is also well established. All the EU states are signatories to a number of existing international treaties covering mutual assistance, extradition and mutual recognition of judgments and decisions. They include the 1959 Convention on Mutual Assistance in Criminal Matters, the 1983 Convention on the Transfer of Sentenced Persons and the 1996 Convention relating to Extradition. But as the Tampere proposals show, the agenda now is to enhance these arrangements:

> Enhanced mutual recognition of judicial decisions and judgments and the necessary approximation of legislation would facilitate co-operation between authorities and the judicial protection of individual rights. The European Council therefore endorses the principle of mutual recognition which, in its view, should become the cornerstone of judicial co-operation in both civil and criminal matters within the EU. (European Council, 1999)

The essential requirement underpinning this is that decisions taken in one member state should be accepted as valid and enforceable in any other member state on a reciprocal basis. This can apply to all aspects of the judicial process – from pre-trial orders such as arrest warrants, witness summons and search and seizure orders to final decisions such as sentences and orders for compensation.

It is proposed that, in the short term, this would be achieved by removing some of the safeguards and procedural requirements that are currently in place under both international treaties and national law. For example, the safeguarding principles of double criminality,[11] double jeopardy[12] and the political offence exception may be removed and the role of those executing requests in the requested state would be substantially reduced. In the longer term, the aim is for certain decisions made in one member state to be directly enforceable in another. It is this process of accepting decisions passed in foreign jurisdictions without necessarily having to question the legitimacy of the decision in another state that has become known as mutual recognition.

While the aim of making current procedures simpler and quicker is understandable, the risk is that human rights standards may be breached in the process. In particular, there are dangers in simply relying on the presumption that there are directly comparable systems of justice and protection in the EU member states. The current safeguards and procedures are designed for two main purposes. First, to ensure that a country does not assist in the prosecution or detention of a person by another state in circumstances which are contrary to human rights standards. Secondly, to ensure that disparities between legal systems do not result in defendants and witnesses who are the subject of a request from another country being placed in a worse position than they would be under the national law of the requested country.

The removal of the safeguards may well therefore affect the right to a fair trial as guaranteed by Article 6 of the ECHR. As this right is safeguarded in different ways and at different points under the varying criminal justice systems, the impact of the Tampere proposals is likely to differ between countries. A recent paper illustrates the removal of the double criminality requirement for the UK, for example (JUSTICE, 2000b).[13] Under current UK law applications for search and seizure warrants require that the offence fall within the definition of being a serious arrestable offence. The abolition of the double criminality requirement would mean that UK courts could be asked by a requesting state to execute a warrant for a non-serious offence for which it would have no jurisdiction under domestic law.

As well as resulting in a two-tier system of justice in domestic jurisdictions, there is the risk that decisions will be taken – particularly in relation to joint investigatory teams carrying out cross-border investigations (see above) – to 'forum shop' in order to obtain evidential and other orders where the requirements are less stringent.

It is suggested that these potential difficulties could be overcome by adopting a set of common minimum standards. However, experience shows that this is extremely difficult to achieve – especially a set of standards that complies with those already being applied in member states.

This is largely because of the differences in criminal justice systems, especially between the inquisatorial and accusatorial systems. It is precisely because of these differences that the European Court of Human Rights has not laid down a set of procedural details for ensuring compliance with the rights to fair trial under Article 6. Apart from recognising that certain practices are unfair – such as not allowing a defendant to challenge the evidence – the procedural rules are largely considered a matter for domestic law to prescribe. It therefore provides little assistance in achieving agreed common standards across EU member states.

The focus of international assistance in criminal matters has primarily been on the police authorities concerned in the investigation of crime and the legal authorities concerned with its prosecution. Recently, some attention has started to be paid to the rights of victims of crime in terms of both assistance and their standing in the criminal process. However, little or no attention has been paid to the needs of the defence of those charged in criminal cases with cross-border dimensions. There are a number of issues including a common system of European bail, access to affordable and competent legal representation and to interpretation services. Any structure for European integration of criminal justice procedures must necessarily therefore take on board the position of the defence as well, including the need for defence lawyers to have access to an independent network of co-operation within the EU.

CONCLUSION

The speed at which co-operation over criminal matters is developing at the EU level has been likened to that of the development of the internal market in the 1980s. The combination of significant new powers for cross-border surveillance policing, the creation of large information databases, and the Tampere agenda for a European legal area for mutually enforceable judicial orders clearly illustrate a rapid move towards a formalised system of judicial and police co-operation in criminal matters.

To what extent these developments are likely to result in the establishment of an EU police force or EU prosecuting authority is difficult to predict. There is clearly support from some member states that bodies such as Europol and the proposed Eurojust be developed into independent, supranational units with separate police and prosecuting powers over EU cross-border crime. For others, this would represent a step too far in relinquishing sovereignty over criminal matters: their support stops at the proposals for radical changes in legal procedures such as the direct enforcement of a Eurowarrant across member states.

Whatever the final outcome, there is no doubt that a layer of criminal justice laws and procedures is being rapidly developed at the EU level. As they are matters that fall under the intergovernmental third pillar rather than the EU legal framework, there are continuing concerns over the adequacy of the democratic controls. At the same time, although the European Court of Justice's jurisdiction has recently been extended to cover these areas, the judicial supervision it may exercise is restricted in several significant ways. The challenge therefore is to ensure that these moves for greater co-operation over criminal matters are matched by a strengthening of the protection of fundamental rights. At one level, this involves institutional reforms so as to ensure proper judicial and democratic controls that can call to account the legitimacy of agreements reached and actions taken. On another, it calls for greater attention to be paid to the impact of such changes on individuals particularly when faced with the divergent standards of criminal law in member states.

There is a danger that member states will simply rely on the fact that they have all signed-up to the European Convention on Human Rights as sufficient proof that individual fundamental rights are protected. However, as the negotiations around the recently signed Charter of Fundamental Rights of the European Union acknowledged, further integration requires further measures if there is to be a common sense of justice and fairness. Although this is presently only to have the status of a political declaration rather than a binding charter, the political acceptance of the need to guarantee rights at the EU level is an important step forward that needs to be built upon in the twenty-first century.

NOTES

1   Convention applying the Schengen Agreement of 14 June 1985 between the Governments of the States of the Benelux Economic Union, the Federal Republic of Germany and the French Republic, on the gradual Abolition of Checks at their Common Borders.
2   Portugal and Spain in 1993; Denmark, Finland and Sweden in 1996 with Iceland and Norway as associate member; Italy, Austria and Greece in 1997.
3   These provisions have been replaced by the *Convention Determining the State Responsible for Examining Applications for Asylum Lodged in One of the Member States of the European Communities* – known as the *Dublin Convention* – signed in June 1990.
4   An extraditable offence is one which is punishable under the law of the requesting state to loss of liberty or a detention order for a maximum period of 12 months and under the law of the requested state for a maximum period of 6 months: Article 2 of the 1996 EU Convention on Extradition.
5   These requirements are set to be extended: see ENFOPOL 19, dated 15 March 1999.
6   On the basis of Article 30(2) TEU.
7   See document 8777/00 (Eurojust 2), 23 June 2000 as to German proposal and document 10355/00 (Eurojust 6) as to the Four Presidencies proposal, 20 July 2000.
8   SIRENE stands for 'Supplementary Information Requests at the National Entry'.
9   Under Articles 39 and 46 of the Schengen Convention.

10   See French Presidency Programme of measures to implement the principle of mutual recognition of decisions in criminal matters, 26 June 2000 (Council, 2000).
11   The principle is that no one should be extradited for an offence which is not criminal in both the country making the request and in the requested country.
12   The double jeopardy or *ne bis in idem* principle ensures that a person is not tried twice for the same offence or for the same criminal conduct.

REFERENCES

Anderson, M. (1989) *Policing the World*. Oxford: Clarendon.

Convention on Mutual Assistance in Criminal Matters (2000), House of Lords Report.

Council (1995) *Memorandum of Understanding on the Lawful Interception of Communications*, JHA Council, 25 October.

Council (2000) *Programme of Measures to Implement the Principle of Mutual Recognition of Decisions in Criminal Matters*, Brussels, 26 June.

Council/Commission (1999) *Action Plan of the Council and the Commission on how best to implement the provisions of the Treaty of Amsterdam on an area of freedom, security and justice*, 1999/C 19/01. OJ, 23 January.

European Council (1999) *Presidency Conclusions*, Tampere, 16 October.

European Parliament (1996) *Second Report on Europol*, Committee on Civil Liberties and Internal Affairs (Rapporteur: Nassauer) A4–0061/96.

European Parliament (2000) *Report on establishing a Secretariat for the Joint Supervisory Data Protection Bodies*, Committee on Citizens' Freedoms and Rights, Justice and Home Affairs (Rapporteur: Jorge Salvador Hernandez Mollar), 6 September.

House of Lords (1998) Report of the Select Committee on the European Communities: *Europol: Third Country Rules*, HL 116, July.

House of Lords (2000) Report of the Select Committee on the European Union: *Convention on Mutual Assistance in Criminal Matters between the Member States of the European Union – the Final Stages*, HL 93, August.

JUSTICE (2000a) *The Schengen Information System: A Human Rights Audit*, London: Justice.

JUSTICE (2000b) *EU Cooperation in Criminal Matters: a human rights agenda*, London: Justice.

Schengen (1998) *Annual Report*, Brussels, 22 June.

6 Towards Network Democracy? The Potential of Flexible Integration

Alex Warleigh

DEMOCRACY AND THE PROBLEM OF THE NATION STATE

Democratising the European Union is proving to be extremely difficult. Obliged after the Second World War to launch a project of political and economic integration in response to their appalling economic circumstances, the need to prevent a further war in (western) Europe, and the foreign policy of the United States of America, the initial member governments of what is now the European Union were nonetheless unable to stomach immediate federation. Instead, they set themselves on a course that was supposed to build 'Europe' gradually, giving member governments (and to some extent the populations of the concerned countries) time to get used to the idea. In any case, the build-up of mutual dependencies that the member governments deliberately set in train would at some point take the choice away from them through the stealthy creation of a European state. Sector by sector, policy by policy, the eventual European federation would acquire its competences. Eventually, all that would remain would be the open recognition of what had become reality, and democratisation would come through a new constitution for the United States of Europe.

This 'community method', designed by Jean Monnet, has been imperfect in many ways, including its failure to reconcile member governments to their interdependence by making them fear abnegation. As predicted by scholars like David Mitrany (1944), governments have actually been unwilling to transfer power to what they consider to be a new state-in-waiting, doing so only as a matter of last resort and preserving as much autonomy as possible. Moreover, popular disquiet about the EU is increasing as its impact and end goal – 'ever closer union' – becomes more widely understood (Everts and Sinnott, 1995). After fifty years of European integration we have no United States of Europe, but rather an unwieldy product of the tension between the desire for national autonomy and the continued need for co-operation. Integration has deepened very considerably; but it has done so when governments have been obliged to deal collectively with a problem too intractable to admit unilateralism. This was the case for the formation of the then-EEC (Forsyth, 1981); the passing of the Single European Act (SEA) (Sandholtz and Zysman, 1989); and the agreement of the Maastricht Treaty on European Union (TEU) (Pryce, 1994). The member governments continue to have very different ideas about how the EU should develop, and, as shown by the principle of 'flexibility', vary in the degree of integration they are prepared to countenance.

The democratisation of the EU is an exceptional example of the difficulties of integration, since it brings the question of state-building into very sharp focus. According to conventional wisdom, 'democracy' comes in only one variant – the liberal democratic (Featherstone, 1994). This is a vital but often overlooked point, since the notion that the EU has a 'democratic deficit' relies heavily on comparison with the institutions and practices of the western nation-state. Paradoxically, it also ignores the fact that the component states of the EU are evolving beyond liberal democracy, relying increasingly on legitimacy-generation through expertise rather than popular representation in the legislature. Moreover, at the national level, power is increasingly centred on the executive, meaning that parliamentary governance is being doubly eroded (Andersen and Burns, 1996). Set alongside any other international organisation, the EU has an impeccable democratic record – given the EU's improving levels of transparency, its directly elected parliament, its status of EU citizenship etc., the United Nations, the World Bank, the International Monetary Fund, and the G8, to name but a few, all pale in comparison. Compared with totalitarian states or dictatorships, the EU is a paragon of democratic virtue.

In other words, and however inexplicitly, democratising the EU is usually seen as a process of making a new superstate which, in order to be democratic, should replicate the institutions and structures with which Europeans are familiar at the national level. Support for democratisation ultimately depends on how much power one is willing to transfer to the EU – witness the member governments' collective lack of desire to make good on their rhetorical commitments to the radical reform of the Commission after its resignation in 1999. There are two related reasons why Eurosceptics oppose such radical change. First, there is the issue of the cost to national sovereignty, which is discussed above. Secondly, there is the question of public opinion. A strategy to make the EU truly democratic, runs the conventional argument, requires that individuals accept the EU as a suitable instrument of government (legitimacy), and also consider that they form a deeply felt community with the nationals of other member states as well as their own (identity). Eurosceptics consider that such a sense of community is normatively unacceptable, given the differences between national publics and traditions, which must for them be preserved at all costs. More neutral voices do not share this view, but do consider that attempting to build such a community would be both unlikely to succeed, and likely to generate resistance. Evidence that the EU has high levels of legitimacy and popular identification is not plentiful. Indeed, voter turn-out rates for the 1999 elections to the European Parliament were the lowest ever despite its growth in power. According to the EU's own opinion surveys, 85 per cent of respondents still consider themselves either solely or primarily to be member state nationals rather than Europeans (Eurobarometer 48, 1998). Thus, for many commentators the EU is in a double bind: it is doomed to lurch from crisis to crisis, while member governments resist as much deepening as they can and the union is itself unable to generate the necessary groundswell of popular support to justify significant change, even if member governments would agree to it.

In this chapter I argue that, normatively at least, such a view is unnecessarily bleak. For all the difficulties of the integration process, it has produced a new multi-level polity, in which actors from all levels – local, regional, national and European – play a part in governance, even if it is usually the national and European actors who predominate. What is necessary is to consider this kind of Euro polity not as unfinished business (the traditional pro-integration view), or as several steps too far (the sceptical view), but as a normative good in its own right. Instead of considering the EU an unfinished exercise in state building, we should view it as a working joint governance system, whose primary virtue lies in avoiding serious (armed) conflict between member states and the ability to provide more general welfare than would be available through individual action by national governments. In other words, it is necessary to separate the 'community method' from its state-building aspects and stress its functional qualities. Democratic reform of the EU is possible if we think 'outside the box', avoid using liberal democracy as a template, and investigate alternative models such as what Jachtenfuchs, Diez and Jung (1998) call 'network democracy'. This theory emphasises the fostering of a culture of dialogue in order to increase popular participation in EU decision-making, thereby both increasing legitimacy and facilitating the development of the currently absent cross-border political culture. In turn, this would help create a sense of common political identity on which to base further reform. Moreover, in network democracy, the EU is seen not as a potential state but as a series of overlapping sectoral agencies akin to the proposals of the functionalists (Mitrany, 1933, 1944). The network model can thus serve to reduce opposition to democratic reform of the EU by assuaging both popular and elite concerns about the development of a superstate.

The plan of the chapter is as follows. First, I set out the concept of network democracy and establish its appropriateness for the EU. Subsequently, I investigate the potential of its institutional baseline – flexible integration – and ask whether it can help produce a network Europe. In order to do this I of course also investigate 'closer co-operation' (the Treaty provision on flexible integration, which allows a subgroup of member states to proceed with integration even without the participation of the full set of member states). Finally, I investigate current issues of democratic reform on the EU agenda. I conclude that despite its normative value, the network democracy concept is not sufficiently central to EU reform efforts. Inability to make a liberal democratic state out of the EU will eventually oblige member governments to investigate network democracy through the use of flexibility. However, the beginning of the twenty-first century will see the necessary pressures for this build-up, rather than being acted upon. As a result, in the early years of the millennium, the EU will continue to be marked by the stain of the democratic deficit.

NETWORK DEMOCRACY

Having become a kind of polity in its own right, the EU is in need of a certain amount of direct legitimacy in order to prosper (Beetham and Lord, 1998): it cannot simply count on the legitimacy of its component states, since the latter is open to question and in any case is bestowed only reluctantly by national governments. The EU's development of legitimacy is difficult for a further reason. To a great extent, EU legitimacy has to derive from policy output, and in this respect it is remarkable that negative integration – the removal of barriers to joint action – is far more in evidence than positive integration – the establishment of new common policies.[1] Furthermore, there is a complex relationship between changes in the role of the state and what the EU's citizens consider it should do about them. Developing the powers of the EU might actually run counter to deliberate national policies; for example, 'rolling back the state' at the national level does not incline most voters of the centre-right to seek strong social policies at the EU level, but rather to oppose them. Even when system need can be demonstrated or at least considered likely, it is not clear that the various publics of the EU support expansion of the Union's remit any more than national elites – there was no mass clamour for a single market as a response to the oil crisis of the 1970s, and today the streets of Madrid, Stockholm and Paris are not noticeably thronging with protesters demanding that the 'economic' be put back into economic and monetary union (EMU).

Perceptions of EU legitimacy, however, do change over time (Duchesne and Frognier, 1995). In the short term, playing to the public gallery by trying to develop support-winning policies is difficult. Nonetheless, in the medium term there is room for manoeuvre. Although citizens do not tend to identify deeply with the EU, they do on the whole accept its place in the general apparatus of governance in Europe (Banchoff and Smith, 1999). According to Eurobarometer polls, the EU is actually seen as the most suitable actor in certain fields; general legitimacy levels may not be high, but in policy areas like development aid and environmental protection, where EU powers tally with popular ideas about what transnational governance should be about, the EU can be confident of at least default public support (Blondel et al., 1998; Sinnott, 1994, 1995). In the long term, this affords grounds for optimism: an EU which reflects, in general, popular conceptions of what transnational governance is for is likely to be supported. Above all, this means not seeking to replace the nation-state, to which most people remain sincerely if perhaps irrationally attached. No matter that nation-states are usually themselves artificial creations born of conquest or revolution, with bogus 'traditions' and more than one 'ethnic group' despite official claims to a single common nationality. The EU has few if any resources to mobilise against these powerful emotional attachments; even were such extreme social engineering ethically acceptable, the EU could not do what many nation-states did and impose a sense of nationality. It simply does not have either the requisite resources or the coercive power.

Instead, the EU must seek legitimacy through constructing itself as a non-state entity, albeit possibly one more closely bound together than at present. This is problematic, since those in favour of integration, and those with institutional interests in its deepening, have often seen state-building and integration as synonymous. They have sought, as 'purposeful opportunists' (Cram, 1997), to build up the range of EU competences wherever possible, responding not primarily to policy need but to opportunities to create new competences whether the EU really needed them or not. From the perspective of orthodox European idealism, such action is a sad necessity: 'Europeans' need to steal a march on retrograde national governments wherever possible in the name of Europa. Changing this perception will be tough, although Commission Presidents Santer and Prodi have both indicated general support for the new perspective.[2]

What is necessary is to recognise that the existence of different traditions and political cultures in the EU makes it difficult, if not impossible, to establish a priori solutions to the problem of what counts as good governance in the EU.[3] In order for the EU system to be seen as legitimate, and for the various national publics to develop greater affinities with each other, not only policies but also principles and ideas must be negotiated over time. An EU value set would eventually emerge from such negotiations; in turn, this could serve as an underpinning for institutional design and policy output of the union. This kind of democracy stresses the role of citizen participation. It envisions the union as a series of overlapping communities, defined both territorially and functionally. Legitimacy arises from citizens' participation, 'ownership' of the union through greater involvement with it, and a sense of affective engagement born of stakeholding – a sense that the EU is important, and that what one does in order to shape it both matters and counts. Identities are not threatened since they are multi-level and plural; individuals can identify as gay, black, female, Islamic and so on, as well as with their town, region, country, Europe or even the world. In 'network democracy', identities are not opposed but rather co-existent. This does not mean that they are never in tension; but network democracy seeks to allow and address such tensions rather than leave them to fester.

The intellectual basis of this model is clearly in the tradition of deliberative democracy, a tradition which is increasingly seen as a source of solutions to the democratic deficit given the existence of a pluralist Euro polity (Eriksen and Fossum, 2000). Fifteen member governments and their publics, plus all the EU institutions, bodies and policy regimes cannot be treated as homogeneous in discussions of democracy or anything else. Differences between them persist, and solutions to difficult problems must come through negotiated compromise in which differences are seen as reasonable rather than perverse, and in which self-interest is considered best served through a recognition of interdependence. Importantly, this means abandoning attempts to secure dominance. If one is in a position of inter-dependence, one's general welfare depends on that of those on whom one is dependent as much as one's own. In other words, differences are seen not as a problem but a starting point for discussions that produce outcomes to which everyone can agree. Importantly, in such views of democracy, interests are not simply bargained, but *negotiated*. Instead of making pack-age deals, member governments would prioritise the seeking of mutually acceptable decisions on any given policy. The emphasis is on democracy as a practice, in which articulated reasons rather than simply power balances shape outcomes (Bellamy and Warleigh, 1998). As pointed out by Eriksen and Fossum '[o]nly deliberation can get political results right as it entails the act of justifying the results to the people who are bound by them' (2000: 48).

Of course, deliberative democracy has its weaknesses. It is heavily idealistic, although practical. As acknowledged by its proponents, its sheer difference from liberal democracy might itself cause a negative reaction: citizens may simply not recognise such a system as democratic given the ideational hegemony of liberal democracy (Jachtenfuchs et al., 1998: 435). Deliberative democracy does not set great store by traditional majoritar-ianism; it considers the process of reaching unanimous agreement through negotiation to be more important than reaching an agreement itself. In the real world, this is not always suitable: if certain decisions have to be made despite an inability to reach a negotiated settlement, then voting may be necessary. Other aspects of liberal democracy may also have lasting popularity. For example, the European Parliament (EP) may prove to be a necessary feature of the future EU, and the existence of this majoritarian institution would have to be squared with the generally more 'deliberative' culture. Moreover, deliberative democracy may simply ask more of states and citizens than they are willing to give; not in terms of sovereignty, but in terms of time and effort. For deliberative democracy to work, states will have to accept long negotiations, and at the individual level citizens will have to be more active and less apathetic than many appear to wish (Blondel et al., 1998: 79). Relatedly, we have as yet only the germ of a Europeanised civil society, which requires careful fostering and institu-tional encouragement.

However, there is no doubt that the EU could benefit from the appli-cation of some kind of deliberative democracy. Although the semantic closeness should not be stretched too far, the fact that the Union functions by networking (Peterson, 1995; Warleigh, 2000a), that is by drawing together pools of concerned actors and developing joint strategies for resolving problems and creating policies, is hopeful. Moreover, it should not be forgotten that 'policy entrepreneurs' – actors willing and able to press their own interests by building coalitions of support amongst the relevant actor communities – can often perform a vital role as brokers of an agreement between parties with ostensibly entrenched, and differing positions, meaning that pushing matters to a vote in order to resolve differences may not always be appropriate, or indeed necessary. Adrienne Héritier (1996) shows how this is already true in the case of the EU regulatory policy-making, and John Peterson (1995) demonstrates the importance of such 'informal politics' across the range of EU decision-making. This complements the apparent culture of the Council of Ministers, in which the search for consensus rather than voting is usually prioritised, even when the Treaty permits the use of the qualified majority voting (QMV) mechanism (Chryssochoou, 1994).

At elite level, at least some of the necessary behavioural prerequisites of network democracy are thus already present. Applying the network democracy model would increase the range of stakeholders involved in EU decision-making, at the very least by increasing the range of available opportunities to contest or support (national) positions with which an individual or group (dis)agrees. Although it would to some extent favour self-selecting individuals and groups, network democracy would represent a significant departure from the often clientelistic, quasi-corporatist current arrangements for consultation of interest groups by the Commission, which often exclude a broader range of societal interests – sometimes to the Commission's cost (Warleigh, 2000b). Moreover – and absolutely crucially – it must be remembered that there is as yet no European *demos*, or people, in any conventional sense (Chryssochoou, 1998). There is thus no reason to suppose that ostensibly appropriate majoritarian, liberal democratic models will be accepted by the publics of the member states, since in the absence of a strong sense of solidarity there is no reason for citizens of, say, France to accept great sacrifices for, say, Finland, or indeed vice versa. However, this is not to say that such a sense of community either should or will never arise. Deliberative democracy – ongoing negotiation of common problems by concerned citizens and groups – is likely over time and to some extent to foster exactly this by iterated contact and communication.

There are even isolated examples of institutional attempts to foster new deliberative practices, and thus move from network governance to network democracy, at the EU level. Héritier (1999) observes that the Commission has attempted to construct policy communities of stakeholders, in order both to increase the legitimacy of its proposals in terms of quality and secure their acceptance by those whom they principally concern. Scott (1998) argues that the 'partnership principle' of cohesion policy constitutes a similar quest for legitimacy through the harnessing of local expertise and the inculcation of a deeper sense of attachment to the EU through engagement with its policy-making processes. However, the most obvious parallel between the EU and the network democracy model is the idea of flexible integration, in which the EU emerges as a gestalt of variable overlapping policy subsystems rather than a federation-in-waiting. In the next section I explore these links more thoroughly.

FLEXIBILITY: ANTITHESIS OF INTEGRATION?

Flexible integration comes in many different guises, as ably summed up by Alexander Stubb (1996). The three principal varieties are set out below. Multi-speed models conceive the EU as a system of several tiers, in which member governments are differentiated not by lack of common vision but by ability to integrate at the same pace. Thus, on a policy-by-policy basis, certain member governments press ahead, and the rest commit to catch up later. For example, Greece joined the single currency as soon as it met the convergence criteria, even though it was unable to participate at the launch of the currency in January 1999. In the concentric circles model, member governments are divided into discrete bands circling around a core group of countries. In each band are member governments that are able or willing to accept the relevant degree of integration, but not more. In this model, the EU set of policies is divided into certain distinct categories, and member governments have to choose which package they are willing or able to accept. Governments may well fail to catch up with the vanguard group, either through deliberate choice or long-term inability to meet entrance criteria. At the moment, this model has not been translated into reality, apart perhaps from the general British and Danish reluctance to join anything. Finally, the à la carte model allows governments to pick and choose from the set of EU policies like so many items on a menu. In this model, there is no implication that governments will catch up with the vanguard group, although such an eventuality is not excluded. In some policy areas, governments could lead the union; in others, they could be far behind. For example, Ireland takes part in EMU, but as a neutral country is on the fringes of the military aspects of the budding EU security policy.

Although none of these models comes without costs – for example, a government consigning itself to the outer rings of the concentric circles is unlikely to wield the same power in the EU as one at the heart of each policy – flexible integration is inherently positive. It allows member governments to integrate as they wish. It allows those who so choose to deepen their co-operation, often significantly – consider as an example the single currency. Often quietly, member governments have always liked flexibility.[4] They have negotiated and imposed long derogation periods from pieces of legislation, which often become unofficially permanent. Through preference for directives rather than regulations as the form of most EU policy, they allow each other to differ significantly in the implementation of joint policy. Moreover, since the 1979 *Cassis-de-Dijon* case,[5] it has been clear that the entire single market is based not on the idea of harmonisation but on approximation grounded in an agreed set of minimum standards and the acceptance as equivalents of different national policy regimes. Looking below the surface of integration, it is clear that flexibility is *necessary* for the EU; without it, integration would never have made progress. However, the first official recognition of the principle as a potential cornerstone of integration is cautious; in the attempt to codify past practice, member governments were confronted by the big question of the EU – is it to become a state or not? – and shied away.

The Amsterdam Treaty provisions on flexibility ('closer cooperation' [CC], Articles K15, K16, K17 and K12, as well as the new Article 5) do not do the principle justice. In all likelihood, they are a recipe for stagnation, so difficult to invoke that their utility is limited (Ehlerman, 1998). Flexible integration will be possible only regarding those policy areas already part of EU competence. As a result, although it can be used to deepen integration in existing areas of EU policy, CC cannot be used to extend the range of EU competence, thus failing to replicate what is theoretically one of flexibility's main virtues. Moreover, much has been made of the judgement that the Amsterdam Treaty makes the first formal (i.e. Treaty-inscribed) recognition of the Luxembourg Compromise, made to bring the French back into the EU system after de Gaulle's walk-out in 1965 (Devuyst, 1998, 1999; Philippart and Edwards, 1999; Moravcsik and Nicolaïdis, 1999). This 'compromise' essentially left any member government able to invoke a veto if it deemed a proposal countered its 'vital national interests' (which it defined itself). Although this undoubtedly contributed to the Eurosclerosis period, the Luxembourg Compromise was never given the formal status of primary or even secondary law, and was deemed to have been thrown into the dustbin of history after the SEA reintroduced qualified majority voting (Wistrich, 1989). CC can thus be represented as part of a challenge to the existing scope and powers of the EU institutions by member governments.[6] The latter appear to be seeking inter alia to repatriate certain powers of the Commission, shift the emphasis from EC legislation to soft law and voluntary agreements, and impose flexibility rather than extending QMV (Devuyst,1999). It might also be added that the German Constitutional Court's judgement in the *Brunner case*[7] does nothing to ensure the safety of the presumed primacy of European law.

But flexibility also needs to be considered in light of the general refashioning of the (nation) state in western Europe: the neo-liberal triumph of the 1980s is shifting to the 'Third Way', and 'the state' as traditionally configured is a beneficiary of neither. Indeed, regulatory and managerial governance is preferred (Majone, 1996). Flexibility is thus in keeping with the rather elusive style of governance in the *Zeitgeist*: integration does not have to head towards a state or be uniform to be deepened. A suitable parallel may instead be with the development of the European Council, created to steer the integration process in a fashion which both partially removed a similar role from the Commission and made such a function acceptable to the member governments, thereby ensuring it was carried out and the integration project continued (Bulmer, 1996). If flexibility is allowed, it potentially delegitimises using non-EU mechanisms to make policy (Philippart and Edwards, 1999), and thereby ensures that the Union remains a viable policy-making instrument. Moreover, it can already be seen as a means of extending the full Community *acquis*: incorporating the Schengen Accords, even at the price of opt-outs for Ireland, Denmark and the UK, gave them the full force of EU law (Shaw, 1998). Indeed, as Philippart and Edwards (1999) point out, even flexibility is flexible: it operates differently in each Pillar of the EU,[8] giving the Commission a substantial role in pillar 1 and an important one in pillar 3. In any case, a government seeking to invoke the veto to block an attempt at flexible integration cannot do so without cost. The Treaty provides for a government thereby frustrated to insist on a kind of peer tribunal in the European Council, which could in theory impose some kind of informal penalty on the recalcitrant state. Moreover, at least in pillar 1, the real veto power is with the Commission, which can simply refuse to make the necessary formal proposal for a flexibility measure proposed to it by the concerned member governments (Article 5a [2], Amsterdam Treaty).

If flexibility is part of an intergovernmental master plan to claw back sovereignty, it is thus at best imperfectly operationalised, itself the product of the need to marry national sovereignty to the functional demands of the system member governments themselves created. Amsterdam is merely a staging post on a gradual journey whose end-point is still as undecided as the means of getting there are disputed. A typical elite bargain, 'closer co-operation' is as much a managerial device as an organising principle for the EU (Shaw, 1998). Failing to make the necessary links with democratic reform, member governments at Amsterdam merely obliged themselves to revisit the issue subsequently.[9]

FLEXIBILITY AND DEMOCRACY

The relationship between flexibility and democracy is open to question, not just because of the shortcomings of CC but also because flexible integration is all about allowing the creation of inequalities. Although according to the Treaty, flexibility is supposed not to damage socio-economic cohesion, it is difficult to see how this can actually be the case. If the government of country A opts out of a given policy area, then the people of that country will clearly have fewer EU rights, or at least fewer benefits from integration, than those of country B, whose government opts in. Moreover, the actions of the government of country A can have effects on the populations of other countries: witness the nationals of most EU states who, despite their country's participation in the Schengen provisions on freedom of movement, have to show their passports to get back into their own country when returning from Britain thanks to the latter's refusal to adopt the relevant *acquis*.[10]

However, this fact can only be considered problematic if viewed from a certain perspective. In the above example, concerns about the inability of the citizens of country A to benefit from rights available to others, and the impact of their government's choice to opt-out on the citizens of other countries, privilege the putative concerns of the EU as a whole over those of country A and its citizens. Where opting-out stems from a government decision in keeping with popular opinion, it cannot be considered undemocratic. Unfortunate side-effects may simply have to be borne as a recognition that democracy must take precedence. The problem of democracy arises solely when government choices (not) to participate in a given policy regime are out of tune with the wishes of their citizens. In any case, opting-out is by definition situation-specific; such choices are about discrete policy areas (or groups of them), not the *acquis* in its entirety. Accordingly, it is far less likely that a government will commit itself to European integration – or fail to do so – in a manner which is generally out of step with public opinion. The latter eventuality is far more likely with the traditional 'community method', which has produced a set of EU policies and powers almost entirely at odds with what EU citizens consider the union should do (Blondel et al., 1998).

Indeed, it was early advocates of flexibility who first pointed out the democratic deficit (Mitrany, 1965). These scholars – the functionalists – always urged the creation of a (global) system of overlapping spheres of governance in which specific policy areas are governed as separately as possible. They argued that no government should be forced to participate in any of these regimes, but that no citizen should be denied membership of the new post-national polity simply as a result of national government intransigence (Hancock, 1941/4).[11] They drew up plans for world governance which saw democracy as a matter of both representation and welfare provision. Instead of a new state, there would be a series of specialised agencies, each with representative parliaments. The agencies would ensure equal distribution of goods between the populations of the various states, since there would be no motive to discriminate on grounds of nationality (Mitrany, 1933, 1944).

Contemporary scholarship on the idea of postnational democracy has some extremely interesting parallels with such models. The central questions explored in this body of work are how to reconcile multiple identities and provide a political system which is both accountable and offers sufficient opportunities for political participation (see inter alia Chryssochoou, 1998; Curtin, 1997; Follesdal and Koslowski, 1998; Lord, 1998). In other words, democracy in a context beyond the nation-state must allow for the needs of the system as a whole as well as the wishes of its particular component parts. In the case of the EU, this means not just acknowledging the fact that the Union 'contains not only multiple layers of community affiliation but also increasingly dispersed and differentiated modes of governance' (Bellamy and Warleigh, 1998: 468), but treating it as a normative good in its own right rather than an unfortunate problem with which we are faced. In this endeavour, flexibility is an extremely helpful tool. It can act as an instrument for the development of network democracy by further breaking down the link between the citizen and the nation-state, while allowing the latter's continuation when popular acceptance of change is insufficient. It can also help show that liberal democracy is not a suitable model for transnational systems such as the EU. As a result, it thereby reduces opposition to democratisation (since the state-building issue is taken off the agenda).[12] It remains to examine the current treatment of democratic reform in the EU in order to assess what progress towards network democracy is likely in the near future.

CONCLUSIONS: TOWARDS NETWORK DEMOCRACY?

Many events which cannot yet be predicted will shape the EU of the early twenty-first century. One intergovernmental conference (IGC) was of course concluded in Nice in December 2000, and it was agreed that another one would take place in 2004. The impact of EMU and enlargement will be evident, but the pace of the former will be greater than that of the latter of the new century. Subsequently, the attendant massive changes to the economic and political natures of the EU will be under way, but by no means complete.

One block to radical reforms may come from the regions of the federal member states such as Germany, and it is likely that future integration will have to pay heed to the pronouncements of the Bundestag, given the Länder's collective ability via that chamber of the German parliament to prevent the ratification of new Treaties. On the other hand, close observation of developments in foreign, and possibly even security, policies will also be required. The Helsinki Summit of 1999 marked a new willingness of the member governments to make progress in integrating this most difficult of areas, agreeing to grant the EU access to its own troops in order to implement the so-called Petersberg tasks (humanitarian and peace-keeping arrangements), which were made the Union's preserve by the Amsterdam Treaty; a competence deepened at Nice. The key variable to investigate, however, is flexibility, since this is the litmus test of two key issues: the willingness of the member governments to make progress, and their willingness to do so as a subgroup if necessary. What follows are suggested as likely maximal changes, not driven by any normative orientation but rather by a reading of the current dynamics of the ongoing union reform process. The actual result will inevitably be somewhat different, and possibly more extensive if exogenous factors combine with the effect of the euro to support this.

In relation to the institutional framework, the European Council and Council of the European Union (Council of Ministers) will remain central, and are likely to be carrying out their existing policy functions. As agreed at Nice, enlargement will result in an increase in the use of QMV, a reweighting of Council votes in favour of the larger states, and one Commissioner per member state until the number of member states exceeds twenty-seven. The 1999 Commission débâcle increased the likelihood of augmenting its accountability to the EP, which process could even go so far as to instigate election of the Commission President by the members of the European Parliament. If this right of election is given, it can be expected to facilitate the development of stronger transnational political parties, or at least reinforce their cohesion in the EP. As a corollary, and despite the fact that it would be a logical consequence of increasing stakeholder participation in policy design and implementation, the Council will not have moved to vote in public. National governments will wish to retain their ability to strike important bargains in secret, considering that reforms to the Commission–EP relationship will distract popular attention from the lack of transparency in their own institution. Continuing to legislate in camera as the Council would also allow member governments to 'balance' the EP's increased access to both legislative power and information about the workings of the Council since the advent of co-decision (and particularly its endgame, the conciliation process).

The most significant changes relative to current status may concern two of the lesser bodies, the Ombudsman and the Committee of the Regions (CoR). The Ombudsman's access to information, powers and status will be improved as both a concession to the Scandinavian bloc and an expression of the member states' intention to 'modernise' Union governance while omitting to legislate in public. Moreover, CoR may come closer to the centre of the stage as a means of placating the German Länder (not to mention those of Austria and the regions of Spain and Belgium). CoR could be given increased resources in order to bring the EU 'message' to the citizens (thus fulfilling one of its primary purposes and acting as a poisoned chalice for the Länder). It might also have gained a special institutional status which allows it extra gravitas as co-guardian of subsidiarity with the Commission, although it would still be a consultative body regarding legislative proposals.

As demonstrated by the limitations of the EU Charter of Fundamental Rights, its failure to add significantly to the rights already enjoyed by EU citizens, and its at best questionable justiciability, 'European' citizenship will probably remain largely 'frozen' in formal terms (Warleigh, 1998). Hints of network democracy will, however, be evident in the EU. With the launch of the civil dialogue project as part of the preparation for the next IGC in 2004, there may well be greater public and NGO awareness of, and participation in, the debate surrounding European integration. This might translate into a sense of greater identification with the Union. If there is sufficient imagination, the 'partnership principle' could be extended to areas other than regional/structural policy: perhaps to the fields of consumer protection and public health, and even that mainstay of experiment in progressive approaches to EU policy-making, environment policy. This

could be very significant as it would couple greater stakeholder consultation with co-decision and often also QMV, creating a model of decision-
making which could subsequently be applied to other areas in the first
pillar. Consequently, there will be changes to the EU's political culture
other than the accommodation of increased diversity thanks to
enlargement.

The major problems of EU democracy will not be solved, however. This
is because such reforms will have failed to make the necessary break with
the nation-state-based, liberal democratic model, even though they will
demonstrate its inapplicability by revealing the continued reluctance of
most member governments effectively to make themselves superfluous. I
argue elsewhere with regard to EU citizenship that behind-the-scenes purposeful opportunism and institutional tinkering sometimes mean that
official stalling masks the potential for future change (Warleigh, 2001).
However, at this fundamental level, it is unlikely that the perceived necessary self-sacrifice will be made in the absence of a massive and unpredicted
threat, such as near total economic collapse.

The provisions for closer co-operation remain insufficient. As a result, to
unleash the potential of flexibility, reform will be necessary. Current indications are that France and Germany will seek to make this a key issue of
the first decade of the millennium, and also that they have different views
about it. As a result, flexibility is likely to be a battleground for some time,
and its potential for reconfiguring integration will be correspondingly
truncated for at least the short–medium term.

I began this chapter with the remark that in the EU, democratisation
has proved extremely difficult. Since this is likely to remain true for some
years yet, I will conclude it in the same way. Although many of the
ingredients of successful reform are visible now – flexibility, the fostering
of public participation in decision-making, the abandonment of state-
building as a model – it is unlikely that they will become explicit guiding
principles of the EU at any point in the near future. This is because, at
heart, member governments do not consider that European integration is
about democracy, even if they claim to be concerned about the democratic deficit. Agents of integration may carry it out with high motives.
Actors both within and outside the member governments often seek to
foster integration, not just for institutional gain but because they consider
it the best way to achieve the goal of maximum public welfare (security,
peace and economic growth) as such is, after all, the 'ethics of integration'
(Bellamy and Warleigh, 1998: 453–6). But in the final analysis, member
governments continue with the integration process because they are
economically dependent upon it and also because they perceive it to be a
potential means of reasserting themselves, albeit as a collective, in a way
impossible for them unilaterally – even Germany. It is worth recollecting
here that the single market and currency were forged not out of idealism
but to enable the EU to rival the USA and Japan (Sandholtz and Zysman,
1989: 95). As a consequence, the problem of democratisation will receive

attention, but not radical surgery. Member governments will prefer to deal with ongoing 'reform' and disaffection rather than confront the issues squarely.

The prospects for real progress in democratisation thus lie further into the future. European integration is anything but static, and the pressures for reform are likely to build despite the possible developments described above. This is because such changes will insufficiently replicate liberal democracy, while also failing adequately to tap the potential of the network alternative. The EU will continue to muddle along until eventually popular disaffection will force further change. This event becomes ever likelier in the context of enlargement, with its related increase in diversity and wealth of the member countries. Not least because of this, a majority of governments will in a few years have reached the point of maximum frustration with the present system, and will decide to unleash flexibility, since not all member states will agree to form a European federation. Instead, a subgroup will federate. The EU will eventually become a kind of network democracy in order to join the laggard group(s) to the vanguard. However, this will not be through idealism or deliberate choice, but through the inability of the 'community method' to reach its goal, at least as far as the total of member governments is concerned.

NOTES

1   However, the single currency may well shift this balance since it is difficult to imagine a more visible 'positive' product of integration.
2   For a brief further discussion of the issue of agency, see Warleigh (2000b).
3   The following paragraph draws on Jachtenfuchs (1998) and Jachtenfuchs et al. (1998).
4   I use 'flexibility' and 'flexible integration' as synonyms for the sake of variety.
5   Case 120/78 ECR (1979: 649).
6   Proponents of this view should note that the national interest clause applied in only two instances: preventing a group of member states from deciding under QMV to adopt measures under the CC provisions; and preventing a QMV implementation decision in pillar 2 (Common Foreign and Security Policy). It may thus be less significant than is often alleged.
7   For a discussion of the legal challenge to the Maastricht Treaty on the grounds that it was an unacceptable challenge to national sovereignty, see 'Brunner versus the European Union Treaty' in Common Market Law Reports 69:2 (1994).
8   The Maastricht Treaty divided the EU into three 'pillars'. Pillar 1 is the European Community, i.e. the vast bulk of what the EU does. In this 'pillar', all the EU institutions have their full range of powers. Pillar 2 (Common Foreign and Security Policy), and pillar 3 (after Amsterdam called Police and Judicial Co-operation in Criminal Matters, but still usually referred to under its Maastricht name, Justice and Home Affairs), are more intergovernmental.
9   The 2000 IGC did not result in a major breakthrough on the issue of flexibility, although the Amsterdam provisions on closer co-operation were modified to ease the restraints on their use, notably by removing the national interest veto

of non-participating states. Furthermore, both France and Germany have made it quite clear that they see some kind of flexibility as the crucial catalyst for the development of the EU, and have pledged to place it at the heart of post-2000 reform negotiations.

10 It should be noted that this particular example of opting-out may not endure much longer, since the UK has recently and quietly decided to accept parts of this *acquis*.

11 The date of publication is subject to dispute. Hancock claimed the book came out in 1941, and thus pre-dated a work by the main functionalist writer, David Mitrany. However, a counter-claim that the two were published in 1944 cannot to my knowledge be disproved.

12 Of course, nothing in theory prevents a subgroup of the member states from federating, although the Treaty presently does. This could easily be a beneficial and democratic result of flexibility – the possibility for the various member governments and publics to differ in their commitment to integration without blocking progress for those who wish it.

REFERENCES

Andersen, S. and Burns, T. (1996) 'The European Union and the Erosion of Parliamentary Democracy: A Study of Post-parliamentary Governance', in S. Andersen and K. Eliassen (eds), *The European Union: How Democratic Is It?* London: Sage.

Banchoff, T. and Smith, M. (1999) 'Introduction: Conceptualisisng Legitimacy in a Contested Polity', in T. Banchoff and M. Smith (eds), *Legitimacy and the European Union*. London: Routledge.

Bellamy, R. and Warleigh, A. (1998) 'From an Ethics of Integration to an Ethics of Participation: Citizenship and the Future of the European Union', *Millennium*, 27 (3): 447–70.

Beetham, D. and Lord, C. (1998) *Legitimacy and the European Union*. Harlow: Longman.

Blondel, J., Sinnott, R. and Svensson, P. (1998) *People and Parliament in the European Union: Participation, Legitimacy and Democracy*. Oxford: Clarendon.

Bulmer, S. (1996) 'The European Council and the Council of the European Union – Shapers of a European Confederation?', *Publius*, 26 (4): 17–42.

Chryssochoou, D. (1994) 'Democracy and Symbiosis in the European Union: Towards a Confederal Consociation?', *West European Politics*, 17 (4): 1–14.

Chryssochoou, D. (1998) *Democracy in the European Union*. London: Tauris.

Cram, L. (1997) *Policy-Making in the European Union: Conceptual Lenses and the Integration Process*. London: Routledge.

Curtin, D. (1997) *Postnational Democracy: The European Union in Search of a Political Philosophy*. The Hague: Kluwer.

Devuyst, Y. (1998) 'Treaty Reform in the European Union: The Amsterdam Process', *Journal of European Public Policy*, 5 (4): 615–31.

Devuyst, Y. (1999) 'The Community Method after Amsterdam', *Journal of Common Market Studies*, 37 (1): 109–20.

Duchesne, S. and Frognier, A.-P. (1995) 'Is There a European Identity?', in O. Niedermayer and R. Sinnott (eds) *Public Opinion and Internationalized Governance*. Oxford: Oxford University Press.

Ehlerman, C.D. (1998) 'Differentiation, Flexibility, Closer Cooperation: The New Provisions of the Amsterdam Treaty', *European Law Journal*, 4 (3): 246–70.

Eriksen, E.O. and Fossum, J.E. (eds) (2000) *Democracy in the European Union: Integration Through Deliberation?* London: Routledge.

Eurobarometer (1998) 'Monitoring Public Opinion in the European Union'. No. 48. DGX. European Commission.

Everts, P. and Sinnott, R. (1995) 'Conclusion: European Publics and Legitimacy of Internationalized Governance', in O. Niedermayer and R. Sinnott (eds) *Public Opinion and Internationalized Governance.* Oxford: Oxford University Press.

Featherstone, K. (1994) 'Jean Monnet and the "Democratic Deficit" of the European Union', *Journal of Common Market Studies*, 32 (2): 149–70.

Follesdal, A. and Koslowski, P. (eds) (1998) *Democracy and the European Union.* London/Heidelberg: Springer.

Forsyth, M. (1981) *Unions of States.* Leicester: Leicester University Press.

Hancock, J.R. (1941/4) *Plan For Action.* London: Whitcombe and Toombs.

Héritier, A. (1996) 'The Accommodation of Diversity in European Policy Making and Its Outcomes: Regulatory Policy as a Patchwork', *European University Institute Working Paper* 96/2. Florence: European University Institute.

Héritier, A. (1999) 'Elements of Democratic Legitimation in Europe: An Alternative Perspective', *Journal of European Public Policy*, 6 (2): 269–82.

Jachtenfuchs, M. (1998) 'Democracy and Governance in the European Union', in A. Follesdal and P. Koslowski (eds) *Democracy and the European Union.* London/Heidelberg: Springer.

Jachtenfuchs, M., Diez, T. and Jung, S. (1998) 'Which Europe? Conflicting Models of Legitimate Political Order', *European Journal of International Relations*, 4 (4): 409–45.

Lord, C. (1998) *Democracy in the European Union.* Sheffield: Sheffield Academic Press.

Majone, G. (1996) *Regulating Europe.* London: Routledge.

Mitrany, D. (1933) *The Progress of International Government.* London: Allen and Unwin.

Mitrany, D. (1944) *A Working Peace System.* London: Royal Institute of International Affairs.

Mitrany, D. (1965) 'The Prospect of Integration – Federal or Functional?', *Journal of Common Market Studies*, 4 (2): 119–49.

Moravcsik, A. and Nicolaïdis, K. (1999) 'Explaining the Treaty of Amsterdam: Interests, Influence, Institutions', *Journal of Common Market Studies*, 37 (1): 59–85.

Peterson, J. (1995) 'Decision-Making in the European Union: Towards a Framework for Analysis', *Journal of European Public Policy*, 2 (1): 69–93.

Philippart, E. and Edwards, G. (1999) 'The Provisions on Closer Cooperation in the Treaty of Amsterdam: The Politics of Flexibility in the European Union', *Journal of Common Market Studies*, 37 (1): 87–108.

Pryce, R. (1994) 'The Maastricht Treaty and the New Europe', in A. Duff, J. Pinder and R. Pryce (eds) *Maastricht and Beyond: Building the European Union.* London: Routledge.

Sandholtz, W. and Zysman, J. (1989) '1992: Recasting the European Bargain', *World Politics*, 42 (1): 95–128.

Scott, J. (1998) 'Law, Legitimacy and EC Governance: Prospects for Partnership', *Journal of Common Market Studies*, 36 (2): 175–94.

Shaw, J. (1998) 'The Treaty of Amsterdam: Challenges of Flexibility and Legitimacy', *European Law Journal*, 4 (2): 63–86.

Sinnott, R. (1994) 'Integration Theory, Subsidiarity and the Internationalization of Issues: The Implications for Legitimacy', *European University Institute Working Paper* 94/3. Florence: European University Institute.

Sinnott, R. (1995) 'Policy, Subsidiarity and Legitimacy', in O. Niedermayer and R.

Sinnott (eds) *Public Opinion and Internationalized Governance*. Oxford: Oxford University Press.

Stubb, A.C.-G. (1996): 'A Categorization of Differentiated Integration', *Journal of Common Market Studies*, 34 (2): 283–95.

Warleigh, A. (1998) 'Frozen: Citizenship and European Unification', *Critical Review of International, Social and Political Philosophy*, 1 (4): 113–51.

Warleigh, A. (2000a) 'History Repeating? Framework Theory and Europe's Multi-level Confederation', *Journal of European Integration*, 22 (2): 173–200.

Warleigh, A. (2000b) 'The Hustle: Citizenship Practice, NGOs and "Policy Coalitions" in the European Union – The Cases of Auto Oil, Drinking Water and Unit Pricing', *Journal of European Public Policy*, 7 (2): 229–43.

Warleigh, A. (2001) 'Purposeful Opportunists? EU Institutions and The Struggle Over European Citizenship', in R. Bellamy and A. Warleigh (eds) *Citizenship and Governance in the European Union*. London: Continuum.

Wistrich, E. (1989) *After 1992: The United States of Europe*. London: Routledge.

7 The Euro: A Future International Currency?

Kevin Boles, Frank McDonald and Nigel Healey

The introduction of the euro adds an extra dimension to the international financial system, introducing a new currency to rival the dollar as an international and reserve currency. Within the European Union, the significance of monetary union for the twelve member states of the euro-zone cannot be overstated, as the mixed reaction among both public and policy-makers can testify. For some members of the EU, the euro is a symbol of the renaissance of Europe as the world leader in commerce and culture (Bergsten and Henning, 1996). For others, it is a necessary convenience that facilitates commercial development and greater competition across borders formerly protected by exchange and interest rate differentials (Baldwin, 1991). For businesses trading within the euro area, the use of the single currency will reduce transaction costs and exchange rate risk, both of which will raise efficiency, increase investment and effect greater competition (Emerson et al., 1992; McDonald, 1997). In some states, however, public disagreements reflected the opposition to the perceived loss of sovereignty and led, in the case of Denmark, to the outright rejection of the proposal in a national referendum.

One of the political attractions of a single currency in Europe is the economic weight it offers to the EU in trade negotiations with the other powerful economies of the US and Asia (Bergsten, 2000). Over time, the euro is likely to become a reserve currency, replacing as it does the former domestic currencies of members of economic and monetary union (EMU) in the foreign reserves of governments. Moreover, the euro may come to rival the US dollar in money and capital markets, altering the nature of the international monetary system. This could engender significant volatility in financial markets, and raise yet again the spectre of trade wars and protectionist practices (Bergsten, 2000). International policy co-ordination and system management take on a much greater significance in this context. Already, a desire to see the euro succeed has prompted internationally co-ordinated intervention to support the European currency in the face of financial market volatility.

Over the longer term, there is a very real possibility that world trade will be characterised by three main trading blocs, each with its own dominant currency: the EU and the euro, US and the dollar and Asia with the Japanese yen or the Chinese yuan. The introduction of the euro therefore increases the desirability of co-operating within the Triad (USA, EU and Asia) in macroeconomic policy decisions. The adoption of the single currency in Europe does indeed present an opportunity for closer co-ordination. However, the political cost to some countries can be high, and the ensuing democratic deficit that global monetary management creates make co-ordination difficult in practice.

This chapter examines the pressures that are likely to arise from these developments, and considers the shortcomings of the existing institutional structures for dealing with these pressures. It evaluates the current institutional structures, the International Monetary Fund and the World Bank, which link the European Union to the USA, Japan and the new industrialised countries of south-east Asia (NICs). The chapter addresses the question whether these institutions can evolve to cope with the evolution of the euro as a reserve currency, and as an international vehicle for business purposes.

THE EURO AND THE INTERNATIONAL MONETARY SYSTEM

The role of the euro as an international currency and its future challenge to the dollar as a reserve and vehicle currency are recurrent topics in the literature. Can this new currency, underpinned by the economic weight of the EU, reach this status? To achieve international status, both as a transaction and a reserve currency, the euro must meet a number of criteria, which Bergsten (1997) summarises under five headings:

1   The size of the underlying economy and the size of its global trade.
2   The underlying economy's independence from external constraints.
3   Avoidance of exchange rate controls.
4   Depth, breadth and liquidity of its capital markets.
5   The strength and stability of the economy and its external position.

The US dollar easily meets all these criteria and despite the frequent volatility of the dollar throughout the 1980s and 1990s, it is still the main currency used in denominating reserves, in international trade and as a vehicle currency (IMF, 2000b). There is no agreement as to the weight to be applied to each of the criteria, with the exception of large, liquid and well-managed equity, bond and capital markets in the issuing economy (Garber, 1996). The consensus is that these have the greatest influence on the role a currency will play in the international monetary system. In the case of the US dollar, for example, it has been the prudent management of the capital markets that has helped to sustain the dollar as the international currency of choice for trade invoicing and official reserves. The New York

Federal Reserve Board (Fed) offers extensive support to foreign central banks in money market transactions. The Fed provides correspondents with services to make US dollar payments, manage dollar portfolios, deposit gold and engage in foreign exchange operations (Garber, 1996). The dollar also gained from the inertia effects of traditional preference, the costs of system changes and the lower information and transaction costs that are a consequence of a widely used currency.

In contrast to the US dollar and despite the size of the underlying economies of Japan and Germany, neither the yen, nor the German mark, have developed to be a truly international currency. The strength and stability of the Japanese economy through the 1980s and early 1990s was insufficient to grant the yen true international status, and the lack of deep, liquid capital markets prevented wider use of the yen in reserves or as a vehicle currency (Bergsten, 1997; Garber, 1996). In Germany, the Bundesbank resisted calls to become a lender of last resort, delaying the development of equity and bond markets, and restricted the circulation of Deutschmark denominated assets through careful management and frequent sterilisation of the money markets.

In terms of GDP, the EU is slightly larger than the US at $8,361 billions to $8,179 billions and has a marginally greater share of world trade, 20 per cent and 18 per cent respectively. Japan follows in third place with a GDP of $3,797 billions and a 10.3 per cent share of word trade (see Table 7.1). The size of the European internal market will provide the euro with a strong base as a domestic currency, but it is trade with countries outside the union that will provide the international dimension for the euro. Just as size grants large countries the opportunity to invoice exports in the domestic currency, shifting any exchange rate risk to the importer, so companies within the EU will be able to denominate trade invoices in euros (Friberg, 1999).

However, domestic usage or the potential to invoice in euros does not guarantee the currency a prominent place in the international monetary system. In 1995, only 40.1 per cent of Japanese exports were denominated in yen and 46.6 per cent in US dollars. The import ratios were even lower with 17.7 per cent in yen and 75 per cent in dollars (Ilzkovitz, 1996). With the passage of time, increased use in global trade and a reputation for stability should provide the euro with economies of scale, positive externalities and network effects, as well as lower transaction and information costs. Ironically, these also create inertia effects in delaying the adoption of the euro in international usage (Ilzkovitz, 1996). With an established market for the dollar, transaction costs are very low, so much so that pre-EMU the dollar was the vehicle of choice for many intra-European trades. The same was true for east and central Europe, where the German mark gained ground only after reunification and trade increased with the former communist bloc countries. In order to challenge the dollar the euro will need to achieve parity in turnover on the exchange markets, in invoice usage and offer exchange stability.

TABLE 7.1   *The European Union and the world economy*

	GDP[1]) (US $bn)	% world GDP	% world trade
EU 15	8,361	29.9	20
USA	8,179	29.3	18
Japan	3,797	13.6	10.3
The rest	7,620	27.2	51.7
World total	27,957	100	100

[1] At current prices and exchange rates excluding intra-EU transactions.
Source: OECD National Statistics, January 1999.

Despite euroland having the potential to be the bigger economy, with the largest external trade, it may well be several years before the euro is equal to the dollar either in invoicing or in vehicle currency terms. The various estimates range from several years to several decades (Alogoskoufis and Portes, 1997). Inertia effects as well as wait-and-see strategies will dominate the rate of change (Tanzi, 1998). Several commentators have cited the slow decline of sterling, from being the dominant international currency to its replacement by the US dollar as an example (Bordo and Jonung, 2000; Vanthoor, 1996). Others suggest a serious shock to the international system would be needed before the euro could possibly dominate the dollar as the key reference currency (Gros and Thygesen, 1998).

However, EMU itself constitutes a significant shock to the world economy that could propel the euro to overtake the dollar very quickly (Buiter, 1999). Despite the early weakness of the euro against the dollar, falling by as much as 30 per cent in the first two years, there are indications that the euro is becoming both an international and reserve currency. Replacing the domestic currencies of member states, increased usage in government and commercial bonds and the growth of European financial markets are the vehicles for its prominence. If all fifteen EU countries join EMU within ten years and enlargement of membership continues, EMU will provide the international monetary system with a series of shocks. Not only will the euro be the currency of choice for a very large domestic economy, but it will also become the key reference and anchor for most of the Mediterranean economies and significant parts of Africa. Around euroland will be an extensive euro-zone where the euro will be used as the anchor or substitute currency, as well as for invoicing in cross-border trade. Table 7.2 lists the possible member states of EMU by the second decade of the twenty-first century.

The size of the underlying economy alone may not by itself qualify a currency for international use, but it does offer economies of scale and recognition that allow exporters to invoice goods in that currency (Hartmann, 1996). An additional hurdle facing the European Union is the

TABLE 7.2   *Possible euroland economy in 2010*[1]

	GDP (US $bn)	% world GDP
EMU 12	6,027	23.63
UK	1,415	4.8
Denmark	160	0.63
Sweden	228	0.82
Poland	163	0.51
Hungary	46	0.17
Czech Republic	49	0.2
Total	8,088	30.76

[1] Using current prices and exchange rates.

Source: OECD National Accounts, January 1999.

creation of large and liquid capital, bond, and equity markets capable of rivaling those offered by the United States.

STABILITY AND CREDIBILITY

While free trade has brought greater independence to the diversified economies of the world, it has brought greater interdependence too, exposing individual economies to sudden shifts in market sentiment (Kenen, 1995). With unrestricted and instantaneous capital flows there is increased likelihood that negative externalities, leading to costs in terms of unemployment and inflation, will spill over to other countries. Globalisation has increased the occurrence of international financial crises through 'herd' and 'contagion' effects (Tanzi, 1998). Sudden shifts of investments, in and out of markets, can and do cause havoc. Innovation, technology, deregulation and the increasing role of the institutional investors have dissolved the boundaries between national financial frontiers. As a result, global capital markets have emerged with consequences that traditional monetary theory is not capable of analysing (Caravelis, 1994). Alan Greenspan, the chairman of the Federal Reserve Board, points out that we do not understand the present-day dynamics of the monetary system and emphasises the need to update and to modify institutions and practices to reduce the risks inherent in the current regime (Greenspan, 1998). There have been repeated calls for greater transparency in financial reporting to add clarity, both for governments and for private portfolios, yet the markets and institutions that experienced the greatest turmoil during the summer of 1998, are the most open and transparent in the world (IMF, 1998b).

The utility of the euro, in trade and as an anchor or as a reserve currency, will depend very much on its stability within the international monetary system. If the currency proves unstable and exhibits a volatile

TABLE 7.3 *Percentage share of national currencies in total identified official holdings of foreign exchange, 1993–99*

All countries	1993	1994	1995	1996	1997	1998	1999
US dollar	56.4	56.4	56.8	60.1	62.1	65.7	66.2
Pound sterling	2.9	3.2	3.1	3.4	3.6	3.8	4.0
Deutschmark	13.4	14.0	13.5	12.8	12.6	12.1	–
French franc	2.2	2.3	2.2	1.7	1.3	1.3	–
Swiss franc	1.1	0.9	0.8	0.8	0.7	0.7	0.7
Dutch guilder	0.6	0.5	0.4	0.3	0.4	0.3	–
Japanese yen	7.6	7.8	6.8	6.0	5.3	5.3	5.1
ECU/euro	8.2	7.7	6.8	5.9	5.0	0.8	12.5

Source: IMF (2000a).

relationship with the dollar and the yen, causing inflationary or deflationary spillover effects, its introduction could further destabilise the already fragile international monetary system. McCauley (1997) suggests that four evolving developments will determine the level and volatility of the exchange rate:

1   The size of the euro area (euroland) could lead to the adoption of the euro as an anchor currency for the exchange rates of smaller countries.
2   An increase in the liquidity of the euro area financial markets could affect the behaviour of private portfolio managers.
3   The effect of the latter could alter the choice of debt denomination made by managers.
4   A unified European exchange rate could increase effective dollar volatility.

We discuss these relationships and the possible effects on the global economy. Currently, the US dollar is the reserve currency of choice for central banks and since 1988 the dollar has maintained more than a 50 per cent share in foreign exchange holdings. The percentage shares of foreign exchange holdings by currency for all countries, as reported by the IMF (2000a) are illustrated in Table 7.3.

Most of the euro-11 countries have large dollar reserves, which were necessary for intervention in the market under the European Monetary System (EMS). Now that exchange rates are fixed and intervention is directed by the ECB, there is less need to hold such high reserves, but governments are likely to manage the disposal of any excess reserves with great care for fear of destabilising the international monetary system (Gros and Thygesen, 1998). However, as illustrated by the figures in Table 7.3, the weight of European currencies in foreign reserves, represented by former national currencies and the ECU, has fallen from 22.8 per cent share, to 12.5 per cent of official exchange holdings. The weight of dollar holding has increased from 60 per cent to 66 per cent. This is to be expected, as the residual EU currencies in becoming euros also become domestic currency in EMU member accounts. It remains an interesting illustration though of the testing time the euro will face in achieving prominence in the reserves of non-EU foreign banks.

The euro has proved more popular on the international bond market, especially with commercial customers, as lower interest rates in euroland and the wider and steadily deepening money markets make borrowing in euros more attractive. With monetary policy managed by the ECB, governments of EMU members now have to raise necessary borrowings through the public capital markets. This in itself will encourage the development of deeper and thicker capital markets, with closely competing government and interest-bearing securities. In fact, within months of the first issue of euro bonds in January 1999 the euro was the currency of choice for half of all international bond issues, with the dollar taking a 40 per cent share, sterling 5 per cent and the yen less than 1 per cent (*Financial Times*, 1999). If the European capital markets develop along the lines of the US model, wide and deep secondary markets for derivatives, swaps and similar instruments are likely to follow.

In their 1998 Annual Report, the directors of the International Monetary Fund (IMF) agreed that the euro would over time constitute an attractive international and reserve currency that might come to rival the dollar. When and how this comes to pass depends on developments in the financial markets in Europe, the regulatory environment and the variety of instruments available (IMF, 1998a). Some restructuring of the European financial markets is certain to accompany the establishment of the euro. However, it is the volume of free-flowing private capital, several times larger than official portfolios, that the IMF considered to be the greatest single threat to the stability of the international monetary system.

In time, if the euro proves a stable currency and euroland delivers steady growth, investors will want to balance their portfolios by buying euro assets. According to estimates from the ECB there has been a steady increase in the share of EU currencies in private portfolios, rising from 13 per cent in 1981 to 37 per cent in 1995. Between the same years there has been a steady decline in the share taken by the US dollar from 67 per cent to 40 per cent. This decline has slowed during the 1990s, but the ECB predicts a continuation and possible acceleration of the trend (Duisenberg, 1998). Portfolio changes could be very large. Cooper (1992) suggests a 'tipping point' may be reached where investors may move their assets into euros in large volumes, a shift that could be sudden given the rapid movement of global capital. Large portfolio shifts could put downward pressure on the dollar and upward pressure on the euro, which would have significant implications for trade competitiveness. Such a scenario could result in strong trade protection pressures within Europe. Others argue that, as the US government securities and bond markets have the advantages of being large, well established and highly liquid, the dollar will maintain its prowess as the currency of choice (Garber, 1996).

Empirical estimates of any trade reducing effects of exchange rate volatility are few and, where they do exist, are rather tentative (De Grauwe, 1988; Gros and Thygesen, 1998). Investment in goods and services, which are subject to a high degree of international competition, may be discouraged by exchange-rate variability and price uncertainty. Trade and investment may well be diverted towards markets that offer the greater stability rather than the greater return. To the extent that these negative forces are mitigated, EMU should encourage investment and raise output (Emerson et al., 1992). Theoretically, trade diverting effects will be greater if the exchange-rate of the euro continues to be volatile, as some researchers predict, although to what extent exchange rate volatility affects trade has not been clearly established (Cooper, 1992). Using a choice of variables, a number of empirical studies have sought to determine the volatility of the euro against the dollar, but they have proved inconclusive. Using a two-country model De Grauwe (1997) suggested volatility would increase and some research has suggested that the ensuing volatility could be on the scale of that between the US dollar and the Japanese yen (Bergsten, 1997; Masson et al., 1997), using the IMF econometric model, MULTIMOD, found that the euro–dollar relationship could be slightly more variable than the former relationship between the dollar and the German mark.

As Gros and Thygesen (1998) have pointed out, none of these models is appropriate for the new era of EMU. First, the EU will be a much more self-sufficient and therefore a more closed economy than was the case pre-EMU. As such, there will be less concern about the external exchange rate. Secondly, the elimination of the intra-European exchange rate buffer means intra-European shocks will have some effect on the exchange rate of the euro. However, this will not automatically mean significant volatility for the international monetary system. Investors, in an attempt to predict policy decisions that may affect the value of investments, will carefully monitor the responses of governments and central banks. Despite intervening to support the euro in October 2000 and again in November of the same year, the ECB has not declared a position on the exchange rate of the euro. This stance of refusing to specify any target range within which the euro is to operate has disappointed some commentators, but as the actions of the ECB demonstrate the Bank intends to monitor the exchange rate as an indicator of monetary policy effects. This is consistent with Article 109 of the Treaty on European Union (TEU), which identifies price stability as the guiding principle for monetary policy decisions taken by the ECB. It is the ECB's intention to take account of any movement in the exchange rate that is likely to impact upon price developments in the euro area (Duisenberg, 1998). Thus independence in monetary policy could result in the global market becoming a theatre dominated by two very large economies, too self-contained and intro-spective to be concerned with international co-ordination. Without an agreed framework for co-ordination and co-operation, the longer-term result could be greater volatility for smaller economies, a repetition of peso and rouble-like crises or a major restructuring of trade agreements around the two or possibly three major trading blocs. In the event, closer co-ordination will benefit trade and contribute to global economic stability.

CONTEMPORARY INTERNATIONAL FINANCIAL ARCHITECTURE

An argument frequently offered in support of EMU is that the euro will create political and economic critical mass giving European nations a greater say in world economic affairs (Bergsten and Henning, 1996). However, the opposite might be just as likely to happen. For example, at the present time, four members of the EU Germany, France, Italy and the UK are members of the G8. Three of these have already signed up for EMU, and with the President of the European Commission also in attendance at G8 meetings, the EMU economy is well represented. European financial integration, like trade integration in the past, has resulted in a single voice for Europe within the international financial architecture. In time, represented by a single negotiator, the individual member states may lose influence in the G8.

A similar picture is emerging at the IMF. Presently the long-term and wealthier members dominate the IMF and voting rights are derived from the tranche of the special drawing rights (SDRs) held in members' accounts. The wealthier countries have by far the largest accounts, with members of the EU commanding 30.5 per cent of the voting power against only 17 per cent for the USA (IMF, 1999). Presently then, the united voting power of the EU is far greater than that of the USA, but its effectiveness depends on the ability of the nation-states to unite behind a single block vote. More recently, there have been strong calls for greater recognition of other IMF members, in particular Japan, as well as Switzerland and Russia, and the newly industrialised countries of the Pacific Rim. While any loss of political status and influence is likely to be resisted by individual states, developments within the structures of the EU may force change. But, there are many potential areas of conflict and disagreements between the EU and the international financial architecture, itself a product of the Bretton Woods system instituted in the mid-1940s.

Under the Bretton Woods agreement, and with the management of the IMF, dollar convertibility became the basis of the new American hegemony. Taking the role as lender of last resort, as well as principal consumer of the world's goods, the US acted as banker in the rebuilding of the postwar economic structures. The global economy was transformed in the half century after the war. Led by the USA, managed through the Bretton Woods vehicles of the International Monetary Fund, the World Bank and the General Agreement on Trade and Tariffs (GATT) the global economy has grown significantly. The institutions too have changed, and their purpose and direction seems less clear now than at the postwar founding (Bergsten and Henning, 1996).

Originally dedicated to the maintenance of currency convertibility for current transactions, the IMF's role has evolved to include surveillance of the economic and exchange rate policies of the 181 states that now constitute its membership. More recently, the IMF has focused its activities on liberalisation, stabilisation and reform in developing countries, a role that has brought it into conflict with the World Bank. The World Bank too has grown enormously. Comprising four institutions, the International Bank for Reconstruction and Development (IBRD), the International Development Association (IDA), the International Finance Corporation (IFC) and the Multilateral Investment Guarantee Agency (MIGA), the Bank was established to be the financial link and mediator between the rich countries of the north and the developing countries around the world (World Bank, 1999). Both institutions have been subjected to scrutiny over their record in meeting the stated objectives, a record that has emerged as somewhat random. The institutions are repeatedly criticised for inefficiency, eroding national sovereignty and for not having clear strategies (Tanzi, 1998). After the collapse of the managed exchange rate system (originally set up as part of the Bretton Woods agreement) in 1971, the first of the G5 meetings, between the US, Germany, France, the UK and Japan tried and failed to find a replacement system. Despite the oil shocks of the 1970s, the dollar devaluations of the 1980s and the major crises of the 1990s, including those in Mexico, Asia, Russia and Brazil, no satisfactory agreement on how to co-ordinate or co-operate within the international arena has been reached. There is little talk of co-ordination when free markets are operating quietly, but as soon as a monetary crisis appears, and threatens volatility in currency values, there are renewed discussions on the urgent need for reforming the institutional structures for international economic co-operation.

PROSPECTS FOR GLOBAL CO-ORDINATION

The developments in the international monetary system over recent years, including financial crises, the heightened exchange rate volatility of a global capital market, and the new European currency, together with the realisation of greater interdependence all combine to suggest a need for international financial and monetary co-ordination. The scale and devastation of the Asian crisis in 1997, with the accompanying threat of capital meltdown, proved to be a catalyst in reawakening the discussion of economic policy co-ordination between the monetary authorities of Asia, the United States, and the European Union (Li and McDonald, 2000). If the need for regulation is accepted, then the question moves on to an evaluation of the prospects for co-operation. The preceding section indicated the limited success of international co-ordination over recent decades, but the calls for intervention continue to be made. One key difficulty, however, is that while there may be agreement on the need for co-ordination, no real consensus regarding the nature and substance of co-ordination has emerged among the financial regulatory authorities.

Bergsten and Henning (1996) identify three sources of unresolved tensions in creating an effective system of co-ordination among the Triad economies. These are the choices between growth and price stability, the difference in attitudes to global and regional interests and the tensions caused by some countries continuously running budget surpluses that are thought to contribute to budget deficits in other economies. Fundamentally, governments disagree on the appropriate target of macroeconomic policies (Alogoskoufis and Portes, 1997). All governments agree that growth is the main objective, but it is in discussions of how to achieve growth that disagreements emerge. For example, the US has preferred to pursue expansionary style policies, while the Germans have pursued price stability. The US tends to run chronic budget and trade deficits, while Japan and now the EU (on balance) have a tendency to maintain a budget surplus. The US is a truly global power with commercial and military interests in every part of the world. The Japanese and the Europeans tend to be regional, perhaps even parochial, in their interests.

In a review of the global economic architecture, the European Commission identified the fundamental mismatch between the institutions of Bretton Woods and the changes that have taken place in the global economy (European Commission, 1998). This is a mismatch that the introduction of the euro is likely to exacerbate. The world has changed fundamentally in the last fifty years, but the international financial architecture has failed to adapt to the changing needs of the system. In particular, certain developments have emerged to challenge the abilities of governments and the scope of policy: globalisation, changes in the economic balance of power and the end of the Cold War. Under the hegemonic leadership of the United States, the global economy grew in strength over the decades until the 1970s, aided by the authorities that adopted the role of lender (and consumer) of last resort. Economic growth and the rise of international trade coincided with the steady erosion of trade barriers, and eventually the emergence of new regional economic powers. The systemic asymmetry of the postwar years was eroded incrementally, with the appearance of regional groupings in Europe and Asia. The end of the Cold War did not end the expansion of trade, but the unevenness of this expansion, and of the distribution of the benefits from trade have elicited calls for greater representation of the peripheral economies. The argument for free trade is that competition leads to a more efficient use of resources and a maximisation of global welfare. Yet very frequently, severe volatility in the markets disrupts trade, reduces confidence and threatens the return of protectionism (McDonald, 1999).

These very real effects are all cited as good reasons for enhanced international co-ordination (Krugman, 1995).

The case for co-ordination remains unchallenged. Yet, fundamental agreement on mechanisms and objectives remains an unreachable goal. The IMF concedes that 'the financial crises of the 1990s exposed weaknesses in the international system, highlighting the fact that globalisation brings risks as well as important benefits' (IMF, 2000a). The response has been some closer co-operation, but more needs to be done. The European Commission (1998) suggests a new and deeper integration is required based on the development of the Bretton Woods institutions, but taking account of the principle of 'global subsidiarity'. Global subsidiarity recognises the role of economic and political regions. Therefore, policies which are more effectively made and realised at the regional level ought not be decided at the international level. But, where co-ordination is required, the available institutions should act together to provide effective mechanisms. Putting the EU forward as an example of how multilateral rules can be effective, the Commission recommends a strengthened and enlarged World Trade Organization (WTO) and a stronger International Monetary Fund (IMF). Reducing barriers to trade ought to remain the principal objective of the WTO and it would still constitute the forum for settling trade disputes, but enlarged membership is identified as a pressing priority. It is argued that consideration be given to empowering the WTO to impose tougher trade sanctions against countries that break trade agreements and to offer aid to developing countries as a positive inducement to lower trade barriers. This will remove any decision-making process from the political arena and further reduce the need and the opportunity for individual countries, and the United States in particular, to take unilateral decisions in imposing sanctions on trading partners. In the longer-term the WTO might evolve as the key regulatory framework in all trade-related areas.

Supported by a commission-like secretariat, the IMF could further its reporting and monitoring role as the global watchdog and work more closely with the World Bank in the developing economies. Fundamental to the effective working of these institutions is a greater transparency in reporting and policy decisions (Buiter, 1999; European Commission, 1998; IMF, 2000b). Markets do not always behave rationally, but keeping the markets well informed will contribute to a more stable economic environment (IMF, 1998c).

Despite its exhortations for stronger international institutions, the European Commission envisages more decision-making at the regional level. However, in addition the three major economies of the US, Japan and the EU would have a special responsibility for agreeing effective international economic co-operation and co-ordination. In effect, the G8 would become the G3, the Triad, with representatives from the three currency zones of the euro, the dollar and probably the yen. Figure 7.1 is a representation of this scenario.

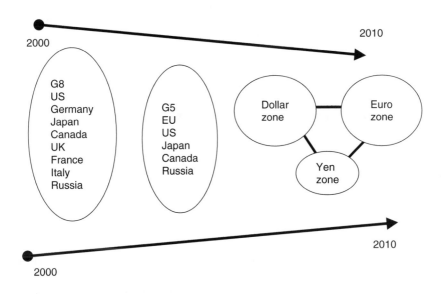

FIGURE 7.1 *International financial architecture for 2010*

CONCLUSION

The present and potential size of the euro-economy lends support to the idea of the euro becoming an international currency. However, the European Union must take a stronger role in global management, to both support the currency and to counter any instability that might occur in an international financial system with competing currencies. The first step towards the development of the international currency is in the use of the euro through trade and invoicing, and then as a vehicle and reserve currency and an alternative to the dollar. How quickly this happens and whether or not parity in usage with the dollar is reached, depends upon the intrinsic stability of the euro and most importantly the development of wide, deep and liquid euro bond and equity markets. Whether the existence of a bipolar world, or tri-polar world, with Asia as a junior or equal partner, brings with it greater volatility for the international monetary system remains to be seen. With three principal currencies to choose between, investment shifts in and out of any one currency could be swift and destabilising. The desire to limit and minimise negative spillover effects and potentially excessive volatility is certainly a concern for many Europeans, and a source of ambivalence for the Americans. The Europeans have a tendency to manage economies, while the US tends towards benign neglect and a belief in the power of market forces.

The scenario of greater regional responsibility, advocated by the European Commission, combined with an IMF and a WTO with more autonomous decision-making powers and greater transparency in reporting does have attractions. Regulation of international trade and the international monetary system by independent technocrats of the world's central bankers, economists at the IMF and World Bank, rather than by politicians may be the future. However, it is questionable whether the member states will want to devolve the decision-making powers or membership advantages of the IMF, the G8 or other international associations to the bureaucrats of the European Commission or the economists of the IMF. Professionally qualified independent technocrats may be able to address the economic problems, yet this tidy solution leaves a number of questions unanswered. For example, what will be the role of central banks in the new financial architecture of the third millennium? Will they or should they be truly independent, democratically accountable, with transparent systems of reporting? The questions are not merely rhetorical, as the experience of European monetary union, with the independent European Central Bank, has already shown. Rather, there is a very real source of conflict in the conduct of independent monetary policy by institutions without any democratic accountability. It is possible that in the not too distant future international monetary issues will be managed by unaccountable technocrats rather than by elected politicians. The tendency for the institutions of the EU to acquire more power as a consequence of the rise of the euro could mean that the only realistic alternative is full federal government in Europe. While an international euro, readily adopted as a reserve currency, may give the EU a greater say in world affairs, the structures required to manage this role may not appeal to all member states. Despite the assurances given to the citizens of the European nation-states, especially to those in the UK, there is a very real prospect that in the twenty-first century, the institutions of the EU, and not sovereign governments, will continue to effect major decisions that impact upon the lives of Europe's citizens.

REFERENCES

Alogoskoufis, G. and Portes, R. (1997) 'The Euro, the Dollar and the International Monetary System', in P.R. Masson, T.H. Kruegger and B.G. Turtleboom (eds) *EMU and the International Monetary System*. Washington, DC: International Monetary Fund.

Baldwin, R.E. (1991) 'On the Microeconomics of the European Monetary Union', *European Economy Special Edition*. Brussels: European Commission.

Bergsten, F.C. (1997) 'The Impact of the Euro on Exchange Rates and International Policy Cooperation', in P.R. Masson, T.H. Kruegger and B.G. Turtleboom (eds) *EMU and the International Monetary System*. Washington, DC: International Monetary Fund.

Bergsten, F.C. (2000) 'East Asian Regionalism', *The Economist*, 15–21 July.

Bergsten, F.C. and Henning, R.C. (1996) *Global Economic Leadership and the Group of Seven*. Washington, DC: Institute of International Economics.

Bordo, M. and Jonung, L. (2000) *Lessons for EMU from the History of Monetary Unions*. London: Institute of Economic Affairs.
Buiter, W.H. (1999) 'Alice in euroland', *Journal of Common Market Studies*, 37 (2): 181–209.
Caravelis, G. (1994) *European Monetary Union*. Aldershot: Avebury.
Cooper, R.N. (1992) 'Will An EC Currency Harm Outsiders?', *Orbis*, 36 (Fall): 517–531.
De Grauwe, P. (1997) *The Economics of Monetary Integration*, 3rd edn. Oxford: Oxford University Press.
De Grauwe, P. (1988) 'Exchange Rate Variability and the Slowdown in the Growth of International Trade', *IMF Staff Papers*, March: 63–84.
Duisenberg, W.F. (1998) 'The Stability-oriented Monetary Policy Strategy of the European System of Central Banks and the International Role of the Euro', speech by the President of the European Central Bank at the Economic Club, New York, 12 November.
Emerson, M., Gros, D., Italianer, A., Pisani-Ferry, J. and Reichenbach, H. (eds) (1992) *One Market, One Money*. Oxford: Oxford University Press.
European Commission (1998) *Towards a More Global Economic Order*, Forward Studies Series. London: Kogan Page.
Financial Times (1999) 2 February: London.
Friberg, R. (1999) *Exchange Rates and the Firm*. London: Macmillan.
Garber, P.M. (1996) 'The Use of the Yen as a Reserve Currency', *Monetary and Economic Studies*, 14: 1–21.
Greenspan, A. (1998) 'Risk Management in the Global Financial System', address to the Annual Financial Markets Conference, Miami, Florida, 27 February.
Gros, D. and Thygesen, N. (1998) *European Monetary Integration*, 2nd edn. Harlow: Addison Wesley Longman.
Hartmann, P. (1996) 'The Future of the Euro as an International Currency: A Transaction Perspective', *CEPR Research Report No. 20*, London.
Healey, N.M. (1999) 'Macroeconomic Policy Cooperation', in F. McDonald and S. Dearden (eds) *European Economic Integration*, 3rd edn. Harlow: Addison Wesley Longman.
Ilzkovitz, F. (1996) 'Prospects for the Internationalization of the Euro', DG-11 doc. 11/362/96-EN. Brussels: European Commission.
IMF (1998a) *Annual Report*. Washington, DC.
IMF (1998b) *IMF Report on Emerging Markets*, Washington, DC.
IMF (1998c) 'Strengthening the Architecture of the International Monetary System', Report of the Managing Director to the Interim Committee of the IMF. October: Washington, DC.
IMF (1999) 'IMF Quotas Increase Enters into Effect', press release No. 99/4, 22 January, http://www.imf.org/external/np/sec/pr/1999/PR9904
IMF (2000a) *Annual Report*. Washington, DC.
IMF (2000b) 'Progress in strengthening the architecture of the international financial system', IMF press release, 30 March 2000. Available at http://www.imf.org/external/np/exr/facts/arcguide.html
Kenen, P.B. (ed.) (1995) *Understanding Interdependence*. New Jersey: Princeton University Press.
Krugman, P. (1995) 'What Do We Need to Know About the International Monetary System?', in P.B. Kenen (ed.) *Understanding Interdependence*. New Jersey: Princeton University Press.
Li, H. and McDonald, F. (2000) 'The End of the Asian Miracle?', in Richard Thorpe and Stephen Little (eds) *Global Change*. London: Macmillan.
Masson, P.R., Kruegger, T.H. and Turtleboom, B.G. (eds) (1997) *European Monetary Union and the International Monetary System*. Washington, DC: International Monetary Fund.

McCauley, R. (1997) *The Euro and the Dollar*. Bank of International Settlement Working Paper: Essays in International Finance, No. 205, November. Princeton, New Jersey.

McDonald, F. (1997) 'EMU: Some Implications for Companies', *Journal of General Management*, 23 (2): 47–64.

McDonald, F. (1999) 'The European Union and the Triad', in Frank McDonald and Stephen Dearden (eds) *European Economic Integration*, 3rd edn. Harlow: Addison Wesley Longman.

Portes, R. and Rey, H. (1998) 'Euro Vs Dollar', *Economic Policy*, April.

Tanzi, V. (1998) 'The Demise of the Nation State?', Working Paper of the International Monetary Fund: WP/98/120. Washington, DC.

Vanthoor, W.F.V. (1996) *European Monetary Union since 1848: A Political and Historical Analysis*. Cheltenham: Edward Elgar.

World Bank (1999) at http://www.worldbank.org/html/extdr/wbgis.ht

8

Social Integration in the European Union: Towards a Single Social Area?

Monica Threlfall

This chapter proposes a discussion of a key but hitherto largely unexplored element in the debate over the EU's social goals: the notion of social integration and the single European social area. It proposes a new definition of these concepts based on the degree to which individuals are locked into the social system of their state of residence. It examines the present level of development of EU social policy in the light of this new perspective, and argues that social integration and parallel development should be seen as separate processes, concluding that new forms of integration creating single social areas are taking place in unplanned ways, not promoted by member states or the Commission. The chapter opens with the background to the two key terms 'social integration' and 'single social area', and then moves on to the main discussion.

SOCIAL INTEGRATION

While the notion of economic integration holds a dominant position in the language of European community-building, and political union between states is an established agenda question, it is something of a paradox that European social integration, which one might suppose to be a parallel concept, is not a part of the European vocabulary. It is only occasionally found, to refer to integration of excluded or vulnerable groups (for instance European Commission, 1994: 49). The concept does not have a clear status in European studies. Much analysis of the social dimension and policy has focused, understandably – and interestingly – on the likelihood of its further development and on its dynamics, on the environment and mechanisms of social policy-making, as well as the pressures which will make new measures more or less likely (Geyer, 2000; Gold, 1993; Hantrais, 1995; Lange, 1992; Leibfried and Pierson, 1995, amongst others). Other approaches focus on issues of sovereignty – the preservation or loss of state authority over welfare (Leibfried 1994; Milward, 1992 amongst others).

Social integration, as posed here, differs from social policy, social quality, social regulation, social dimension, and especially social inclusion.[1] The EU's social *policy*, it is safe to say, is a collection of steps, provisions and laws, some of which lead towards, or provide elements of, a genuine process of integration as defined in this chapter, while others merely narrow the differences that exist between discrete member states. The social *quality* of Europe is the goal of high social standards forwarded by a number of social scientists because they believe it is neglected by the EU (Beck et al., 1998: 1). Social *regulation* as used by Majone (1993), refers to the regulatory regime which constrains or reinforces member state law-making. The fact that a term as imprecise as 'the social *dimension*' is used officially in the EU to refer to a far-ranging area of the institutions' activities indicates the uncertainty surrounding the development of *l'espace social* towards social integration. Social integration of the EU, as discussed here, should not be confused with social inclusion in a well-integrated state with few citizens living on the fringes of society. Even when the term social integration is mentioned, as by Leibfried and Pierson (1995) and Leibfried (1994), it is only occasionally so, despite their extensive work on EU social policy, and then it is without discussing it as a process that may or may not be taking place in the EU. In brief, what is absent in the above-mentioned discussions is an analysis of the effects and consequences on European societies of the adoption of such social policy, social quality and regulation, as well as a discussion of the transformations that the societies would undergo as a result. Is such a transformation, however gradual and uneven, to be termed social integration, and if so, what exactly is meant by this?

SINGLE SOCIAL AREA

As the process of European social integration cannot readily be understood by reference to previous usage, a new understanding is needed. What might social integration, hypothetically, consist of? One should start with a primary definition, building on the literal meaning of integration: to integrate is to make parts into a whole. Making up a single whole from parts is a key characteristic of an integration process, and gives the term its full and strict meaning. Ergo, an integrated labour market is a barrier-free single labour market with external boundaries but no internal ones. Therefore, the EU would be integrating socially if its component societies were losing the geographical boundaries of social institutions and practices and functioning instead as a single social area in an increasingly similar manner to the formally 'single' societies of nation-states (setting aside the fact that these of themselves may be contested concepts). On this basis, social integration clearly differs from mere social convergence which means growing *similarity* between member states, a phenomenon which can and has occurred without the removal of boundaries or geographical barriers (for instance, each country adopting the same age of retirement or each experiencing falling infant mortality rates; see Eurostat/European Commission, 2000). Policies, trends, indicators may converge without the processes they refer to taking place in an integrated social environment; they may converge simply as the result of policies implemented in each society separately or through uncontrolled social trends.

As well as the strict meaning of integration, the current discussion on EU social matters requires a looser meaning to be available too, which would be akin to 'fully harmonised'. Harmonisation is a key term in EU social policy field given its extensive usage, but it is also meagrely defined. To harmonise most often actually means to reform laws so that legal provisions are as similar as possible (hence the term approximation of laws), while accepting that, owing to the process of transposition of directives into domestic law, there is bound to be some slippage between member states. To understand processes and practices that are occurring in the EU, it is useful also to consider a fully harmonised field of activity as if it were 'integrated', even though it may not actually be barrier-free. An example of a field which approaches full harmonisation is occupational health and safety law. The *Daily Express* in Britain showed a surprising grasp of social integration in the context of shopping, when it approved the 'harmonisation' of consumer law (referring to the Commission's proposals to fix a common guarantee period against faulty goods) and advocated that any goods bought abroad be returnable to the manufacturer's outlets in the buyer's home country (Editorial, 29 April 1999: 10). Unwittingly, it was calling for an integrated, frontier-free right for consumers in a single, pan-European retail area – an example of a single social area – and all highly *communautaire*.

Thus defined, it is appropriate to first discuss how much such social integration has already taken place. It is argued here that although *strictu sensu*, it has been a limited phenomenon, new forms of integration are currently taking place in unplanned ways. This is not to say that EU social policy is weak or underdeveloped. On the contrary, Leibfried and Pierson's (1996:186) view that a significant transfer of sovereignty has taken place, and their claim that the dynamics of market-making have led the EC to invade the domain of social policy over several decades, as a result of policy 'spillover', is correct. It is not the degree of supranationalism achieved that is questioned here, nor the extent of nation-state's loss of sovereignty in favour of the EU institutions.

Instead, what is examined here is the degree of integration achieved by those legal and policy instruments irrespective of the institutional tier at which they are adopted. The present discussion focuses on the levels or depth of transnational and pan-European interpenetration, positing that social integration results from the abolition of the legal and institutional barriers that lock individuals into the social system of their current state of residence. Therefore, this chapter analyses the degree to which such barriers have been removed in practice, from the point of view of EU citizens, in order to facilitate their transnational access to social institutions, to cross-national consumption of social services, and to the enjoyment of social practices of other member states.

It is important to consider these questions because integration is such an inherent concept in the European project, and because, as argued here, social integration and limited single social areas are emerging in unexpected ways yet not taking place as planned. Curiously, these questions, though closely affecting the European public, remain veiled in some confusion, which is why the chapter will attempt to clarify certain key aspects.

BOUNDARIES AND DIVERSITY

The discussion just introduced immediately raises issues about boundaries, about homogeneity and diversity within and outside boundaries. The very notion of a single social area or even single society may appear ominously monolithic. Even a 'social union' sounds potentially homogenising. In fact any discussion about social integration is arguably about wider rights and further choice for European publics, about pushing out and removing boundaries rather than affirming them, and about ensuring that citizens get the most out of the European Union. Depending on how we understand and fashion a socially integrated Europe, it would be no less diverse than member states themselves are. In fact, it would be *less homogeneous* than a nation-state by virtue of enlarged boundaries, and the removal of the institutional and legal barriers that currently prevent citizens from enjoying wider choice and from experiencing the greater diversity present in Europe. In the European context, any larger entity is bound to be socially less homogeneous than a smaller one. Nonetheless, the question of losses deriving from integration and harmonisation has to be confronted. If historically constituted nation-states come together, having highly developed national social institutions (in the workplace, in health, education, social protection etc.), do they not lose some characteristic traits? And does it matter, and to whom? Are they merely small sacrifices or of a higher order? The question of social integration can raise hackles and set off fears of loss, particularly of well-loved institutions and practices. The 'ever-closer union of European peoples' which policy-makers are fond of quoting can be experienced as a threat as well as an opportunity.

Such considerations highlight how little thought was given to the social aspect of the integration project by the founding fathers, and how the current designers of the new European architecture continue to shy away from envisioning the future of an integrated Europe for ordinary citizens, possibly fearing adverse, even xenophobic reactions. The chapter presents a fresh examination, particularly from the point of view of EU citizens' access to diversity and choice in the field of social institutions, systems, services and goods.

This chapter examines several areas of social policy: the original social goals of the EEC; the single labour market; joint adoption of regulatory labour policies and the creation of a floor of minimum standards of working conditions; integration of social security systems between member states, and member state co-ordination of their macroeconomic policies, focusing on the degree of integration achieved. The evidence indicates that, despite the emergence of a clear body of supranational competence in the broad area of social policy including employee relations, there are still many fields which are not harmonised, and even in harmonised fields integration is not always evident. This leads to the conclusion that social integration in the full sense proposed here is still an incipient phenomenon. The chapter then explores the ways in which incremental social integration is taking place as a result of citizen initiatives and the practical need to resolve the contradictions that sometimes arise from the application of European laws.

SOCIAL INTEGRATION: A GOAL OF THE EEC?

Whereas some authors argued there was always a social dimension to the EC (George, 1991), others noted its subordinate position (Betten, 1991), and how limited, albeit specific, its scope was (Hantrais, 1995). Despite recent recognition that this is no longer the case, there appears to be a consensus among scholars that the early European architecture was 'founded on a liberal vision that did not embrace supranational social programs' (Ross, 1995: 357).

The reasons most frequently given for the lack of early consideration of the social consequences of creating a common market are that, at the time when the Treaty of Rome was signed, the dominant economic philosophy was one of laissez-faire. Once trade barriers were removed, the free market would ensure the optimum distribution of resources together with optimum social development; therefore the need for social policy was not perceived.[2] The earliest social measures were 'defensive': to prevent accidents in the coal and nuclear industries, and to retrain redundant workers in declining industries (Shanks, 1977: 1–3).

While such accounts of the delayed birth and hesitant growth of social policy are well-known, with the benefit of hindsight the remarkable phenomenon is that the social consequences of the European project were not considered. Certainly social integration was not planned – a mere sprinkling of social policies as an adjunct to economic or market integration is not tantamount to a plan – and blueprints for an integrated European society or social area are wholly absent.[3] Indeed, some fields which might be considered crucial for the original European project, such as education, were pointedly excluded from the purview of the Treaty of Rome.

Despite this there was an expectation that the European project would bring social benefits, but instead of predictions of transformed social institutions, the carrot dangled in front of the public of 1957 as the spin-off from market integration was a simple improvement of working and living conditions.[4] Moreover, the brief yet convoluted Article 117 of the Treaty of Rome allows such improvements to take place both spontaneously and in a politically synchronised way, but is unclear as to whether they would occur only within each member state or across member states. Nor are there any real pointers regarding the meaning of harmonisation of living conditions: these might be achieved through economic convergence while maintaining a different system of social security, housing, personal finance, health care and education in each of the member states. Given these silences, the inclusion of a section on free movement of labour stands out as a major initiative, at once far-sighted and daring.

AN INTEGRATED LABOUR MARKET THROUGH FREE MOVEMENT OF WORKERS

There was one clear project of what would fit the proposed definition of social integration in the original new Europe: the single labour market and the free movement of workers. The right of workers to take up employment in another member state was always one of the basic four freedoms (of capital, goods, professional and other business services, and workers) enshrined in Articles 48–52 of the Treaty of Rome and multiple subsequent Regulations and Directives.

The removal of barriers in all countries, simultaneously and subject to the same regulations, recognisably transforms several markets into a single one. The clear prohibition of discrimination or unequal treatment of EU migrant workers encourages integration by removing some of the many potential disadvantages to working in another country. In addition, the arrangement for aggregation of social security rights accumulated through employment in one country after another, culminating in the provision for pensions to be paid out by the last country of employment at the end of a working life, with member states sharing the costs on a pro-rata basis, are arguably clear indications of an emergent integrated social security system for migrants, notwithstanding the fact that each social security entitlement is at the rate pertaining to each national system the free mover has worked in. While no member states challenge the concept of free movement, it is not always well applied in practice: by the mid-1990s, the European Court of Justice (ECJ) had had 323 cases on the co-ordination of social security arrangements referred to it (cited in Leibfried and Pierson, 1996: 194).

So one should ask whether an integrated labour market with cross-national and cross-frontier supply and demand for labour has effectively come into being in Europe. In theory it has, since freedom of movement and bona fide EU administrative provisions are up and running (Ireland, 1995: 232), but in numerical terms it has been very slow in developing. Before the introduction of the Citizen's Europe measures agreed by member states at Maastricht in December 1991, official calculations indicated that the number of intra-community migrant workers was small and growing at an insignificant rate (CEC, 1985, 1991). The oft quoted round figure of EC nationals *residing* in other EC countries was five million, only just over a third of all foreign residents.[5] In the 1990s it started to rise a little faster, reaching 5,122,000 in 1996 (Eurostat, 1997: Table 012), but it still only made up 1.4 per cent of the total EU population (Eurostat, 2000: Table 2a).

As to EU migrants active in the labour force and *employed* in another EU country – the real indicator of free movement of labour – the 1996 figure was 3,247,000, still representing only 1.9 per cent of the EU work-force (Eurostat, 1997: Tables 001, 005, 012), whereas the 1998 proportion was given as only 1.7 per cent of the workforce aged 15–64 (Eurostat, 2000: Table 8). No wonder it was termed 'limping labour market integration' (Leibfried, 1994: 242). Furthermore the position of third-country nationals resident in the EU who are barred from free movement also undermines the reality and the project of an integrated labour market, since eleven million of them, including 6.45 million workers, are not part of the *mobile* labour market (Eurostat, 1997: Tables 005, 012).[6]

One of the reasons for such lack of momentum is, arguably, that the project assumed the jobseeker to be individually mobile and the attraction of far-away labour markets to be great. The familiar migrant is a worker moving from a distinctly poorer member state to a richer one – Irish to the UK, Spaniard to Germany, Portuguese to France, Italian to London, but these migrants with the exception of Italy, mainly moved *before* their countries became members of the EC. Indeed the Spanish case indicates there have been less, not more, migrants out of Spain since it joined the EC. As the original Community workers were heads of household whose spouses and offspring were not accorded the same rights in the host country but only enjoyed derived rights as dependants, it can be said that the EU's vision of free movement was hampered by gender-blindness and lacked an understanding of the conditions needed for people to move. Crucial aspects of social integration – moving as a family, effects on children, language barriers, and access to housing amongst other public and 'merit goods' (Majone, 1993) – were not taken on board at the time. It has remained 'structurally incomplete' (Leibfried, 1994: 244). And although the EU's 1992 Citizen's Europe initiative may eventually accelerate trends, some believe it will remain limited to corporate executives and low-skilled, low-paid migrant workers (Rhodes, 1995: 395).

The limitations of this aspect of social integration so far[7] should not of themselves be surprising since many people who are free to move within their own country of residence never do so, despite facing far fewer barriers. Arguably, European social integration will only be achieved if free movement between member states becomes as easy, as practicable and as frequent for those with the relevant language skills, as mobility within a nation-state, entailing no more paperwork than any change of residence or employer. The removal of barriers such as work permits and the introduction of European-wide job advertisements through the EU's EURES database has evidently been insufficient as a push/pull factor. It appears that people also need the functional integration of many social institutions that govern their lives before they move. Clearly, this has not been the path followed, and the integration of social institutions is hardly on the agenda.[8]

UNEXPECTED CONSEQUENCES

Yet it is argued here that the free movement framework has produced a complicated mesh of unexpected consequences with knock-on effects for social integration, which are gradually leading the EU into greater realms of supranationalism than originally intended. The following report of a case illustrates the risks attendant on the incautious venturer into foreign territory. A Dutch woman moved to the UK with her British partner and had a child. When the child was still under school age she separated from her partner, was left with no financial support, and claimed income support. Soon afterwards, she received a letter from the then Home Secretary Michael Howard stating that as she was not working (as a proper community *worker* should do), she had become 'a burden on public funds' and should either leave the country, or find paid employment. Her income support was stopped. The Home Secretary was entitled to do this on a narrow interpretation of EU law, and had done so to several thousand EU migrants. Precisely because of the lack of integration of social welfare institutions, member states had no duty to maintain other EU nationals from public funds as opposed to entitlements from earned/in-work social insurance contributions.

But the case also illustrates the unforeseeable consequences of the gender-blind concept of free movement and how its proper application affects family law and the court system. The Dutch mother had simultaneously been ordered to remain in Britain by a family court in order for the child's father to be able to see him – finding herself in the impossible situation of being asked to leave by one institution and to stay by another. Moreover, because she was not a real 'immigrant' subject to a formal deportation order, she was not entitled to appeal to the Home Office. Eventually the House of Lords ruled that she was entitled to income support (Bosely, 1997).

As such cases become more frequent, the rights of EU citizens living in another country are extended incrementally. In countries where benefits for parents and children are extensive, the effects will be greater. Clearly there are implications not only for harmonisation of welfare systems but also for family court procedures and for fathers' statutory rights, amongst other aspects. Indeed, a Council Regulation on the mutual recognition and enforcement of judgements on parental rights of access to children was being discussed in November 2000 (European Parliament, 2000c: 20).

'Free movement' of court judgments

Free-movers faced so many problems arising from intra-EU marriage, divorce and alimony, that a convention on parental and matrimonial matters was signed in Brussels in May 1998, making civil and commercial judgments by courts binding in other member states, so that alimony and child-support payments became enforceable throughout the EU. Commissioner Mario Monti had hailed it as 'a first step in a new single market policy in the field of procedural law', adding that 'the free movement of judgments is an important corollary to the basic freedoms of the EU treaty' (Walker, 1997). The Commission followed this with a proposal that the 1998 Brussels Convention be replaced by a binding Council of Ministers Regulation[9] adopted in May 2000, introducing uniform rules relating to the annulment of marriage, divorce and separation and aiming to facilitate the rapid and automatic recognition by one member state of decisions adopted in another. Former Commissioner Anita Gradin explained that 'a Regulation would enable the application of *harmonised* rules [my emphasis] to jurisdiction, otherwise cross-border recognition of decisions would not function' (European Commission DGV, 1999b: 3). Notably, the directly enforceable Regulation also applies to child custody judgments, hopefully deterring the practice of child abductions (European Parliament, 1999b: 6).

This raises two matters of note. First, that a family court order enforceable EU-wide is an illustration of social integration as a single area of jurisdiction is created, and citizens involved in the deeply personal as well as social problems of divorce and parental rights find that, for practical purposes, they are living in the EU as in one country. Secondly, had harmonisation in this field been proposed as a goal by the Commission in the name of social integration, *before* the practical need to sort out complicated human situations had become manifest, it would doubtless have faced trenchant criticisms of interference. Instead, free movement rights created de facto situations for which harmonisation then provided a solution which member states have gone along with. The issues have not been wrapped in ideology nor in the language of citizenship rights, and have drawn little attention.

A single jurisdiction

A further illustration of the single European jurisdiction is the Europe-wide driving ban agreed by ministers in 1998 – a driving disqualification will apply equally in all member states, who will maintain a common Europe-wide list of disqualified drivers (*Guardian*, 25 May 1998: 2). This is also a case of social integration, in so far as it affects the actual experience of citizens. Even though the driving laws are not harmonised, and continue to be of varying severity in each country, the EU has become a single country from the disqualified driver's point of view.

A similar example is the Directive under discussion at the time of writing aimed at extending the protection of victims of road accidents, which would help around half a million drivers each year who are involved in accidents while abroad (European Parliament, 1999a; 2000b: 9). It entails a further rupture of national frontiers, breaking down barriers to the application of insurance and compensation schemes, so that from the drivers' point of view it may eventually make no difference which country they have an accident in.

Paradoxically, such questions of jurisdiction have advanced integration more easily than if the subject to which they apply had been discussed head on by the politicians. Outright proposals for common alimony payments or driving tests would probably have been unthinkable, but supranational application and enforcement of a variety of laws is not. Thus the integration process is, ironically, carried along on the back of the chauvinism of certain publics who believe their country's laws are better and therefore welcome them being enforced elsewhere without fully taking on board that the reverse also applies.

A SINGLE PLAYING FIELD OF LABOUR STANDARDS?

The chapter will now briefly discuss the existing legislation on working conditions. The purpose is not to question the EU's contribution to raising labour standards in individual member states, nor to discuss the degree of transfer of sovereignty that has taken place in this area, but to assess how far legislation already adopted harmonises and/or integrates working conditions. More than a *level* playing field, is it a *single* playing field?

The Treaty of Rome did not actually stipulate any integration of working conditions. For instance, the articles affecting Community migrant workers only stipulate that they may not be treated differently from nationals of other member states, but do not lay down any pan-European standards. The well-known Article 119 (now 141) on equal pay between the sexes stipulates that workers of both sexes should be paid the same for work of equal value, but the level of the equal pay can vary from one member state to another. The point is often overlooked that the general conditions under which male and female employees work were *not* integrated across countries by the Treaty of Rome. It was only the later adoption of Directives and ECJ decisions which started the process of harmonising certain aspects of working conditions.

The first Directive affecting employees' rights across the board in all member states was the one on collective redundancies (75/129/EEC). It meant that workers' representatives would receive similar (harmonised) treatment in the advent of redundancies in all member states in so far as they would be informed and consulted in advance. But in the increasing number of companies where employees have no unions to represent them, the Directive can be ignored. Apart from this, it is not designed to prevent redundancies, merely to soften their effect through negotiation.

The Directive on the Transfer of Undertakings (77/187/EEC) aimed to protect employees' rights and conditions when their company is taken over by another, so that takeovers should not be used to declare collective agreements or hard-won concessions null and void. In practice this applies mainly in unionised firms. The 1980 Directive on Insolvency of Employers (80/987/EEC) provided for a fund out of which employees' unpaid wages could be paid in case of insolvency of the employer. A 1990s Directive stipulates the obligation of employers to give employees a contract or letter indicating the employment relationship and setting out who they are employed by and the nature of their duties (91/533/EEC).

Another whole set of Directives is aimed at preventing businesses from discriminating against or abusing more vulnerable groups of workers, such as women, young people and part-time workers, and ethnic minorities[10] while treating male, prime-age full-time workers better. But this does not harmonise their actual working conditions across countries. Though the 1997 Amsterdam Treaty introduced a general right to non-discrimination and the subsequent Directive was adopted in 2000, equal treatment is always relative and comparisons are made within individual countries. Arguably, there is a lack of European integration in the very concept of equality of treatment, since the comparator is not another member state but another social group. Only a border-free absolute right to the *same* treatment in each country, implemented in the EU as a single jurisdiction or single social area of application would be tantamount to true integration.

Other Directives do not claim to harmonise conditions, but merely to prevent the continued disparity between member states from becoming too great, by establishing a floor of minimum standards, a process involving what could be called 'disparity-limitation'. The Working Time Directive (93/104/EC) sets limits to the working day and week, but the maximum weekly average working hours per person is still high at 48 per week. Actual times of work and patterns of holidays can and do continue to vary from state to state, but the intention is to constrain the disparity with the upper limit.

The Parental Leave Directive stipulating three months of unpaid leave to look after children, when some member states already offered three years' paid leave (Germany), is another example of mere disparity-limitation. And the Directive on Information and Consultation of Workers' Representatives in European multinationals cannot claim to bring member states' businesses into line with each other as it only affects European multinationals, not all firms. Statutory provisions and the tradition of information and consultation of employees range from very weak or virtually non-existent, to widespread but weak (Spain), and widespread and strong (Germany), where they go as far as co-determination by employees and managers on company boards.

Despite this picture of patchy coverage, there is one aspect of working conditions which is of a different order. Health and safety in the workplace has been ever more regulated at EU level from 1974 onwards, with an important extension made with the 1989 'Framework' Directive on health and safety at work, which was followed by a burgeoning of specific Directives affecting particular sectors, currently 29 Council Directives among 48 legal instruments.[11] Health and safety is numerically the most conspicuous of regulatory social policies (Cram, 1993: 139). But even though it is certainly the most extensively covered area, it is still an open question whether it can be said that workplace health and safety is fully harmonised. Only very few of the 1978 health and safety action programme directives were actually fully enacted according to Ross (1995: 369 and fn36). and 'a wide variety of different fits' between the EU texts and national arrangements still exist (Ross, 1995: 373 fn44).

Interestingly, health and safety is one area where a clear project for integration of workplace conditions appears to exist, not only because of the breadth of the Framework Directive and its seven 'daughter' Directives, but also because the field is governed by QMV and because Article 118a (ToR, SEA, TEU) specifies 'a high level of protection' as a base – much more than just a minimum floor. In this field the scene is set for widespread upward harmonisation, for 'a race to the top' (Ross 1995: 371), achieving pan-European standards, though perhaps not of a single standard since variations are still allowed. It is the area which comes closest to social integration through regulation, with an employee able to expect something close to a pan-European level of risk – though in practice this depends on domestic enforcement.

So are working conditions a good example of social integration? An important part of the employment relationship remains unregulated by European law, especially when compared to the sheer volume and detail of legislation found in some national labour codes.[12] And even where European law bring domestic laws into line with each other, such harmonisation is often leaky.[13] The array of existing Directives does represent a move in the general direction of harmonisation, and does institute steps towards *more similar* conditions for employees in each member state, but one should not presume their impact or coverage is comprehensive. Aspects of working life such as employment protection from dismissal and redundancy and the ensuing compensation are not touched upon.[14] In addition the EU treaties expressly rule out the areas of pay, and the conditions governing strikes and employer lock-outs as well as the law governing the operation of trade unions including collective bargaining procedures (Teague, 1994: 10). All in all, as Teague states 'a real limit exists to any project aimed at increasing the uniformity of industrial relations systems' (1994: 7). It is all the more unlikely to develop now that EU thinking is far less concerned with general labour market regulation (Grahl and Teague, 1996: 2) and more with labour market flexibility. In addition, the whole issue of uneven compliance or poor implementation in varying degrees by member states further undermines the idea of employees being subject to the uniform conditions of a pan-European system. While there is agreement that from the member states' point of view, national sovereignty over workplace health and safety has been surrendered, often unwittingly (Rhodes, 1998), employees are still far from experiencing a single system of working conditions.

EUROPEAN COLLECTIVE BARGAINING?

The argument regarding bargaining over working conditions should be looked at with care since there are already well-established European level organisations representing national institutions: the European Union of Industries (UNICE, of which the British CBI is a member), the smaller European Confederation of Public Enterprises (CEEP) and the European Trades Union Confederation (ETUC), as well as about seventeen sectoral international trade unions who have European representation. Both sides of industry (the 'social partners') have long had an official procedure for regular meetings and the prerogative of issuing Joint Opinions which the Commission takes into consideration. Therefore it could be said that each social partner speaks at a pan-European level with an 'integrated' voice.[15]

The Single European Act (1986) formalised the 'social dialogue' and the Social Agreement of the TEU[16] specified a new procedure whereby the social partners at EU level could reach framework agreements that would be accepted at the intergovernmental level, creating the possibility for European-level bargains. For instance, the social partners negotiated but failed to reach agreement over the European Works Council proposal for a Directive, but later concluded framework agreements on parental leave and part-time work which were adopted by the Council of Ministers and became Directives.

As a result of all these measures affecting employment, analysts have asked whether the member states are moving towards European-level collective bargaining. Ross suggested they have resulted in no more than an expanded policy legacy which future Commissions can use to promote European collective bargaining (Ross, 1995: 384). Arguably, it is still an incipient form of integration despite the presence of stable partners and the long-established status of the social dialogue in the EC's concerns. Extended European-level collective bargaining could only replace member states' industrial relations systems with difficulty, because of features such as their heterogeneity (Due et al., 1991), their continued vitality, and the investment of resources made in them by unions and employers (Ross, 1995: 385). Others have suggested that collective agreements concluded at European level would only be effective if a proper European labour market developed (Leibfried, 1994: 243). Aside from the fact that pay bargaining is excluded from the purview of EU social policy, there seems to be no strong belief that European economic convergence is producing sufficiently 'converged' pay levels to enable bargains to be made that would cross national boundaries.

INTEGRATION OF SOCIAL SECURITY SYSTEMS?

The continued heterogeneity of labour market institutions also applies to social security and welfare policy. The Rome Treaty carried conflicting messages about the harmonisation of social policy: from the outset social security policy was primarily a matter for individual member states to determine, except in the case of migrant workers (Hantrais, 1995: 20). But the principle of free movement of workers led the member states to undertake some limited co-ordination of national social security systems in order to safeguard arrangements for migrant workers.[17]

While the French government argued at an early stage that 'harmonization of social protection, particularly in terms of funding, was a desirable objective and even a precondition for fair competition' (Hantrais, 1995: 22), other policy-makers tended to view the welfare state as essentially 'anti-international' (ibid.: 22, citing De Swaan 1990) and as not prone to be integrated nor harmonised. The fiscal, budgetary and expenditure implications for member states were considered politically too sensitive, particularly in their potential knock-on effects on tax-raising.[18] The Commission was aware that funding arrangements were not only extremely complex, but were also anchored in national traditions and cultures (Hantrais, 1995: 9).[19] Thus by the 1990s the Commission had already withdrawn from spearheading an attempt at approximation of laws or harmonisation of the actual social security institutions and financing systems on the grounds of non-interference in the competencies of member states (Vobruba, 1995: 304).

Social protection policy convergence

Even without integration of social security systems, it is possible to encourage their gradual convergence through the co-ordination of their goals, outcomes and effects. National policies for social protection can 'converge over a number of precisely defined common objectives without encroaching on systems which have developed from quite different traditions' (Hantrais, 1995: 24). The view is that if the Commission successfully co-ordinates member states in an effort of co-operation through the Social Affairs Councils, ministers will develop convergent and even common goals and can, separately, use their national systems to produce outcomes which are increasingly similar to those in other member states. Thus the Council of Ministers in July 1992 adopted two non-binding Recommendations on the convergence of social protection objectives, requiring member states (including the UK) to have in place or to set up social protection schemes to provide minimum resources 'in keeping with human dignity' to all citizens and legal residents who are unable to do so for themselves – access to free health care, minimum subsistence incomes and help to access the labour market (European Commission DGV, 1994: Ch. 4.).[20]

Where does this leave the issue of social integration? First, it can be said that if something like the 'Thirteenth State' model (Pieters, 1996) had been adopted, through which the then twelve member states would have created a thirteenth (European) social security fund, producing a single system from the users' and beneficiaries' point of view, then such harmonisation of social security systems would most clearly have amounted to transnational integration. But this and other proposals for different schemes were rejected (Begg and Nectoux, 1995). Secondly, in their absence, can one suppose that an integrated system has nonetheless been built for some workers through the existing arrangements for migrant workers? Research would be needed about the user-friendliness of current arrangements for EU migrants in order to judge whether the practice of aggregation, though technically amounting to a form of transnational integration, is actually experienced by migrants as a single social system rather than as a complicated process of adding up entitlements from several regimes instead of one.

Regarding basic social assistance however, it can be envisaged that successive member state governments will gradually adopt similar approaches and policies, eroding the uniqueness of national welfare traditions. This is because European-level joint discussion of possible solutions to common problems already take place, and the political advantages of adopting potentially unpopular decisions jointly are evident. Moving towards broadly identical policies would amount to a case of policy and programme convergence, though policy implementation would still be *compartmentalised* – occurring separately in each country, with the nation-state controlling the pace and the means without any binding obligations. However, as an overall project it is still a conjecture. Indeed, general analyses of welfare state development in the EC have found little evidence of convergence (Rhodes, 1995: 398) and the research on the 'southern European syndrome', highlighting the difficulties facing the welfare states of Italy, Spain, Greece and Portugal (see Ferrera, 1996; Rhodes, 1996) suggests that convergence of social protection, measured in *outcomes* rather than spending, is a remote prospect.

A rather different question involves what we shall call the consumption of social protection benefits by free movers, as illustrated earlier by the case of the Dutch woman caught in the tentacles of bureaucracy. It has been argued that 'the walls of the welfare state have also been cracked' (Leibfried, 1994: 241), to which one could add that states are no longer protected from claims from a series of new groups (Community non-workers: unemployed, spouses and dependants, students, pensioners), nor more recently from legally resident non-EU nationals too, as some barriers to free movement have fallen since Maastricht. The issue of 'welfare tourism' or 'benefit tourism' has raised public awareness about the disadvantages of having very diverse levels of social protection across member states, but British politicians who feared the possibility of strong flows of EU migrants towards countries with generous social provision (Brindle, 1999) – believing Britain to be one of these – may by now have changed their minds in view of the convenience of having this additional source of cheap labour. The advantage of such free movement of EU citizens may lead national governments to decide that the integration of certain aspects of social protection is desirable, undermining the more common argument, such as Cram's, that precisely because social protection involves the state in statutory obligations, member states' governments have been reluctant to address it (for example Cram, 1993: 142).

At the same time, portability of pensions, while supporting pensioners who prefer to move to another country under free movement rights, has implications for health care systems. When it was launched in the wake of the 1992 Treaty on European Union, pensioners were not supposed to become a burden on their host countries, but the difficulty of sending frail older long-term residents of one country back to the one in which they earned their entitlements soon made the maintenance of such compartmentalised healthcare non-viable, not to say impossible in urgent cases. From 1997, all people residing or staying in another Community country became entitled to all medical benefits *in kind* as if they were insured there, irrespective of whether these were more or less favourable (i.e. applying the equal treatment principle). Cash benefits remain to be paid by the state in which a person is or was 'insured', i.e. earned the entitlement (European Commission DGV, 2000). It will not be long before citizens push out this particular boundary, such as when elderly free-movers need social assistance cash benefits not subject to the insurance principle; or before they break down the remaining access barriers to other benefits in kind, such as education, housing, and social services such as, for example, free internet training to help the elderly to keep in touch with their families.[21] A further extension of rights creating single European areas of social provision will increase de facto social integration.

A SINGLE MARKET FOR USERS OF EDUCATION SERVICES AND HEALTH TREATMENTS?

Two important new fields of social policy competence were agreed at Maastricht and introduced in the TEU: education and healthcare, in which the Commission gained the right to play a co-ordination role.[22] Even though harmonisation is expressly ruled out, these two fields nevertheless present new examples of barriers coming down and of choice being extended for ordinary citizens in a way which is relevant to this discussion.

Free movement in higher education and mutual recognition of qualifications is an established practice. The outcome of equal treatment principles has been to open up access to higher education institutions for EU students irrespective of their state of permanent residence. Interestingly, it has occurred without any harmonisation of the curriculum or of academic structures or the education systems themselves. The point is that cross-national consumption of this social good is feasible without users having to place themselves in the category of EU migrant, and they remain students, not workers. They become consumers/users of such goods and services in a single higher education area. And the university degree obtained, by becoming portable, acquires a pan-European, cross-national validity. Education provision, especially at the primary and secondary levels, nevertheless remains ring-fenced by national frontiers.

There is no reason to suppose that this will remain so in the future. Given the ever-increasing ease of travel, parents may soon be demanding cross-national user rights in secondary education without changing their residence or paying extra fees, sending their children to school in another member state on a weekly or even a daily basis. For the moment qualifications are merely mutually recognised, not harmonised, but if future demand for the international baccalaureate increased to the point of becoming the norm – given that it is a more portable qualification – secondary education will have become integrated. Thus European social integration could occur as a result of user demand rather than high politics.

The health field is even more complex. While healthcare itself is subsumed under social security issues, the Commission acquired a competency for public health under Article 129 of the TEU, which allows it to support public authorities in their duties. There are no proposed measures to harmonise standards per se, nor to integrate systems, since the ambit of Commission action is to improve the 'environment' for health, rather than individual health.

What type of healthcare integration would be of interest to citizens? Harmonisation measures could bring undeniable benefits if they made member states whose health care performance is lagging improve their range of services, standards of care and management of health services. But like the field of employment, healthcare is so vast a domain that a wide array of Directives would be required before anything like a harmonised healthcare environment was created, and still more to achieve a state of affairs resembling healthcare integration. And yet, perhaps even more than employment, harmonisation of healthcare standards and partial upward alignment through the introduction of minimum standards in health are goals that European citizens would willingly agree to. Here the fear of loss of sovereignty might not raise its head so prominently. Regarding future developments, this is a field to watch.

In fact, the answer to the rhetorical headline 'Towards a Europe of Patients?' (European Commission DGV, 1999a: 1) is that the creation of a single market place of health services has already arrived, at least legally. Two 1998 ECJ judgments (*Kohll* and *Decker*)[23] ruled that citizens purchasing treatments, in this case spectacles, in another member state did not have to seek prior authorisation from their insurance fund in order to get their medical expenses reimbursed on return home. And an important Council Regulation issued in 1997 clarified that citizens have the possibility to travel to another member state in order to receive treatment, the cost of which will be reimbursed by their own health insurance institution, but only with prior authorisation. Such authorisation cannot be refused if the type of treatment needed is provided by the country in which the person is insured, but is not available within a time limit compatible with their state of health (European Commission DGV, 1999a: 2). This obviously goes well beyond the idea of the old form E111 allowing people to be treated if taken ill on holiday abroad; it is a new phenomenon of patient mobility (Wavell, 1998). While the financial and legal implications arising from patients circumventing waiting lists and rationed treatments by going to another member state are as yet untested,[24] a single market in health treatments has already been created de jure. From the citizens' point of view, a clear benefit of such social integration or single health area, would be increased access to a wider range of care services and products. While this is not generally on offer at the moment, individuals have taken initiatives and pushed out their rights beyond national boundaries under the umbrella of free movement law.

CONCLUSION

Up to now, EU citizens have been recognised as having agency as foreign workers, foreign residents, tourists, consumers and shoppers in a single market for products and jobs, but hardly as citizens or as users of services, particularly not social services. They have so far been trapped in their social systems, which are far less integrated than might have been anticipated given the pace of development of economic integration and notwithstanding a number of social laws over four decades. They have been prevented from benefiting directly from their general right of free movement by constraints placed on them by an unavoidable involvement in a complex series of national social systems ranging from housing, to schools, to health care, to pensions, to formal and informal family and social contracts and even to systems of personal finance, all of which remain to a large extent ring-fenced by state boundaries.

Future solutions appear to be emerging, from claims arising from the practical application of free movement rights, from user and consumer behaviours and also from the demand for fundamental rights. Even though the Charter of Fundamental Rights adopted by the EU at the Nice summit has not been given full legal status, new forms of socio-legal integration can emerge if there is acceptance and selective application of concepts such as the indivisibility and justiciability of civil and social rights as proposed by the Expert Group on Fundamental Rights appointed by the Commission (European Commission DGV, 1999b: 21).

Should the Charter be judicially invoked, the protection afforded to women in the EU could be widely enhanced, since it affirms that gender equality 'must be ensured in all areas' (Article 23). Already a new area such as the prevention of trafficking of women is under discussion. MEPs have called for a harmonised definition of trafficking to cover slavery, forced labour, forced prostitution, sexual exploitation, forced marriage and the harmonisation of measures to detect traffickers and bring them to justice (European Parliament, 2000b). But if, say, freedom from sexual violence is recognised as a fundamental right, as the European Women's Lobby pressed for, then in a context where the single jurisdiction concept is also being applied, much more integration measures could follow, because women's organisations will undoubtedly seek to exploit the new legal avenues.[25]

Even with only selective endorsement from the Council, it can be surmised that EU competencies in healthcare, education and employment, family law and child protection will eventually be enhanced. And even without waiting for governments to act, ordinary citizens are already finding new ways to improve their ability to access a variety of public social goods transnationally, creating specific Union-wide social areas of integration and developing the Treaty of Rome's promise of improving living conditions in advance of governments.

NOTES

I wish to thank Linda Hantrais, Donald Sassoon, Donald Share and Michael H. Smith for their helpful comments on earlier versions of this text.

1   DGVs brief ranges from 'employment and labour policy to all aspects of social policy, including health and safety standards and some of the key issues in today's society such as equal opportunities, social exclusion and immigration' (European Commission DGV, 1996).

2   This dominant version is under challenge by Moravcsik's account, in which social policy was a high level issue in 1955–56 because businesses feared competition. French industry in particular demanded social harmonisation and common standards but the government finally agreed this could take pace at a second stage (Moravcsik, 1998: 136, 141, 144).

3   Even Shanks' concluding analysis of the 'unsolved problems' of the EEC's social dimension does not address any prospects for social integration, only surmising that 'The Community is not yet ready for the harmonization of social systems' (Shanks, 1977: 79–83).

4   Article 117 provided what was virtually the only indication in the whole Treaty of what was intended to happen: 'MS agree upon the need to promote better conditions of living and of work for workers, so as to lead to their progressive harmonization and improvement. They believe that such a development will ensue not only from the operation of the common market but also from the procedures provided for in this Treaty and from the approximation of provisions imposed by law, regulation and administrative action.'

5   Eurostat figures for 1991 were only 4,955,600 people (Fontaine, 1993: 39).

6   A fact that governments take little account of in enlargement negotiations since they wish to impose years of limitation on the right of free movement on applicant states (Helen Wallace, seminar communication, Loughborough University, 18.2.98).

7   Wallace (1997) takes a more optimistic view, partly on the basis of research showing the rise of second-home ownership by British in France and Spain – an interesting aspect of free movement not monitored by Eurostat.

8   Of course, for many individuals, lack of relevant language skills would still form a barrier – an issue too complex to address here.

9   Council Regulation (EC) No. 1347/2000 of 29 May 2000 on 'jurisdiction and the recognition and enforcement of judgments in matrimonial matters and in responsibility for children of both spouses' Official Journal L160, 30/06/2000, pp. 0019–0029.

10 The sex equality Directives aim to prevent cutting of labour costs by paying women workers less, or by treating them differently from male workers in matters such as social security. Pregnant workers are specifically protected regarding the kind of work they may undertake. Maternity leave is established by a minimum entitlement of 14 weeks, paid at no less than statutory sick pay. Employers are no longer legally able to dismiss pregnant employees regardless of their length of employment. Employment of young workers is harmonised in so far as there are limits to the number of hours per week during the school term, and they require greater health and safety protection. A step towards the harmonisation of conditions for part-time workers was taken by the social partners and adopted as a Directive in 1997.

11 Council Directive 89/391/EEC of 12 June 1989 on the introduction of measures to encourage improvements in the safety and health of workers at work. Details displayed on Eur-Lex Directory of Community Legislation in force 05.20.20.10 Safety at work, Secondary Legislation, http://www.europa.eu.int. Application is monitored by the Commission, e.g. European Commission 1996, Annex 2.

12 For instance, the Spanish *Estatuto de los Trabajadores* or the German labour code.

13 For instance, the exemptions (derogations) to the Working Time Directive are so extensive that the Confederation of British Industry (CBI) went along with it even while the British government was objecting, taking the view that the law would have little effect on their members' businesses (personal communication).

14 There may be developments in this area, as the Charter of Fundamental Rights of the European Union adopted at Nice in December 2000 states in Article 30 that 'Every worker has the right to protection against unjustified dismissal, in accordance with Community law and national laws and practices.'

15 The Joint Opinion on Training, though not binding, is considered to have had considerable impact in some member states such as Spain. But there is neither an integrated training system nor a formally integrated approach to the training to be provided by member-state governments, employers or trade unions.

16 The Agreement was only appended to, rather than incorporated into, the TEU owing to UK objections and its agreed opt-out, formalised in a Social Protocol. In 1997 after the Labour Party came into government and withdrew its opt-out, the contents of the Social Agreement were incorporated into the main body of the Amsterdam Treaty.

17 This was the subject of one of the very first Regulations adopted by the Council of Ministers in 1958 (Hantrais, 1995: 21).

18 Already in 1975 an International Labour Organisation (ILO) report concluded that there were no clear grounds for the harmonisation of social security costs throughout the EC (Cram, 1993: 142).

19   Underpinning this, the typologies and analysis of welfare states created by Esping-Anderson, Leibfried, Ferrera and Rhodes underline the diversity of national institutions.
20   The documents were signed by Norman Lamont, the UK Chancellor of the Exchequer in the then Conservative government which held the Presidency of the Council at the time.
21   For instance, in the UK a charity, Age Concern, offers these, and in Switzerland it is the local council.
22   The Commission had already been able to launch and support Erasmus and Socrates as part of its youth exchanges spending programmes, but had no policy competence in the field of education until then.
23   *Kohll* case C-120/95 and *Decker* case C-158/96, of 28 May 1998 (not to be confused with the well-known *Dekker* case).
24   The ECJ in *Kohll* and in *Decker* recognised that a barrier to the principles of the internal market (i.e. inability to obtain treatment anywhere in the EU) could be justified 'where the financial balance of the social security system might be seriously undermined' (European Commission DGV, 1999a: 1).
25   The European Women's Lobby pressed the committee drafting the Charter to include a ban on gender-related violence and persecution, including rape, domestic violence, forced marriage, prostitution, and 'honour' killings, believing these to constitute a form of torture. See their policy statements on http://www.womenlobby.org

REFERENCES

Beck, W., Van der Maesen, L. and Walker, A. (eds) (1998) *The Social Quality of Europe*. Bristol: The Policy Press.

Begg, I. and Nectoux, F. (1995) 'Economic Union and Social Protection', *Journal of European Social Policy*, 5 (4): 285–302.

Betten, L. (ed.) (1991) *The Future of European Social Policy: Views and Comments*. Deventer: Kluwer.

Bosely, S. (1997) 'Mother Gets Lords to Ban Benefits Ruse', *Guardian*, 28 November.

Brindle, D. (1999) 'DSS Officers Told to Drop the "Benefit Tourist" Test', *Guardian*, 31 May.

Cram, L. (1993) 'Calling the Tune Without Paying the Piper?', *Policy and Politics*, 21 (2): 135–46.

De Swaan, A. (1990) 'Perspectives for Transnational Social Policy', *Cross-National Research Papers*, 2 (2): 7–22.

Due, D., Madsen, S. and Jensen, C. (1991) 'The Social Dimension: Convergence or Diversification of Industrial Relations?', *Industrial Relations Journal*, 2 (2): 85–102.

European Commission DGV (1994) White Paper: *European Social Policy: A Way Forward for the Future*.

European Commission DGV (1995) *Medium-term Social Action Programme 1995–7* (COM(95) 134) Social Europe, 1/1995: 7–32.

European Commission DGV (1996a) 'State of Communication of National Measures Implementing Community Law', 15.01.1997, Annex 2, *Social Europe Supplement* 1996/4.

European Commission DGV (1996b) *Social Europe Magazine*, No. 4, July.

European Commission DGV (1999a) *Free Movement and Social Security: Citizens' Rights When Moving Within the EU*, Bulletin No. 2.

European Commission DGV (1999b) *Women of Europe Newsletter*, No. 87, July/August.

European Parliament (E.C 1999a) *Session News, 15–19 November*, Brussels: 22 November.

European Parliament (1999b) *Session News, 13–17 December*, Brussels: 20 December.

European Parliament (2000a) *Session News, 15–21 May*, Brussels.

European Parliament (2000b) *Session News, 12–16 June*, Brussels.

European Parliament (2000c) *Session News, The Week, 13–17 November*, Brussels.

European Union Convention to draft a Charter of Fundamental Rights of the EU, draft text, Charte 4487/00, Brussels 28 September 2000, http://www.fundamental.rights@consilium.eu.int.

Eurostat (1997) *Labour Force Survey Results 1996*. Luxembourg: OOPEC.

Eurostat (2000) *Labour Force Survey Results 1998*. Luxembourg: OOPEC.

Eurostat/European Commission (2000) *The Social Situation in the European Union 2000*. Luxembourg: OOPEC.

Expert Group on Fundamental Rights (1999) *Affirming Fundamental Rights in the EU*, report. Luxembourg: OOPEC.

Ferrera, M. (1996) 'The "Southern Model" of Welfare in Social Europe', *Journal of European Social Policy*, 6 (1): 17–37.

Fontaine, P. (1993) *A Citizen's Europe: Europe on the Move Series*. Luxembourg: OOPEC.

George, S. (1991) *Politics and Policy in the European Community*. Oxford: Oxford University Press.

Geyer, R. (2000) *Exploring European Social Policy*. Cambridge: Polity Press.

Gold, M. (ed.) (1993) *The Social Dimension: Employment Policy in the EC*. Basingstoke: Macmillan.

Grahl, J. and Teague, P. (1996) *Crisis or Opportunity? Employment and competitiveness*. Discussion paper for Jean Monnet Group of Experts, Hull: Centre for European Union Studies, University of Hull.

Hantrais, L. (1995) *Social Policy in the European Union*. London: Macmillan.

Ireland, P.R. (1995) 'Migration, Free Movement and Immigrant Integration in the EU: A Bifurcated Policy Response', in S. Leibfried and P. Pierson (eds) *European Social Policy: Between Fragmentation and Integration*. Washington, DC: Brookings Institution.

Lange P. (1992) 'The Politics of the Social Dimension', in A. Sbragia (ed.) *Europolitics: Institutions and Policy-making in the 'New' European Community*. Washington, DC: Brookings Institution.

Leibfried, S. (1994) 'The Social Dimension of the European Union: En Route to Positively Joint Sovereignty?', *Journal of European Social Policy*, 4 (4): 239–62.

Leibfried, S. and Pierson, P. (eds) (1995) *European Social Policy: Between Fragmentation and Integration*. Washington, DC: Brookings Institution.

Leibfried, S. and Pierson, P. (1996) 'Social policy', in H. Wallace and W. Wallace (eds) *Policy-making in the European Union*. Oxford: Oxford University Press.

Majone, G. (1993) 'The European Community Between Social Policy and Social Regulation', *Journal of Common Market Studies*, 31 (June): 153–70.

Milward, A.S. (1992) *The European Rescue of the Nation-state*. London: Routledge.

Moravcsik, A. (1998) *The Choice for Europe: Social Purpose and State Power from Messina to Maastricht*. London: UCL Press.

Pieters, D. (1996) 'Problems of Comparison of Social Protection and a Strategy for Harmonisation: the Thirteenth State', in J. Pacolet (ed.) *European Economic and Monetary Union*. Aldershot: Avebury. pp. 24–34.

Rhodes, M. (1992) 'The Future of the Social Dimension: Labour Market Regulation in post-1992 Europe', *Journal of Common Market Studies*, 30 (1): 23–51.

Rhodes, M. (1995) 'Subversive Liberalism: Market Integration, Globalization and the European Welfare State', *Journal of European Public Policy*, 2 (3): 384–406.

Rhodes, M. (1996) 'Southern European Welfare States: Identity, Problems and Prospects for Refom', *South European Society and Politics*, 1 (3): 1–22.

Rhodes, M. (1998) 'Defending the Social Contract: The EU Between Global Constraints and Domestic Imperatives', in D. Hine and H. Kassim (eds) *Beyond the Market: The European Union and National Social Policy*. London: Routledge.

Ross, G. (1995) 'The Delors Era and Social Policy', in S. Leibfried and P. Pierson (eds) *European Social Policy: Between Fragmentation and Integration*. Washington, DC: Brookings Institution.

Shanks, M. (1977) *European Social Policy Today and Tomorrow*. Oxford: Pergamon Press.

Streeck, W. (1995) 'From Market-making to State-building? Reflections on the Political Economy of European Social Policy', in S. Leibfried and P. Pierson (eds) *European Social Policy: Between Fragmentation and Integration*. Washington, DC: Brookings Institution.

Teague, P. (1994) 'The Evolution of EU social policy', *Employee Relations*, 16 (6): 5–11.

Teague, P. and Grahl, J. (1992) *Industrial Relations and European Integration*. London: Lawrence and Wishart.

Vobruba, G. (1995) 'Social Policy on Tomorrow's Euro-corporatist Stage', *Journal of European Social Policy*, 5 (4): 303–15.

Walker, M. (1997) 'Europe's Will May Become Law in UK', *Guardian*, 27 November: 15.

Wallace, W. (1997) 'Rescue or Retreat? The Nation-state in Western Europe 1945–96', in P. Gowan and P. Anderson (eds) *The Question of Europe*. London: Verso.

Wavell, S. (1998) 'Your Very Good Health – In a Foreign Body', *Sunday Times*, 31 May: 11.

9

Cultural Policy in the EU and the European Identity

Enrique Banús

CULTURAL POLICY AND CULTURAL IDENTITY

'If we were beginning the European Community all over again, we should begin with culture.' These words are attributed to Jean Monnet, one of the founding fathers of the European Communities. However, at the end of the 1990s, a high level official in the German cultural administration expressed the opinion that 'there will never be a European culture coordinated in all respects' (Maurus, 1998: 87). And Wolfgang Mickel, a well-known educationalist on European issues, endorsed this view when he stated that the EU had no cultural policy of its own (Mickel, 1998). Whether Monnet actually pronounced this phrase is of small importance. Its extraordinary impact shows that there is a high level of identification with it. We should ask ourselves the reasons for this.

Cultural policy in a modern sense is relatively new. The first Minister of Culture was named in France in 1959. Cultural policy was linked to the welfare state after the war (Linde, 1995). Culture was understood as part of public service. While all of the European states devote part of their budgets to culture, important differences lie behind this common attitude. In countries with more liberal traditions, culture is considered as a matter of choice, determined by individual freedom, where the state should interfere as little as possible. Therefore, there is little tradition of Ministries of Culture in the United Kingdom or in Scandinavian countries. Elsewhere on the continent, in contrast to the Anglo-Saxon system and following the French model, the state not only awards direct subsidies but also plays a role in cultural management. It controls important cultural institutions. While nearly all the member states have witnessed decentralisation processes since the 1980s, the administration of culture is handled in very different ways in the individual states. In Germany and Austria, culture falls within the almost exclusive competence of the 'Länder'; in Spain, it has to a large extent become the responsibility of the Autonomous Communities, while in France, the Ministry of Culture is still very important.

Within the European Union there are considerable differences between what is understood as 'cultural policy' and what action is taken in different states, which raises an interesting problem for any consideration of cultural policy within the EU.

But the acceptance of Jean Monnet's words is possibly related to a phenomenon that pre-dates the cultural policy in the welfare state. It hints at an appeal to the link between 'culture' and 'identity' that was closely related to the genesis and the development of the nation-state, particularly in the nineteenth century. In fact, states have tended to consider cultural unity (and linguistic unity[1]) as an important part of political unity.[2] Inherent to the process of nation building seems to have been cultural homogenisation, forging a 'cultural identity' (Birnbaum, 1996; Wenturis, 1998). This link between a political entity, an identity as member of this entity, and culture as way of expressing or aquiring this identity seems to be the background for the acceptance of Jean Monnet's word.[3]

Probably in line with it, the influential Tindemans Report establishes relationships between European identity and progress in political integration when it stated that 'Europe cannot proceed to a greater degree of political integration without the underlying structure of a unifying European identity'.[4] A decade later, in 1987, a Commission document indicated the importance of cultural belonging as a prior condition for the Internal Market,[5] the core of the new political entity. The same idea was expressed in an Opinion of the Committee of the Regions of 13 March 1998: 'Only by strengthening "cultural citizenship" will it be possible to consolidate the Union and build external relations on a lasting basis'.[6] In many areas, the concept of European identity seems to be accepted. There was even a document approved by the foreign ministers of the member states, following a summit meeting that was explicitly devoted to European identity.[7]

Nevertheless, in official declarations about Europe, or more precisely, about that part of Europe that we call the 'European Union', the link between identity and culture is rarely made explicit. But many other times it appears implicitly, for example, when the Parliament not only state that cultural elements are part of that identity but that 'the concept of European citizenship and identity is linked to an awareness of cultural interdependence . . . and the capacity to identify and recognize the common elements of the various European cultural traditions, even in their most disparate forms'.[8]

The official documents appear to suggest the important role that identity can play in attaining the objectives,[9] and furthermore they underline the fact that culture forms a part of this identity. It only remains to be established whether a cultural policy also exists within the European Union.

CULTURAL POLICY IN THE EU? THE CURRENT LEGAL SITUATION

From the legal point of view, a cultural policy can exist since there is a clear legal base for it: Article 151 (formerly 128) of the EC-Treaty grants the Community a certain competence in the cultural sphere (Forrest, 1994). And indeed, there are hard facts indicating the existence of something like a cultural policy. Within the European Commission, there exists a Directorate General for Culture and a member of the Commission with special responsibilities for Culture; and, there is a specific programme with clear objectives and conditions for participating, supported by a budgetary allocation (Culture 2000). This is important, because political actions normally depend upon budgetary provision. Community budgets include an endowment for culture, although it is not very relevant in financial terms since only 0.033 per cent of the European Union budget is earmarked for it. This percentage falls far short of what the public powers in the member states spend on culture; it is in fact a tenth of what the least generous of the states set aside. But we must not forget that the lion's share of cultural spending is at regional and local levels, so it is hardly surprising that community activities are not given a high priority in the budget. But it is significant that this percentage has been gradually increased, although it is far from the optimistic forecast of the European Parliament in 1983 that 'the allocation of 1 per cent of the Community budget to the cultural sector would constitute a realistic objective to attain within a reasonable period'.

Large budget increases are not foreseen for the coming years either – in the period 2000–4, the figures are anticipated to remain stable between 32.3 and 34 million euros. This budgetary item is dedicated almost entirely to the new cultural instrument, the Culture 2000 Programme.

This Programme follows a Council resolution of September 1997, made in response to growing pressure for some initiative in this area.[10] Since the 1970s, it was acknowledged that the creation of the common market also affected cultural life, that the concept of merchandise also included 'cultural goods', and that cultural and artistic activities fell under the concept of 'services'. Since the 1970s, the Parliament had been asking for some degree of cultural action. In the 1980s, a number of institutional decisions in the realm of culture were adopted, with regular meetings of the Council and of the Ministers of Culture of the member states, and with the creation of the Directorate General of Culture in the Commission.[11] From the early 1980s, there were numerous (but dispersed) actions in several sectors, beginning with the protection of architectural and archaeological heritage. In the 1980s, the audio-visual sector received particular attention (although it is not clear whether the motives were cultural or commercial) followed by initiatives to protect the heritage, and to promote books and reading. And in the 1990s – after Maastricht – three specific programmes were created (Ariane for books and reading, Raphaël for protecting the heritage, and Kaleidoscope for various actions organised by partners from different countries).

Up to this point, the substance of 'cultural policy' basically comprised a system of direct grants to certain institutions or cultural projects, and a system of granting subsidies to projects presented under one of the available headings. It was a policy, moreover, that seemed to follow the well-known 'watering-can principle': little money distributed over quite disparate projects selected for support by the Commission itself. The latter held to the view that the broad scope of the concept of culture prohibited a focus upon specific priorities. So these funds financed measures to protect the architectural and archaeological heritage; support for archives; the choice of a cultural capital and cultural month; grants to train cultural advisers and other professions related to culture (particularly translators and restorers); promoting theatre and music; European literature and translation awards; support for translations, particularly of works in minority languages, and the network of European Translation Colleges; financing the European Youth Orchestra and the Baroque Orchestra; exhibitions for young artists; promoting reading for youth; library co-operation.

Ultimately, however, the policy was criticised for its dispersion and its lack of impact on citizens.[12] Culture 2000 was intended to contribute 'to the promotion of a cultural area common to the European peoples' in the following ways:[13]

- specific innovative and/or experimental actions,
- integrated actions, covered by structured, multiannual transnational cultural co-operation agreements,
- special cultural events with a European or international dimension, such as the European Capital of Culture and the Cultural Month.

The programme declared the objectives of 'highlighting the cultural diversity' and the 'sharing and highlighting' of 'the common cultural heritage of European significance'. And, in the spirit of Article 151 of the Treaty of Rome, it comprised 'a single financing and programming instrument for cultural cooperation'. The European Parliament had intended an amendment to this title that would insert the term 'cultural policy', but this was not finally adopted. Even the European Commision seemed to accept that a cultural policy does not exist or, at least, would not be accepted by the Council.

THE PROBLEMS OF A 'CULTURAL POLICY' IN THE EU

The ambivalent attitude towards cultural policy was identifiable long before this programme. The founding article relating to the cultural responsibility of the Union – Article 151 – made no mention of a European Union cultural policy, but to a Community's contribution to the flowering of the cultures of its member states. Therefore, these responsibilities are subsidiary to those of the states and can only reinforce and complement them. The verbs used in Article 151 are very expressive: 'contribute to the flowering of the cultures of the member states', 'encourage' (of course, only the co-operation between member states) and 'support' and 'supplement' (their action and, of course, only if necessary). These statements are in line with the new subsidiarity philosophy of the EC-Treaty but also follow the thread of all previous documents.

Therefore, the cultural activities of the Community are for the most part at the service of the states. This becomes clear if we consider the two areas of action established in Article 151. Cultural diversity is treated in both a negative sense (the Community must 'respect it' in its cultural activities) and also in a positive sense (in its global concern for culture it should 'encourage' diversity). In relation to diversity, mention is explicitly made of the national and regional levels. This aspect of cultural diversity remains a key concern of the member states, because the only reform that the Amsterdam Treaty introduces in the 'cultural chapter' is a new obligation of the Community to respect and promote diversity. And the original version of Article 151 (then 128) excluded all harmonisation and established a particularly protected decision-making system, unique in the Treaty: unanimity in the Council must be safeguarded throughout the whole decision procedure. This remains the case under the Amsterdam Treaty.

The second aim of Article 151 relates to the common cultural heritage, which has to be brought to the fore, at the same time as contributing to the flowering of the cultures of the member states. The issue then is to bring about 'the delicate balance between a promotion of shared values and the protection of cultural diversity' (Perez-Solorzano and Longman, 1998: 124).

There are different significant aspects in the historical and contemporary cultural action at EU level: on the one hand, the Parliament has been prominent in its attempt to include cultural issues in Community activities and also in the proposal that there had to be a real Community cultural policy, while on the other hand it has taken some time to initiate activities in the field. Hence, the most relevant achievements have been activities in support of cultural co-operation between member states, not a real cultural policy. Why? After the first informal meeting of the Ministers of Culture, in September 1982, we can read in the 'Rapport général' of the Commission that there were differences of opinion regarding the opportunity for a true European cultural action.[14] The problems came from the member states. But the states were not the only protagonists of cultural life, and regions and municipalities have become more and more important. The regions in some states (particularly in Germany) were worried by the perceived greater centralisation and they feared the loss of influence to a new European centralism. In this regard they found allies in those member states who held the view that the European Union should not extend its activities to non-economic areas. Member states' concern with cultural issues and their obsession with diversity combined to produce an acceptance, however unwilling, of a new partner to share the responsibility for the promotion of national cultures, even though this might have the secondary effect of fomenting the common heritage.

But what was specifically European in the different measures financed with Community funds? Mainly two elements: either projects were funded (especially in the field of heritage protection) for representative buildings – supposedly European precisely because they encapsulated the common heritage – or (as in Kaleidoscope) partners from the various member states were required as a condition for the project – in which case the project was European through addition.[15] The approach adopted was therefore a response to the deep underlying problem: for the institutions that used the term, it was not clear what European culture or common heritage was/is – so they used the 'par excellence' or 'addition' model.

The Culture 2000 programme includes all the previous methods through which access was provided to community funds. The criteria for awarding these grants were maintained, and reinforced. For the integrated measures, co-operation among partners from five member states is encouraged. On the other hand, although it seems that the tendency is to grant larger subsidies to fewer projects, the conceptual framework is broadened: the 'cultural heritage' concept is now wider – to embrace the so-called 'non-material heritage' (traditions, customs, etc.).[16] The programme did not cover all the problem interpretations of what was an already difficult term, culture;[17] the Commission's first proposal referred to those 'new forms of cultural expression', and included environment, science, pacifism, among an extremely broad range of interpretations and attitudes.[18] Even so, the Programme contained a great many aims, many of which are to be found in national cultural policies, including the promotion of creativity, citizens' access to culture, support of new forms of expression, special attention to the young.

So the essence of the EU's cultural activities has been and will continue to be the provision of funds with no guarantee of elements that help to configure an awareness of a common heritage. In the past, direct grants would appear to have been the result of commitments acquired rather than an in-depth consideration of Article 151. In the activities financed by the Culture 2000 programme (and in the past by the former programmes), the nature of the activities depends on the organisers and the projects that are supported. The idea is that the beneficiaries (those who overcome the far from simple administrative formalities) organise and collaborate on a cross-border basis, highlighting the logic of establishing a multinational organisation followed by an exchange and the presentation of something in common. It is very similar to the application of the 'principle of the four fundamental freedoms' to culture. If broadening the market means exchange and contact, co-operation will presumably also have a unifying effect here, and maybe bring the common heritage to the fore.

COMMON HERITAGE: THE UNKNOWN FACTOR

It is through the forging of a common heritage that a contribution could be made to European identity, since (on a national level) the definition of a common heritage has been one of the classic instruments to manifest or build an identity.[19] It is true that 'the collective identity finds its expression in symbols' (Wenturis, 1998: 188): it requires shared symbols, 'iconic devices' (Perez-Solorzano and Longman 1998: 118) and a common history (Smith, 1991). And heritage is no more than a collection of objects with symbolic values that are links to a common history.

Do the institutions think that this European cultural heritage exists? The important final document of the Stuttgart summit held in 1983, the Solemn Declaration on the European Union contains a chapter devoted to cultural cooperation,[20] and the document on the European identity from the Copenhagen Summit speaks about 'the diversity of cultures'.[21] It is noteworthy that the highest level documents talk, as does Article 151 of the Treaty, about cultural co-operation on the Community level and about cultures, in plural, although they are located 'within the framework of common European civilisation'.[22] But other documents do in fact talk about European culture: the European Parliament does,[23] the Economic and Social Committee proposed the creation of 'a European cultural area'[24] clearly stating that 'the idea of "European culture" should be fostered', the Committee of the Regions speaks about 'European culture, which is older than the division of our continent into nation-states' and adds that 'It is Europe's cultural heritage which makes us Europeans',[25] and the Commission speaks about the sense of being part of European Culture.[26] Here again, significant differences crop up between the institutions. The representatives of the member states take great care not to talk about European culture and so they use the 'politically correct' plural form.[27]

But do the institutions that accept a European culture in the singular define it? Do they identify the common heritage? The Treaty makes no further mention of it. And attempts made by institutions to describe the specificity of European culture are not very convincing (Banús, 1996). In many cases, diversity is highlighted. So the Commission states that 'Europe's cultural richness' is 'represented by the diversity',[28] the Ministers responsible for Cultural Affairs talk about 'a richness born of diversity';[29] the 'Europeanness' would be a 'sum', like the 'Comité des consultants culturels' say: 'la culture européenne est une réalité . . . faite de la somme de toutes les cultures nationales, régionales et même locales et de leur interaction';[30] also the member of the Commission responsible for Culture in 1995 indicated that 'la cultura europea es la suma de las distintas culturas europeas, de las que existen en los distintos Estados, incluso de las que existen dentro de cada Estado y que constituyen unas identidades culturales propias'.[31] The Parliament goes a little bit further when it establishes that the European cultural identity is 'the product of interaction between a civilization and a plurality of national, regional and local cultures'.[32]

Now then, just a sum? Is that all?[33] In that case, Article 151 of the Treaty on European Union – the Magna Carta of attribution of competences in the cultural field – would be tautological. But the institutions believe there is something more: some 'common roots' (European Commission[34]), a

'European Cultural heritage' (European Parliament[35] and European Council[36]), a 'common cultural heritage' (Parliament,[37] Council[38]), some 'certain common characteristics that transcend national or regional differences' (Commission[39]), a 'cultural continuum' ('Comité des consultants culturels'[40]). It would be futile to look for more precise definitions. It might be preferable not to, for when some institution goes further, it often falls into banality. For example, it seems banal to declare, as the Parliament did in February 1993, that European culture is 'el conjunto complejo de culturas'.[41] In another Resolution, the European Parliament replaces an unknown element with other unknown elements, when it says that cultural identity is 'the product of interaction between a civilization and a plurality of national, regional and local cultures',[42] which then remits to new elements which are equally difficult to define.[43]

There is much difficulty in describing what constitutes the common heritage in European culture, while at the same time lauding (and promoting) the diversity of cultures. However, this may not be the greatest problem, as the intellectual debate calls into question concepts that are much more basic to all of these considerations.

THE CRISIS OF CULTURAL IDENTITY

Indeed, even the concept of collective identity seems problematic (Szalo, 1998). And, of course, in recent years the origins of collective identities have been undergoing a process of deconstruction. In fact, in contrast to the essentialism common in earlier periods, it is now argued rather that we are dealing with 'inventions', that is, 'realities' which are present solely in the imaginary, with 'constructs',[44] which are the result of a cultural, or socio-economic process (Anderson, 1983; Hobsbawm and Ranger, 1983; Sørensen, 1995; Spiering, 1996). They are often even self-interested constructs – ideas, imagined and devoid of any real basis, which some authors do not hesitate to call myths.[45] In summing up the debate, Helly could state categorically 'all writers concur to say that the notion of the nation as a community of people of common origin . . . is fictional' (Helly, 1998: 36).[46]

Nevertheless, there can be no doubt that, in recent years, the topic of nationalism is once more in vogue in the theoretical debate, public rhetoric, and social reality[47] and there can also be no doubt that 'mit der Frage nach der Identität . . . das elementare Konstruktionsprinzip moderner Gesellschaften thematisiert (ist)' (Weidenfeld, 1985: 14), so 'Identität und Orientierung sind . . . zwei Seiten der gleichen Medaille' (ibid.: 15).[48]

ON EUROPEAN IDENTITY AND CULTURE

In this context, it should be remembered that the citizens' attachment to Europe (48 per cent) is lower than to village (85 per cent), region (87 per cent) or country (88 per cent) (Reif, 1993). It would seem then that there is a lack of orientation within Europe which is perhaps inherent to this project generally, at least if Jelin is right: 'the space for identity is always local, whereas the space for function is always more universal' (1999: 110). Furthermore, the rhetoric of the institutions about the need for a European identity has not escaped deconstruction and has been described as 'a European mystique in order to galvanize popular support' (Seton-Watson, 1985: 13) or as an attempt to create 'a single, binding European cultural identity from above' (Fulbrook, 1993: 266).[49]

This criticism may be excessive even if the institutions calling for this identity seemed to do so in order to capitalise on it, and even though the institutions are not very adept at defining this identity or culture. Thus, the aforementioned document of the Summit Conference devoted to European identity is very vague and, although it mentions the common heritage, has no reference to cultural factors, with the exception – once again – of 'the diversity of cultures'. And the European Commission's official dictum of the 'unity in diversity' can easily be criticised as 'empty rhetoric' (Wintle, 1996a: 5).[50]

But the theoretical debate on European identity is not very productive either (Wittal-Düerkop, 1998). Although the literature is abundant, many still seem to be 'auf der Suche nach europäischer Identität'.[51] Of course, there are attempts to define European identity and link it to certain attitudes or one in particular.

In some cases, this European specificity is linked to socio-economic, or politico-economic aspects (Kaelble, 1994; Weidenfeld, 1985). In other cases, it is cultural aspects that prevail. It is not necessary to insist on the well-known and topical opinion that sees European identity as the result of the mixture of Greek, Roman and Judaeo-Christian elements (Joll, 1969; Wintle, 1996b). In some cases these different perspectives become mixed, for instance, when modernity is emphasised and the inherent civic values are seen as an essential characteristic. The search for intellectual or cultural factors that make up the countenance of Europe is particularly prominent amongst French authors. Paul Hazard (1935), for whom the essential aspect of Europeanness is that way of thinking that is never satisfied, may be considered as an important precursor of this effort. A well known analysis was made years later by Edgar Morin (1987a), when he examined the nature of European identity through the medium of a character dialogue. Fernand Braudel (1989) relates European identity to exchange, but in exceedingly commercial terms, while the Swiss writer, François Bondy (1985) links it to the capacity and availability for universality and the rejection of caesaropapism. The problem with these models is that they end up becoming absolute and what starts out being a description ends up as a prescription, which is what happens to Morin after his extraordinary analysis.[52]

Michael Wintle concludes in regard to the essays collected in his *Culture and Identity in Europe*: 'These attempts to isolate and define European identity or essence make clear that it is elusive and equivocal' (Wintle,

1996b: 1). Cultural identity then is not clear, neither is the common heritage. Could all these considerations be left aside and another basis for European integration sought?

THE ALTERNATIVE AND ITS PROBLEM

There are, in fact, authors who disregard heritage as a factor in cohesion and, following the line of Habermas, choose to look to civic values for the element of identity. In this case, European citizenship would be the magic formula, directed not towards the past, but rather towards the future. From this point of view, one can believe the other elements that are usually considered part of collective identity 'belong to myths, but not to realities' (Salazar, 1998: 767). The institutional documents which speak of a common civilisation and, above all, the document which speaks of European identity, for which, the 'fundamental elements of the European Identity' are all political: 'representative democracy, . . . the rule of law, . . . social justice . . . and . . . respect for human rights'[53] seem to be in keeping with this line which emphasises civic aspects.

However, it should not be forgotten that 'collective memory, social environment and culture have a direct influence on the image that a social group has of itself' (Salazar, 1998: 771) and that 'one country's image of another is likely to depend on its image of itself' (Aldridge, 1969: 278).[54] Therefore, in European integration – in which it is also essential to replace very deep-rooted images of oneself and of the 'Other' – faced with the current reluctance to acknowledge the importance of those aspects which belong to the imaginary, precautions should be taken to avoid the risk of constructing a 'laboratory Europe', without taking into consideration all of the elements that play a part in the shaping of a space for co-existence. There can be no doubt that, especially in recent years, culture has become a significant source of identity for many groups (Smith, 1998: 321). It is recognised that culture is not only a collection of goods, but also a set of symbols (Cassirer, 1954).

On the other hand, Habermas and his followers seem not to realise that their proposal is also part of a tradition, for – as Braun points out – 'Habermas' post-traditional identity . . . is no less historical than any other ideology he challenges. It is a different narrative of the past . . . but a history or even a metahistory nonetheless' (Braun, 1998: 244). It would therefore seem necessary to continue thinking about the inclusion of European culture within the consciousness of Europeans and to perhaps find a bridge between both positions.[55]

EUROPEAN 'CULTURAL CITIZENSHIP'?[56]

The Commission states that 'Europe's cultural dimension is deeply rooted in the collective consciousness of its inhabitants'.[57] But there can be no doubt that the awareness of many Europeans is much more national, and increasingly regional, than European. Among the most effective instruments for transmitting national identity, education has been and is still being used to good effect. Education, even among the European Union member states, is still basically national: much more national than European history is studied and (a high cohesion-building element) much more national than European literature is being studied.[58] The national view is not only emphasised in the content, but also in the approach itself: this is evident from a look at manuals and text books (Banús, 1998). Taking into account the importance of education for forming mental categories, it is not surprising that a lot of people's 'forma mentis' is essentially 'national', which within the predominantly simplified vision of 'identity', tends to think in terms of antithesis, and a barrier to a European vision.[59]

But the predominance of national awareness has caused too many evils in Europe's recent history – and goes on causing them. In his emotional last speech to the European Parliament, François Mitterrand pronounced those words in which for Europe, he associated nationalism with war.[60] And nationalism is not a phenomenon of the past; nor is it limited to the post-communist countries whose assertion of national identity is blossoming after decades of repression. It is a phenomenon that is evident in western societies, often in the guise of protection against globalisation and its homogenising effects. This comes about, paradoxically, in the wake of a widespread perception of crisis facing the nation-state, as sub-state levels emerge and many societies become ever more pluri-cultural. However, nationalism is now presented as an attitude which can refer to sub-state levels. Pluri-culturalism has led to, amongst others, ethnocentric reactions.

The strength of this withdrawal towards nationalism stems from a very potent mixture: the atavistic fear of losing what is one's own when it comes in contact with what is someone else's, and its use to drive the formation of the modern state. Indeed, the configuration of 'we-groups' is often achieved through differentiation with respect to the Other. And 'every We-group implies necessarily the existence of the others, and it is based upon the distinction between us and the others' (Skiljan, 1998: 828). Thus, the 'establishment of group identity' is often achieved 'by means of differentiation from other group identities' (Firchow, 1986: 185),[61] so that often 'the notion of *alterity* became synonymous to that of *antagonism*' (Jenkins and Sofos, 1996d: 286). Internal cohesion, in the ideal nation-state model, required not only cultural and, if possible, linguistic unity, but also the referent 'foreign' as a screen to reflect that cohesion. A people's unity that may be immersed in internal squabbles can achieve cohesion by rallying against the common enemy. This is how the concept of 'cultural identity' became consecrated over a long period as a synonym of 'national identity'. This awareness of the importance of cultural identity appears also at an international level, in the UNESCO Conference on Cultural

Policies, held in Mexico in 1982. At the conference, 126 states accepted a final Declaration which included a chapter (the first) on cultural identity that recognised each culture represents a unique and irreplaceable set of values,[62] and acknowledged that the traditions and means of expression of each nation are the way it manifests its presence in the world.[63] This concept has been understood in two different ways: in the frame of an essentialism, by which identity cannot be changed, or in the frame of a more dynamic model in which changes of identity are considered as possible. The first vision embodies risks – one is that of immobilisation; another one is to consider every influence as a risk. The second vision often leads to the conclusion that 'the Other' has to change when he/she enters one's own space. In both cases, the conclusion is the same: immobilisation and the rejection of the 'Other' (Burow, 1998).

There is no need to highlight the fact that the defence of what is national in the sense of 'one's own', the incorporation of other – supposedly one's own – territories into the national territory or the purging from the territory of what is not one's own is at the root of most of modern Europe's wars. It is difficult to wage a war without the popular fervour of defending one's own from a common enemy often considered a threat to identity.

And European awareness must counteract this. To oppose bull-headed nationalism – sometimes revealed under the mask of regionalism – European awareness should be reinforced, because it means an 'opening of horizons'. It corresponds to the reality of cultures, where continual inter-changes have produced the phenomena of blending races, changed habits and mentalities, while yet maintained identities. 'Encounters', in Europe, have contributed to forming 'identities', in a way which is appreciated neither by the static (immobilised) view, nor the naive approximation of the Committee of the Regions when it states that 'living together, cooperation and cultural interaction increase the possibilities and the creativity of each people, and they do not cause changes to any culture, let alone threaten any language, nationality or culture with extinction'.[64] It is evident that, where there are contacts, dialogue, interchange, there can be change. But not every change means risking the loss of identity. Because 'identity' is a more flexible and multi-level entity, and not a monolithic one in which different elements are unable to co-exist.

More than twenty-five centuries of encounters and interactions have forged the patchwork map of Europe that combines local, regional and European elements. And these demonstrate that 'cultural identity' must be seen in a dynamic form, as a complex that changes over time and is made up of elements that come from different experiences: personal 'cultural identity' is moulded by parents' and grandparents' stories, by interchanges with friends, by the first readings in school, by childhood fables and legends, by secondary school experiences, by the mass media, by the cultural life of the place where one resides, by experiences gleaned from travel – by a multitude of mediation processes in a highly structured world of global communication. And the collective cultural identity – if it exists – is also formed as the result of numerous influences.

Europe especially has been living for many centuries in continual interchange, in a 'continuous interaction between the cultures' – as the European Parliament quite correctly says[65] – in assuming elements that have become common without, thereby, losing diversity. Indeed, between Andalusia and Scotland, between Alentejo in Portugal and Carintia in Austria, the differences are obvious. Even so, they have been in the flux of movements, of epochs, of styles, of 'authorities' and 'canonical' texts, signs of 'les courants culturels communs aux Européens'[66] – from Petrarchism to Wertherism, through Dandyism and symbolism – randomly quoting from different centuries. In fact, it is very difficult to find any strictly national movement over the centuries (Banús, 1999). Without the Italian, Petrarch, or the Frenchmen, Ronsard for example, it is impossible to imagine Shakespeare's sonnets; without a theological debate of Spanish Baroque it would be impossible to imagine a European phenomenon like Mozart's *Don Giovanni*; without the Schlegel brothers in Germany – 'transferred' to Spain by the consul of Hamburg in Cadiz, Johann Nikolas Böhl von Faber – Spain would not have rediscovered its own baroque drama; and a long etcetera that can turn the hero of an eighth century BC song into the protagonist – of course, deconstructed and altered – of one of the twentieth century novels said to be decisive for the history of literature (James Joyce's *Ulysses*); the New Testament prophet, John the Baptist, into a character in a morbid opera representative of nineteenth-century 'decadentism'; Strauss' *Salome*, sublime example of the 'femme fatale' that delighted so many at that time; the Mediaeval Castilian, Rodrigo Diaz de Vivar, the Cid, into the protagonist of one of the peak works of French neo-classical drama. While, during the Baroque era, Italian architects not only built churches in Prague, Vienna or Madrid, they also prepared the scenery for plays in the Spanish Court of Aranjuez; a Greek painter sojourned in Italy and set himself up in Spain (Domenicos Theotocopuli, better known as El Greco); Goethe's work would be unthinkable without his trip to Italy; from his native Hamburg, Brahms moved to Vienna, where he discovered the Hungarian world; and the Viennese, Mahler, in the third movement of his First symphony, uses the theme of a French children's song ('Frère Jacques, Frère Jacques, dormez-vous?'). And we are not surprised to find in the Gachina-Palais near Saint Petersburg a tapestry of Sancho Panza that the king of France gave to the tsars in the eighteenth century.

The results of these changes have been fixed in the conscience of the citizens like so many characters – Antigone, Faust, Don Juan, Ulysses and many others – while many stories, books, buildings, landscapes, towns and so on, are 'living' in the 'mental home' of Europeans. This presence of characters and stories from different national sources in the cultural life of so many citizens has presented no problem for plurality, rather it has been undoubtedly 'an enriching factor and a distinguishing mark of the People's Europe'.[67]

AN ALTERNATIVE TO NATIONALISM AND GLOBALISATION

The risk for this richness and plurality does not lie with the extremely limited possibilities of the Community cultural action[68] nor does that threat arise from the increased interchange of open borders (because, in culture, borders have never played the role they played in politics).[69] Many authors think that the risk could be globalisation.

The globalisation issue – a real intellectual fashion – has many sides and is a very diversified reality. It is without doubt a threat, due to its harmonisation of the cultural experiences of a good part of the population and the loss of a great many referents, but it is also an opportunity.[70] It is doubtless also something of an 'object of symbolic constructions' (Robertson, 1996: 62), and it has caused ethnocentric reactions, which are much more nationalist than European in nature, although it can also be used as an argument for 'Eurocentrism', supporting a 'fortress Europe'. This would follow the line of one of the basic directions which, according to Wittal-Düerkop, the negative form of defining European identity usually adopts: Europe 'definiert sich (. . .) in Abwehr konstruierter außereuropäischer Bedrohungen als Schutzdefinition' (Wittal-Düerkop, 1998: 207).[71]

This 'cultural fortress Europe' and the nationalist reactions could be opposed by highlighting the history of Europe as a laboratory especially equipped for cultural interchange, with the incidence of multiple extra-European elements, all historically consolidated and forming part of the 'cultural identity' of Europeans. Of course, not all relationships have been open. There are also relationships of outright rejection, critical acceptance, cross-breeding, syncretism.[72] What is European could be a necessary, balancing complement to these tendencies only if presented as cultures that have been immersed for centuries in processes of interchange, that have often been European – and, in other cases, of course, extra-European. The most absolute example is that of one of the cultural forces that configured European culture: Christianity has undoubtedly extra-European origins, but it was to revolutionise Europe, not only in terms of religion but also in terms of culture.[73] There are many more examples: Aristotle was received through the Arabs, originating a great European debate in the thirteenth century. Non-European continents account for – among many other things – the arrival of products like tea, coffee or chocolate, which were to mark European life time-wise and space-wise: cafés are part not only of urban scenery but have also facilitated the literary encounters of writers and artists.

The awareness of the common cultural heritage marks the way between nationalism and globalisation; that is, between confronting the 'Other' and disappearing in it, between the narrow-mindedness of the nationalist world and the loss of horizon and roots and increasing uniformity; between the cave and the desert.

DOES THE 'EU CULTURAL POLICY' CONTRIBUTE TO EUROPEAN AWARENESS?

It may be difficult for the European Union cultural action to tend in the direction of European awareness if the first priority in the 'cultural article' of the Treaty is linked with the cultures of the member states and the obligation of the Community to respect and promote diversity. In this preoccupation with the cultural diversity of the states and their regions, the EU joins with those other actors that are already busy making those cultures blossom. Furthermore, creating a European awareness may be difficult if valid descriptions of 'common cultural heritage' are not to be found. This has been resolved in the past – as we have said, by 'par excellence' or by addition – and probably will be resolved in the future in the same way.

The European dimension, quoted in Culture 2000 – just like another very interesting dimension of this programme, 'the mutual knowledge'[74] – will, therefore, depend more on the initiative of the applicants than on a political action directed by the European institutions. Against this clumsy action, a much clearer action could be postulated – theoretically, because in practice, it will not be able to overcome national and regional reticence – by European institutions. It could concentrate more on transversal action, on transmitting common elements and, in the dynamic sense, on mutual knowledge.

The theoretical basis for this could stem from the following reflection: perhaps more than the insistence on the concept of 'identity', more than the requirement that 'European identity' be built in an environment of speeches on political theory and integration strategies in politics, we should focus on the world of the imaginary, a complex world in which a great deal of the content is shared, and shared at very different levels.[75] Here, there are also a great many shared components at European level. This would be the principal 'European heritage', that which exists in the citizens' interior world. And faced with the tendencies that choose only positive elements,[76] the whole of this heritage should be taken into consideration, and properly evaluated. Here, science and politics merge in a common responsibility for the considered transmission of this heritage.

Reinforcing consciousness of the European elements in this world – the life of the citizens – is what European cultural policy, with all the limitations of any cultural policy, should be concerned with. From an open vision of culture as an ongoing process of dialogue, it could reinforce the awareness of the European elements as a way between nationalism and globalisation, fostering a view of Europe as a 'region in continual universal dialogue'. The European Union should be united around a cultural policy with a clear profile, with no 'euro-nationalist' designs, with the conviction that, to propose a European model, is to combat nationalism with its 'Macht der Mythen'[77] ('power of myths') and its loss of plural richness, and is to remain open to dialogue, interchange, acknowledgement of otherness.

The perspectives are not very promising, because the EU has no cultural policy of its own, but to configure a society it is necessary to attend to the citizens' culture. With the current cultural policy, we may remain confined to the conclusion arrived at by Alan Milward, in his historico-economic analysis: that European integration has done no more than to reinforce the interests of the states.

NOTES

1   It is interesting to compare the Constitution of the French Republic, Article 2 of which specifies that the official language is French, the more open Spanish Constitution of 1978, which says that Spanish is the official language and should be known by all Spanish citizens but that there may be co-official languages in some Autonomous Communities, and the Belgian Constitution of 1994, which establishes the federal model and confirms that the languages in common usage are official languages. This is a reflection on the entire evolution of the concept of Nation-State in Europe. There are significant examples of the relevance of language for the state in very recent history: when France signed the European Regional or Minority Languages Charter in 1999, the need to reform the Constitution was considered. It has not been done (and France has not ratified the Charter), because President Chirac and many other politicians believe that the change to the Constitution 'questions the unity of the nation' (see *Le Monde*, 25 June 1999).

2   'El Estado nacional ha nacido a través de una lógica impuesta sobre la contraposición entre una mayoría étnica, identificada por una historia común, una cultura común y lengua . . . y las llamadas "minorías étnicas", consideradas como marginales y peligrosas para un desarrollo armonioso del Estado. El Estado nacional ha sido construido sobre la base de una explícita e intencional negación del Estado-multinacional' (Donati, 1999: 14). In any case the view that only by means of violence have nation-states been established seems rather excessive, because the segregation of these states has also been realised by violent means.

3   This exactly seems to be the sense of Cuisenier's words: 'How can a European community or something alike be established without examining . . . the mechanisms at the root of their cultural identity' (1979: 3). Simone Veil also establishes this relationship when she speaks about 'la dimension culturelle de l'Europe, élément fondamental de cette identité européenne' (Veil, 1987: I – 'the cultural dimension of Europe, a fundamental element of the European identity').

4   The Report is from 29.12.1975, published in the Bull. CE, suppl. 1/76.

5   Document COM (87) 603, p. 5.

6   Brigitte Boyce points out that in recent years 'it has been argued variously that the construction of a common European identity has become indispensable, if the dynamics of economic and political integration are to be sustained' (1998: 306). This could go hand in hand with the risks that some authors warn

against: 'the increasingly openly propagated nationalization of the European continent' (Wenturis, 1998: 182). Delanty regards, with irony, the fact that the European Community, in trying to overcome nationalism, does so 'using the very tools of nationalism: the flag, anthem, passport, group name and sense of common history' (Delanty, 1995: 128). On the use of European symbols, see Odermatt (1991).

7   'Declaration on European Identity' from the Copenhagen Summit Conference, see Bull. EC 12-1973, Point 2501. The European Commission speaks about 'une identité européenne profonde' (Réponse à la question écrite no 752/89, OJ of 29.10.1990; the expression is not so clear in the English version). Furthermore, for some years, in WEU circles, it has become common to speak of a European Security and Defence Identity. An analysis of the use of the term European identity in recent official documents can be found in Boxhoorn (1996: 138).

8   OJ C 72 from 15.3.1993, p. 163. The same link between culture and European identity is given in the Resolution of the Parliament from 18.1.1979 (OJ C 39 vol. 12.2.1979, p. 50), and in the Second Report from the ad hoc Committee 'A People's Europe', adopted by the European Council in Milan (28–29 June 1985) when it establishes that 'the areas of culture and communication . . . are essential to European identity' (see Bulletin of the European Communities, Supplement 7/85, p. 21), and in many other documents.

9   It is worth noting that this call for reinforcement of identity is, at each historical moment, associated with the priority goal: in 1987, shortly after the Single European Act, with the attainment of the Internal Market; in the Tindemans Report, with political objectives and in the opinion of the 1998 Committee of Regions, with foreign affairs. However, many authors, when dealing with the issue of European identity, take as their starting point a transposition of the categories of the state to those of the European Union as if the aim were to create a European super-state: some are sorry that this will not be possible (De Witte), others are glad (for example, Boxhoorn, for whom unity can only be reached by a dramatic restriction of the variety of cultures). Wintle points out the limitations of this attempt at transposition, given that the political project is completely different.

10 Council Decision of 22 September 1997 regarding the future of European cultural action (OJ C 305. 7.10.1997, p. 1). See also Banús (1997), Lulé (1996), Perez (1996), and Thuriot (1998).

11 The first formal meeting of the Council and the Ministers of Culture of the member states was held in Luxembourg in June 1984. In 1986, Commission General Directorate X, until then only responsible for information, also took on competence in cultural issues. On 27 May 1988, the Council and the Ministers of Culture created a special Commission for cultural affairs.

12 In its Resolution from February 1993, the Parliament stated that 'the failure to adopt a coordinated approach owing to the lack of a legal basis and the limited resources . . . have meant that the measures taken by the Commission . . . are inadequate and have no real impact on society' (OJ 72 from 15.3.1993, p. 162).

13 Document COM (1998) 266. This Commission document issued on 6 May 1998 presented two proposals: The First European Community framework programme in support of culture (2000–4) and the Proposal for a European Parliament and Council Decision establishing a single financing and programming instrument for cultural co-operation (Culture 2000 programme). The second was also published in the Official Journal (Series C 211 from 7.7.1998, p. 18). It was approved under Decision No. 508/2000 of the European Parliament and of the Council of 14 February 2000 (see OJ L 63 10.3.2000).

14 This is in agreement with Margue's comment on the Council's unwillingness to support cultural activities: 'Le Conseil et le Conseil européen sont . . . restés plus en retrait dans la promotion de telles actions' ('The Council and the European Council are behind in promoting activities of this kind'; Margue, 1993: 173).

15 A special case is that of the 'European Cultural Capital', in which the European nature is achieved through 'migration': a different country every year. This is finally attained in the proposal for the 2005–19 period, in which turns are taken by the member states.

16 It follows the guidelines set out by the UNESCO Conference in Mexico in 1982.

17 In 1952 two authors gathered no less than 164 definitions of culture (see Kroeber and Kluckhohn, 1952). For an examination of recent concepts and definitions of culture, see Moreno (1998).

18 The words of Heiner Flohr could be applied to that proposal: 'I fear that the tendency of the term "culture" to encompass more and more goes hand in hand with its meaning becoming progressively indistinct. If the word stops being distinctive, everything is culture – a pyrrhic victory that ought to be rejected' (Flohr, 1998: 67). So, what is European could become one more element in an enlarged catalogue of objectives for the European Union's cultural action.

19 Since the end of the nineteenth century, the context of modern cultural policy is the state's interest in protecting its historic, artistic and, above all, architectural heritage. Normally, specialised departments were created within Ministries of Education. It is symptomatic that in the United Kingdom, what is now known as the Department of Culture began as Department of National Heritage, loyal to this tradition. One interesting example of the intent by the state to establish common symbols is Cologne Cathedral, a building that was thought would never be completed, and that was finished at the time of German unification thanks to the decisive encouragement of the Kaiser who, following German Pre-romantic and Romantic tradition, considered gothic architecture to be a national art and the cathedral to be a symbol. And state funding appeared at the height of Kulturkampf, the fight of the state with the Catholic Church. In fact, when the Cathedral was inaugurated the Archbishop was in exile.

20 Bull-CE 12-1983.

21 Bull-CE 12-1973, p. 119. In French: 'la *riche* variété de leurs cultures *nationales*'.

22 Bull-CE 12-1973, p. 119. Similarly, the Parliament's opinion is that European cultural identity is 'the product of interaction between a civilization and a plurality of national, regional and local cultures' (Resolution on 20 January 1994. See OJ C 44 from 14.2.1994, p. 185; this formula is drawn verbatim from the Canavarro Report of December 1 1993 (A3-0386/93), point A, p. 5).

23 It affirms that ''European culture' must be viewed as an intricate nexus of cultures, each of which is distinguished by a rich variety of geniuses and identities which find expression, regardless of geography, in the intellectual traditions which have taken root everywhere' (Resolution of 21 January 1993, OJ C 42 , 15.2.93, p. 174).

24 Opinion of the Economic and Social Committee on the Communication on a fresh boost for culture in the European Community (OJ C 175 from 4.7.88, p. 40).

25 Opinion of the Committee of the Regions of 13 March 1998 on culture and cultural differences and their significance for the future of Europe.

26 Document COM (87) 603, p. 5.

27   But, surprisingly, in the Conclusions of the Presidency at the meeting at Fontainebleau (25–26.6.1984), the expression 'people of Europe' is used (see Bulletin of the European Communities, Supplement 7/85, p. 5). In its first proposal to Culture 2000, the Commission was also, at least in some linguistic versions, quite outspoken, referring to 'culture and history of the European people', later changed to 'European peoples'!

28   From the 'Conditions for participating in the 'Platform Europe' award scheme by the Commission of the European Communities' (OJ C 167 from 10.7.1990, p. 2).

29   Resolution of 13 June 1985 concerning the annual event 'European City of Culture' (OJ C 153 from 22.6.1985, p. 2).

30   Report 'Une culture pour le citoyen européen de l'an 2000', from November 1989, p. 7 ('European culture is a reality, comprised of the sum of all the national, regional and even local cultures and of their interaction').

31   Marcelino Oreja, at the European Parliament, session of 14.3.95, DOCE Anexo 4-460, p. 64 ('European culture is the sum of the different European cultures, of those that exist in the different States, even of those that exist within each State and that constitute cultural identities in their own right').

32   Resolution on 20 January 1994. See OJ C 44 from 14.2.1994, p. 185.

33   In this sense, see Reif (1993: 132). Kleinsteuber (quoted in Shelly et al., 1995: 171) expressly rejected the idea of European cultural identity; while Wintle commented 'one of the conclusions of this book is that the more inclusive and accommodating of diversity that cultural projection, the better' (Wintle, 1996b: 6). In a similar way can be understood the paradox which Koslowski argues: 'Je mehr die europäische Einheit verwirklicht wird, um so mehr tritt das bisher Europäische an Europa, die Vielheit der Nationen, in seiner Bedeutung zurück' (Koslowski, 1992: 1): 'The greater European unity is, the less importance is given to what was previously European, the variety among its nations'.

34   'Condiciones para la participación en la distinción "Plataforma Europea" de la Comisión de las Comunidades Europeas' (DO Serie C 167, p. 2).

35   Resolutions from 18 January 1979 (OJ C 39 from 12.2.1979, p. 50) and 3 May 1974 (OJ C 62 from 30.5.1974, p. 5).

36   Second Report from the ad hoc Committee 'A People's Europe', adopted by the European Council in Milan, 28–29 June 1985; see Bulletin of the European Communities, Supplement 7/85, p. 21.

37   Resolution from 10 September 1991, OJ C 267 from 14.10.1991, p. 46.

38   Council conclusions of 17 June 1994 concerning children and culture (OJ C 235 from 23.8.1994, p. 2).

39   Communication from the Comission, from 29.3.1995 (COM(95)110), p. 1.

40   Report 'Une culture pour le citoyen européen de l'an 2000', from November 1989, p. 9.

41   ('the complex set of cultures'); Resolution of 21.1.1993, DOCE, C 42 from 15.2.93, p. 174.

42   Resolution on 20 January 1994. See OJ C 44 from 14.2.1994, p. 185.

43   And for surprising solutions, the documents of the Economic and Social Committee and the Committee of the Regions are particularly apt. The former indicates that 'the European "cultural model" is not all exclusive, still less a "melting pot", but rather a multi-various, multi-ethnic plurality of culture, the sum total of which enriches each individual culture' (OJ C 62 from 12.3.1990, p. 29) and the Economic and Social Committee argues in 1996 that the European cultural policy 'is not "Eurocentric", but rather general, multi-cultural, multi-ethnic and multi-lingual' (OJ, C 153 from 28.5.96, p. 27). And the representatives of the regions arrive at a curious and illogical ennumeration of elements that make up Europe: 'If Europe is essentially

Judeo-Christian, it is also pagan, Muslim, Slav and African' (OJ C 100 from 2.4.1996, p. 87).

44 For an example of the construction of a nation (France) with its symbols, see Nora (1986).

45 The title of Citron (1987) is paradigmatic.

46 The 'essentialism' versus 'inventionism' positions can be summed up as follows: 'There would seem to be two extremes in the historiography of nationalism. Either you trace back "Englishness" (or "Danishness", or whatever) to time immemorial, blaming its long dormant periods on the pernicious influence of foreigners succeeding, in alliance with an a-national upper class, in suppressing popular national feeling for centuries until the people finally "awaken". Or . . . you see the whole idea as a modern one, with national identities being "invented" or "imagined" by intellectuals who, through education and the media, indoctrinate them into "the people". The latter perspective is today widely adopted' (Rasmussen, 1995: 24).

47 See details in Braun (1998). On the 'resilience' of nationalism in contemporary Europe, see Jenkins and Sofos (1996a).

48 'the issue of identity is being used as the theme behind the fundamental principle on which modern societies are based'; 'identity and orientation are two sides of the same coin'.

49 According to Bruno De Witte it is 'no more then an effort to spread a more favourable image of Europe, without any substance backing it' (1987: 137). Nevertheless, it appears to be completely accepted in Koslowski: 'Wenn die Mitgliedsnationen der EG die Integration ihrer Länder zu einem Binnenmarkt und Währungsraum vollenden wollen, müssen sie eine weitergehende Einheit ihrer Kultur erreichen, als dies bisher der Fall ist' (Koslowski, 1992: 11; 'if the member nations of the EC wish to complete their integration to obtain an internal market and a monetary area, they must become more unified from a cultural perspective').

50 'The idea of *unity in diversity* stems from the work of Guizot and his contemporaries in the nineteenth century, with their romantic nationalism combined with an idealistic pan-Europeanism' (Wintle, 1996b: 4). Smith offers as alternative the formula 'family of cultures' (Smith, 1992: 71).

51 'Searching the European Identity': as in the title of Heinrichsmeyer (1995).

52 'L'essentiel est de concevoir et d'assumer la dialogique' ('what is essential is to conceive and assume dialogue'), says Morin in the quoted lecture. And the conclusion for him, formulated as moral prescription, is: 'Nous devons abandonner tout Salut, toute Idée-Messie', which he repeats: 'Nous devons abandonner tout "Messie" . . . . Nous devons . . . abandonner toute idée, tout esprit de salut' ('we must leave Salvation, all the Messiah-Idea, aside'; 'we must abandon the Messiah idea. We must abandon all thoughts and the spirit of salvation'; Morin, 1988: 22).

53 Bull. EC 12-1973, p. 119. The Declaration also speaks about 'the civilization which they have in common' (Bull. EC 12-1973, p. 119).

54 'Identity construction is a matter of a very fragile balance . . . between "inward" and "outward"' (Strath, 1995: 41).

55 Between them there is a fracture similar to that indicated by Alain Touraine when he points out that 'technology and cultural identity have grown even further apart' (1999: 57). In a way, Habermas' Europe is a technical Europe, the Europe of the heritage, a cultural Europe. It is obvious that looking to the past has led to excesses, in trying to find precedents even for European integration. Wintle states that 'All the authors agree that it is a mistake to view past instances of common European experience and shared culture, the building blocks of identity, as some sort of pre-history of the EU' (1996b: 1),

but the 'civic Europe', is also a construct which ignores essential elements of the person.

56 The expression is taken from the Opinion of the Committee of the Regions of 13 March 1998 on culture and cultural differences and their significance for the future of Europe.

57 Document COM (87) 603, p. 5.

58 And this when a full understanding of one's own literature is impossible without placing it in the European framework. See the interesting proposal for a European history of literature in Felten and Valcarcel (1992).

59 For the national cultural identities as barriers to European integration, see Zetterholm (1994).

60 See OJ, Annex Debates of the European Parliament, session from 17.1.1995, Number 4-456. p. 53.

61 This leads to the use of definitions, framed in negative terms (Boyce, 1998: 306), that is, by indicating what 'we are not' and by excluding those who 'are not'. Indeed, 'concepts like nationhood . . . have an inherent capacity to "exclude" as much as to 'include" (Jenkins and Sofos, 1996b: 2).

62 A good summary of the topic and the results is found in Harvey (1990: 89ff).

63 See UNESCO (1982: 43). This concept naively evokes the thesis of the best of all possible worlds and ignores the idea that, in all cultural identities, what is human and what is inhuman are expressed in both their positive and negative, their kind and brutal, their generous and mean aspects. And neither inhumanity, nor brutality, nor avarice turn into virtues simply because they are traditional.

64 Opinion of the Committee of the Regions of 13 March 1998 on Culture and cultural differences and their significance for the future of Europe.

65 Resolution of 12 February 1993 (OJ C 72 from 15.3.1993, p. 163). In the Spanish version the more expressive word 'ósmosis' is used.

66 'the cultural currents common to Europeans'. This is clearer then the English version, 'artistic movements and styles shared by Europeans' (Committee of the Regions: Opinion of 13 March 1998 on a Proposal establishing 'The European City of Culture' event/Avis . . . sur la 'Proposition . . . concernant . . . la manifestation Ville européenne de la culture'; OJ C 180 from 11.6.1998, p. 71).

67 Resolution of the Council and the Representatives of Member States' Governments on the response of educational systems to the problems of racism and xenophobia (OJ C 312 from 23.11.95, p. 2).

68 With a 0.33 per cent share of a total Community budget that is itself restricted to 1.27 per cent of the member states' GDP, no threatening action can be launched.

69 Even in the most national of all centuries, the nineteenth, throughout a great part of Europe, cultural beats kept time together and moved from a late and sweetened Enlightenment towards a multiform Romanticism, a more or less poetic Realism, a brief Naturalism, brother of positivism and scientism and the anti-naturalist movements like symbolist, dandyist, decandentist, femmefatalist, etc.

70 For an eloquent example of how globalisation may become an opportunity for a 'small culture', see De Meyer (2000).

71 Europe 'is defined in the rejection of threats from outside Europe; this is a protective definition'.

72 Even cultural phenomena considered especially representative of one region can contain extra-European elements: flamenco, representative of Spain in her image abroad, although really only comprehensible in one single region of Spain, Andalusia, possibly comes from outside of Europe, from India. It has taken on Arabic, and Byzantine elements and elements from Gregorian chant.

It has been influenced by the Portuguese fado (giving rise to a type of flamenco called 'fandango') and, of course, by Latin American music.

73   The Christians in the first centuries were responsible for the availability of the documents that were to come down to us from that other great source of culture, the Greek-Roman tradition; more details in Banús (2000c).

74   'Die Kulturpolitik der Europäischen Gemeinschaft muß vor allem darauf aus sein, solche Abschottungen gegen die andere Nationalkultur durch ein europäisches Gemeinbewußtsein aufzubrechen' (Koslowski, 1992: 12; 'the cultural policy of the European Community must be primarily designed to create a common European conscience to prevent the rejection of other national cultures').

75   This formula seems more complex than that offered by Kaelble, which links the political construction of Europe with the integration of European societies and the 'prise en conscience d'une identité européenne' (Kaelble, 1994: 27; 'awareness of European identity'). It is more sceptical than Miguel Siguan's categorical statement: the cultures in Europe – he affirms – 'share many features that are the result of a common history . . . – a history that makes it possible to speak of a European culture' (Siguan, 1998: 29). In that sense we can agree with Wintle when he establishes 'that identity is complex and made up of many layers interacting at different and changing levels, that to manipulate it is by no means impossible but unpredictable and potentially even dangerous' (Wintle, 1996b: 1). And 'there is indeed a European cultural identity, and it consists mainly of a partially shared historical heritage and experience . . . . It is not, however, some sort of blueprint for the EU, which in terms of the shared heritage is as yet only a flash in the pan, or more correctly, a very short and selective part of that shared experience' (Wintle, 1996c: 24).

76   Bondy (1985: 69), warns against this risk and also points out the contrary models, those that have only highlighted the negative elements in the 'European heritage'.

77   Hence, the expressive title of Brusis (1997) with an impressive description of the problems of these myths in the Slovac-Hungarian relations.

REFERENCES

Aldridge, Alfred Owen (1969) *Comparative Literature: Matter and Method.* Urbana: University of Illinois Press.

Anderson, Benedict (1983) *Imagined Communities: Reflections on the Origin and Spread of Nationalism.* London: Verso.

Banús, Enrique (1996) 'The Cultural Policy of the European Union: Problems and Possibilities', in *Report of Sixth Symposium on Cultural Politics.* Copenhagen: The Danish Cultural Institute.

Banús, Enrique (1997) 'Some Remarks about the Cultural Policy of the European Union' in Nada Svob-Dokic (ed.) *The Cultural Identity of Central Europe.* Zagreb: Culturelink.

Banús, Enrique (1998) 'European Identity–National Identity: The Case of the Histories of Literature', in Enrique Banús and Beatriz Elío (eds) *Actas del V Congreso 'Cultura Europea'.* Pamplona: Aranzadi.

Banús, Enrique (1999) 'Europäische Literatur: Mittlungen und Intertextualität', in Hans Felten and David Nelting (eds) *Contemporary European Literature.* Frankfurt am Main: Peter Lang.

Banús, Enrique (2000a) 'Algunas tesis simples para un tema complejo: "Cultura europea"', in Enrique Banús and Beatriz Elío (eds) *Actas del V Congreso 'Cultura Europea'*. Pamplona: Aranzadi.

Banús, Enrique (ed.) (2000b) *Subsidiariedad: historia y aplicación – Subsidiarity: history and application*. Pamplona: Newbook.

Banús, Enrique (2000c) 'Los Padres de la Iglesia, ¿'padres de Europa'?', in E. Reinhardt (ed.) *Tempus implendi promissa. Homenaje al Prof. Dr. Domingo Ramos-Lissón*. Pamplona: Eunsa.

Birnbaum, Pierre (1996) 'From Multiculturalism to Nationalism', in *Political Theory*, 24 (1): 33–45.

Bondy, François (1985) 'Selbstbesinnung, Selbstbestimmung: Kultur und Integration', in Werner Weidenfeld (ed.) *Die Identität Europas*. München-Wien: Hanser.

Boxhoorn, Bram (1996) 'European Identity and the Process of European Unification: Compatible Notions?', in Michael Wintle (ed.) *Culture and Identity in Europe: Perceptions of Divergence and Unity in Past and Present*. Aldershot: Ashgate.

Boyce, Brigitte (1998) 'The Role of Islam in Europe's Search for a Common Cultural Identity', in Enrique Banús and Beatriz Elío (eds) *Actas del IV Congreso 'Cultura Europea'*. Pamplona: Aranzadi.

Braudel, Fernand (1989) 'Europa außerhalb Europas', in Fernand Braudel (ed.) *Europa: Bausteine seiner Geschichte*. Frankfurt am Main: Fischer.

Braun, Robert (1998) 'Nationalism and Post-traditional Identity', in Csaba Szaló (ed.) *On European Identity, Nationalism, Culture and History*. Brno: Masaryk University.

Brusis, Martin (1997) *Macht der Mythen. Geschichtsdeutungen im slowakisch-ungarischen Verhältnis*. Sonderheft von Südosteuropa. Zeitschrift für Gegenwartsforschung.

Burow, D. (1998) 'Lebensentwürfe am Schnittpunkt zweier Kreise', in Enrique Banús and Beatriz Elío (eds) *Actas del IV Congreso 'Cultura Europea'*. Pamplona: Aranzadi.

Cassirer, Ernst (1954) *Philosophie der symbolischen Formen*. Oxford: Cassirer.

Citron, Suzanne (1987) *Le mythe national. L'histoire de France en question*. Paris: Éditions Ouvrières.

Cuisenier, Jean (ed.) (1979) *Europe as a Cultural Area*. The Hague: Mouton.

Davies, Norman (1996) *Europe: A History*. Oxford: Oxford University Press.

Delanty, Gerard (1995) *Inventing Europe: Idea, Identity, Reality*. New York: St Martin's Press.

De Meyer, Gust (2000) 'Cultural Globalization and Local Identity: The Case of (Belgian) Popular Music', in Enrique Banús and Beatriz Elío (eds) *Actas del V Congreso 'Cultura Europea'*. Pamplona: Aranzadi.

De Witte, Bruno (1987) 'Building Europe's Image and Identity', in Albert Rijksbaron, Willem Hendrik Roobol and Max Weisglas (eds) *Europe From a Cultural Perspective*. The Hague: Nijgh & Van Ditmar Universitair.

Donati, Pierpaolo (1999) 'El desafío del multiculturalismo en una sociedad multicultural postmoderna: un planteamiento relacional', in Enrique Banús and Alejandro Llano (eds) *Razón práctica y multiculturalismo*. Pamplona: Newbook.

Felten, Hans and Valcarcel, Agustín (1992) 'Literatura europea – Unidad de referencias intertextuales', in Enrique Banús (ed.) *Actas del I Congreso 'Cultura Europea'*. Pamplona: Aranzadi.

Firchow, Peter Edgerly (1986) *The Death of the German Cousin*. Lewisburg-London: Backwell University Press-Associated University Press.

Flohr, Heiner (1998) 'Teaching High Culture to the Masses or Adjusting Culture to Mass Standards?', in Enrique Banús and Beatriz Elío (eds) *Actas del IV Congreso 'Cultura Europea'*. Pamplona: Aranzadi.

Forrest, Alan (1994) 'A New Start for Cultural Action in the European Community:

Genesis and Implications of Article 128 of the Treaty on European Union', *International Journal of Cultural Policy*, 1: 11–20.

Fulbrook, Mary (ed.) (1993) *National Histories and European History*. London: UCL Press.

Habermas, Jürgen (1991) *Staatsbürgerschaft und nationale Identität: Überlegungen zur europäischen Zukunft*. St Gallen: Erker.

Harvey, Edwin R. (1990) *Políticas culturales en Iberoamérica y el mundo*. Madrid: Tecnos.

Hazard, Paul (1935) *La Crise de la conscience Européenne*. Paris: Boivin & Cie.

Henrichsmeyer, Wilhelm, Hildebrand, Klaus and May, Bernhard (eds) (1995) *Auf der Suche nach europäischer Identität*. Bonn: Institut für europäische Integrationsforschung.

Helly, Denise (1998) 'The Transformation of an Idea: The Nation', in Anna Krasteva (ed.) *Communities and Identities*. Sofia: Petekston.

Hobsbawm, Eric J. and Ranger, Terence (eds) (1983) *The Invention of Tradition*. Cambridge: Cambridge University Press.

Jelin, Elizabeth (1999) 'Ciudades, cultura y globalización', in UNESCO (ed.) *Informe mundial sobre la cultura*. Madrid: UNESCO.

Jenkins, Brian and Sofos, Spyros A. (1996a) *Nation and Identity in Contemporary Europe*. London: Routledge.

Jenkins, Brian and Sofos, Spyros A. (1996b) 'Introduction', in Brian Jenkins and Spyros A. Sofos (eds) *Nation and Identity in Contemporary Europe*. London: Routledge.

Jenkins, Brian and Sofos, Spyros A. (1996c) 'Nation and Nationalism in Contemporary Europe', in Brian Jenkins and Spyros A. Sofos, *Nation and Identity in Contemporary Europe*. London: Routledge.

Jenkins, Brian and Sofos, Spyros A. (1996d) 'Conclusion', in Brian Jenkins and Spyros A. Sofos (eds) *Nation and Identity in Contemporary Europe*. London: Routledge.

Joll, James (1969) *Europe: A Historian's View*. Leeds: Leeds University Press.

Kaelble, Hartmut (1994) 'L'Europe "vécue" et l'Europe "pensée" au XXe siècle: les spécificités sociales de l'Europe', in René Girault (ed.) *Identité et conscience européennes au XXe siècle*. Paris: Hachette.

Koslowski, Peter (1992) 'Sich Europa vorstellen', in Peter Koslowski (ed.) *Europa imaginieren*. Berlin-Heildeberg: Springer.

Kroeber, Alfred Louis and Kluckhohn, Clyde (1952) *Culture: a Critical Review of Concepts and Definitions*. Cambridge, MA: The Museum.

Linde, Enrique (1995) 'Cultura y desarrollo', in *Cultura y desarrollo*. Madrid: Ministerio de Cultura.

Lulé, Marie-Laure (1996) 'Les objectifs fondamentaux de l'action culturelle', in Enrique Banús (ed.) *Actas del III Congreso Cultura Europea*. Pamplona: Aranzadi.

Margue, T.L. (1993) 'L'action culturelle de la Communauté européenne. Bilan et perspectives', in *Revue du Marché Unique Européen*, vol. 2. pp. 171–84

Martín y Pérez de Nanclares, José (1996) 'La operatividad del principio de subsidiariedad del TUE en materia cultural: Especial referencia a la política audiovisual de la UE', in Enrique Banús (ed.) *Actas del III Congreso Cultura Europea*. Pamplona: Aranzadi.

Maurus, Wolfgang (1998) 'The Importance of Culture for the Future of Europe', in Enrique Banús and Beatriz Elío (eds) *Actas del IV Congreso 'Cultura Europea'*. Pamplona: Aranzadi.

Mickel, Wolfgang (1998) 'Kulturpolitik in Europa unter besonderer Berücksichtigung internationaler Institutionen', in Enrique Banús and Beatriz Elío (eds) *Actas del IV Congreso 'Cultura Europea'*. Pamplona: Aranzadi.

Milward, Alan (1992) *The European Rescue of the Nation-state*. London: Routledge.

Moreno, Almudena (1998) 'Valores materialistas y postmaterialistas en la cultura cívica de los europeos', in Enrique Banús and Beatriz Elío (eds) *Actas del IV Congreso 'Cultura Europea'*. Pamplona: Aranzadi.

Morin, Edgar (1987a) *Penser l'Europe*. Paris: Gallimard.

Morin, Edgar (1987b) 'La politique culturelle dans la société complexe', in Jacques Delcourt and Roberto Papini (eds) *Pour une Politique Européenne de la Culture*. Paris: Economica.

Morin, Edgar (1988) *Edgar Morin, Lauréat du Prix Européen de l'Essai Charles Veillon 1987*. Bussigny: Fondation Charles Veillon.

Nora, Pierre (1986) *Les lieux de la mémoire. La nation*. Paris: Gallimard.

Odermatt, P. (1991) 'The Use of Symbols in the Drive for European Integration', *Yearbook of European Studies*, 4: 217–40.

Perez, Laurent (1996) 'Le principe de subsidiarité et les compétences en matière culturelle – L'emergence de un "nouvel ordre culturel européen"', in Enrique Banús (ed.) *Actas del III Congreso Cultura Europea*. Pamplona: Aranzadi.

Perez-Solorzano, Nieves and Longman, Christopher (1998) 'European Cultural Identity: Unity in Diversity or Family of Cultures?', in Enrique Banús and Beatriz Elío (eds) *Actas del IV Congreso 'Cultura Europea'*. Pamplona: Aranzadi.

Rasmussen, Jens Rahbek (1995) 'The Danish Monarchy as a Composite State', in Nils Arne Sørensen (ed.) *European Identities: Cultural Diversity and Integration in Europe since 1700*. Odense: Odense University Press.

Reif, Karlheinz (1993) 'Cultural Convergence and Cultural Identity as Factors in European Identity', in Soledad Garcia (ed.) *European Identity and the Search for Legitimacy*. London: Pinter.

Robertson, Roland (1996) *Globalization: Social Theory and Global Culture*. London: Sage.

Salazar, Gonzalo de (1998) 'Multiculturalism, Statehood and Territory: Integration versus Conflict', in Enrique Banús and Beatriz Elío (eds) *Actas del IV Congreso 'Cultura Europea'*. Pamplona: Aranzadi.

Seton-Watson, Hugh (1985) 'What is Europe, Where is Europe? From Mystique to Politique', *Encounter*, 64–5: 9–17.

Shelly, Monica and Winck, Margaret (eds) (1995) *Aspects of European Cultural Diversity*. London: Routledge.

Siguan, Miguel (1998) 'Linguistic Nationalism and European Identity', in Csaba Szaló (ed.) *On European Identity, Nationalism, Culture and History*. Brno: Masaryk University.

Skiljan, Dubravko (1998) 'Language of Identity and Language of Distinction', in Enrique Banús and Beatriz Elío (eds) *Actas del IV Congreso 'Cultura Europea'*. Pamplona: Aranzadi.

Smith, Anthony D. (1991) *National Identity*. London: Penguin.

Smith, Anthony D. (1992) 'National Identity and the Idea of European Unity', *International Affairs*, 68: 55–76.

Smith, Jim (1998) 'Nacionalismo, globalización y movimientos sociales', in Pedro Ibarra and Benjamín Tejerina, *Los movimientos sociales. Transformaciones políticas y cambio cultural*. Madrid: Trotta, pp. 321–36.

Sørensen, Nils Arne (1995) 'European Identities: An Introduction', in Nils Arne Sørensen (ed.) *European Identities: Cultural Diversity and Integration in Europe since 1700*. Odense: Odense University Press.

Spiering, M. (1996) 'National Identity and European Unity', in Michael Wintle (ed.) *Culture and Identity in Europe: Perceptions of Divergence and Unity in Past and Present*. London: Ashgate.

Strath, Bo (1995) 'Scandinavian Identity. A mythical Reality', in Nils Arne Sørensen (ed.) *European Identities: Cultural Diversity and Integration in Europe since 1700*. Odense: Odense University Press.

Strath, Bo (ed.) (2000) *Europe and the Other and Europe as the Other*. Brussels: Peter Lang.

Szalo, Csaba (1998) 'European Identity, Nationalism and the Dynamics of Identity Construction', in Csaba Szaló (ed.) *On European Identity, Nationalism, Culture and History*. Brno: Masaryk University.

Thuriot, Fabrice (1998) 'L'influence de l'Unione Européenne sur les politiques culturelles internes et en particulier en France'; in Enrique Banús and Beatriz Elío (eds) *Actas del IV Congreso 'Cultura Europea'*. Pamplona: Aranzadi.

Touraine, Alain (1999) 'Iguales y diferentes', in UNESCO (ed.) *Informe mundial sobre la cultura*. Madrid: Unesco.

UNESCO (ed.) (1982) *Conferencia Mundial sobre las Políticas Culturales. Informe Final*. Paris: UNESCO.

Veil, Simone (1987) 'Préface', in Jacques Delcourt and Roberto Papini (eds) *Pour une Politique Européenne de la Culture*. Paris: Economica.

Weidenfeld, Werner (1985) 'Europa – aber wo liegt es?', in Werner Weidenfeld (ed.) *Die Identität Europas*. München-Wien: Hanser.

Wenturis, Nikolaus (1998) 'A Europe without Identity? Ethnicity, Nation-State and EU-Integration', in Enrique Banús and Beatriz Elío (eds) *Actas del IV Congreso 'Cultura Europea'*. Pamplona: Aranzadi.

Wintle, Michael (ed.) (1996a) *Culture and Identity in Europe: Perceptions of Divergence and Unity in Past and Present*. London: Ashgate.

Wintle, Michael (1996b) 'Introduction: Cultural Diversity and Identity in Europe', in Michael Wintle (ed.) *Culture and Identity in Europe: Perceptions of Divergence and Unity in Past and Present*. London: Ashgate.

Wintle, Michael (1996c) 'Cultural Identity in Europe: Shared Experience', in Michael Wintle (ed.) *Culture and Identity in Europe: Perceptions of Divergence and Unity in Past and Present*. London: Ashgate.

Wittal-Düerkop, Tanya-Elizabeth (1998) 'Diskurse europäischer Identität. Europäische Identitätsmuster im Spannungsfeld von Gesellschaftskritik und Kulturtheorie', in Enrique Banús and Beatriz Elío (eds) *Actas del IV Congreso 'Cultura Europea'*. Pamplona: Aranzadi.

Zetterholm, Staffan (ed.) (1994) *National Cultures and European Integration*. Oxford: Berg.

10   Towards a European Language Policy

Christina Julios

English is currently spoken by a quarter of the world's population. In the European Union alone its widespread use has de facto eclipsed the other existing official tongues. Within the context of an increasingly complex and linguistically diverse EU, the present chapter explores the scope of the Union's language policy strategy. As a starting point, an overview of the ideology behind it and the existing European educational programmes is provided. This is followed by an analysis of two major obstacles challenging the EU's multilingual ideal. First, the development of hierarchical relationships between supposedly co-equal official languages. Secondly, a conflict of interests between the union's supranational pluralistic discourse and individual member states' nationalistic agendas. In the light of these trends, the chapter considers likely future developments. In particular the threat that EU enlargement poses to the long-term viability of its pluralistic communication system. Finally, pragmatic alternatives to the increasingly unattainable European Babel ideal are suggested.

GLOBALISATION OF THE ENGLISH LANGUAGE

Hegemony of the English language as the widest spoken tongue in the world is undisputed. A breakdown of the major world languages easily places English (with 1,400 million speakers) at the top of the list far ahead of its nearest rival: Chinese (with 1,000 million speakers) (Edwards, 1995: 32). As David Crystal (1995: 106) has indicated, it is both the number of English speakers worldwide as well as their global geographical distribution that makes the application of the term 'world language' a reality. The ubiquitous presence of English in every sphere of society's life furthermore attests to its powerful international cultural dominance. In 1994, for instance, data compiled in the *Encyclopaedia Britannica* (1995) indicated that about a third of the world's newspapers were being published in those countries where the English language has an official status, and it is reasonable to assume that the majority of these would be in English. Similarly, the *Book of Lists* 1997 reported that the top five papers in the world were all in English, including: *The New York Times, The*

Washington Post, The Wall Street Journal, The Times and *The Sunday Times*. (Crystal, 1995) It would seem that about a quarter of the world's periodicals, literary and technical reviews, scholarly journals, comics, and pornographic material are published in English (Crystal, 1995: 18). English is also the language of the film industry – 85 per cent of the world's entertainment market is controlled by the United States, with Hollywood films dominating box offices in most countries. While the Oscar system has traditionally been English-language oriented, there is a strong English-language presence in most other film festivals too. Half of the Best Film awards ever given at the Cannes Film Festival, for example, have been awarded to English-language productions (Crystal, 1995: 91). The pop music world has also felt the international power of the English language. The 1990 edition of *The Penguin Encyclopaedia of Popular Music*, which includes 557 pop groups, indicates that 549 (99 per cent) of them work entirely or predominantly in English. Of the 1,219 solo vocalists, 1,156 (95 per cent) sing in English. The mother tongue of the artists appears to be irrelevant. The entire international career of ABBA, the Swedish group, was based on English, with over twenty hit records in the 1970s and 1980s having been recorded and performed in English.

Perhaps the most direct evidence of the English US-led world supremacy has been its almost automatic transformation into the internet's lingua franca. From the outset an English-speaking North American invention, the World Wide Web has become a universal tool for accessing knowledge and exchanging information. A truly multilingual internet remains impracticable, for servers and clients must be able to intelligently communicate with each other, whatever the data source. Most browsers are still unable to handle multilingual data presentation including writing systems such as Arabic, Chinese, Korean, Thai and Indi. If the pitfalls of a technological Babel are to be avoided, English language remains the only viable alternative. Here, the unparalleled domination of the US-led international software market personified by the US giant Microsoft seems to indicate the establishment of a growing trend. Significantly Microsoft refused to translate its Windows 95 software package into Icelandic, alleging a 'limited market' for such a service.[1] While the director of the Icelandic Language Institute, Ari Pall Kristinsson, accused Microsoft of 'destroying' Iceland's linguistic heritage, the fact remains that every school child in his country is taught English as a first foreign language. Microsoft did not consider it necessary to translate its Windows 95 applications into Icelandic when the standard English version could be sold instead (Walsh, 1998: 15). Michael Specter (1996), writing in the *New York Times* has reflected on the influence of English on the internet market. In an article entitled 'World, Wide, Web: Three English Words' he concludes that 'if you want to take full advantage of the internet there is only one way to do it: learn English, which has more than ever become America's greatest and most efficient export' (Specter, 1996). The world's current economic situation as well as the consequences of the technological revolution in the communications sector will almost certainly reinforce the global role of English.

THE EUROPEAN BABEL IDEAL

Against the background of English domination, the EU stands as a heterogeneous entity comprised of a myriad of multilingual societies, with their particular ethnic and cultural heritage. Inherently pluralist and multicultural in its outlook, the EU seems to thrive in its own inner diversity. With a total population of about 370 million people, the EU is certainly a collectivity that aims at being 'broad as well as deep' (*Economist*, 2–8 January 1999: 16; Nugent, 1999: 52) In the words of Jacques Santer, the former President of the European Commission:

> Europe is made up of a number of different cultural identities: languages, schools of thought and art vary considerably from North to South. . . . This multicultural heritage colours the way in which we see society at large and the meaning we give to our lives. . . . Our common cultural heritage is Shakespeare, Cervantes, Rimbaud, Mozart; but it is also Tolstoy, Moussorgski, Durrenmatt and Kundera. . . . One can therefore speak of a common cultural heritage of pluralistic humanism reflected in the diversity of Europe's individual cultures . . . our cultural heritage plays an ever increasing role in our *multicultural global village*, in which everyone's race, creed, sex and ideas must be fully respected. The Treaty of Maastricht bears this out. (Santer, 1996)

From an original EC membership of six, the EU now numbers fifteen member states. In addition to the latter, a further thirteen countries have lodged applications to join the Union: ten from central and eastern European countries, plus Cyprus, Malta and Turkey (see Introduction). Since its inception, such a mosaic of nations has transformed the EU into an influential international organisation as well as the world's principal commercial power, accounting for around one-fifth of the planet's imports and exports (Nugent, 1999: 525).[2] Above all, the sheer variety of the EU's membership has afforded it an extraordinary cultural and linguistic wealth which, as Jacques Santer indicated, is at the very core of the European project. The EU has not only flourished through the fragmented nature of its member states; it positively relishes their distinctiveness. More significantly, it has done so in the spirit of pluralism and co-operation. The existing eleven official EU languages which pervade the Union's institutions, policies and policy processes attest to this equitable ideal. Here, the votes and opinions of the different EU member states find expression in the shared use of their individual national languages. Within the context of a pluralistic European Babel, the official status jointly conferred on the French, Dutch, German, Danish, Italian, Swedish, Finnish, Spanish,

Portuguese and Greek languages stands in stark contrast with the predominant position enjoyed by the powerful English tongue.

EUROPE'S LANGUAGE POLICY STRATEGY

In policy terms, the EU's multilingual ideal translates into a variety of educational and training programmes aimed at nurturing the maintenance and development of the Union's many languages. The White Paper 'Teaching and Learning Towards the Learning Society' presented by the EU Commission in 1995 encapsulates the essence of the European language strategy: 'proficiency in several Community languages has become a precondition, if citizens of the European Union are to benefit from the occupational and personal opportunities open to them in the border-free Single Market' (European Commission, 1997b, 1: 2–3). The EU has indeed been built upon the cultural diversity of its member states, and respect for such diversity finds expression in, among other things, its great linguistic wealth. The protection of the latter as well as the promotion of diversity has therefore become one of the cornerstones of Europe's pluralist construction (European Commission, 1997b, 1: 2–3).

Both the Treaty of Amsterdam and the EU's Agenda 2000 document have placed the greatest emphasis on the development of a 'Europe of knowledge' and the promotion of lifelong learning (Nugent, 1999; European Commission, 1999, 8: 6–7). Within this context, SOCRATES, Europe's education programme, seeks to promote the quality of education by furthering co-operation, increasing mobility and developing the European dimension in all sectors of education. SOCRATES comprises a number of subschemes each concerned with a different area of education. They include: COMENIUS – school education; ERASMUS – higher education; GRUNDTVIG – adult education and other educational pathways; MINERVA – Information and Communication Technology (ICT); and LINGUA – teaching and learning European languages. Although LINGUA specialises in the field of language education, the COMENIUS, ERASMUS and GRUNDTVIG programmes are also engaged in providing opportunities to learn European languages.[3] Indeed, SOCRATES on the whole aims to: 'promote a quantitative and qualitative improvement of knowledge of the languages of the European Union, in particular those which are less widely used and less taught, leading to greater understanding and solidarity between the peoples of the European Union and the promotion of the intercultural dimension of education' (European Council, 1998, 430: 1–7). In turn, the LINGUA scheme endeavours to achieve three individual objectives: first, to raise EU citizens' awareness of the Union's multilingual wealth by encouraging them to learn languages throughout their lifetime; secondly, to develop and disseminate innovative techniques and good practices in language teaching; and thirdly, to ensure that a sufficient range of language learning tools is available to language learners (EUROPA,

2000). So far, around thirty European countries, half a million university students and 10,000 schools have already taken part in the various SOCRATES schemes (European Council, 1999, 378: 1–8) Indeed, data from the Commission attests to the success of these programmes, for it shows that 'demand is far beyond available financial means' (European Commission, 1990: 14).

In addition to SOCRATES, there are a number of further EU programmes aimed at achieving the Union's goal of promoting language learning. They include, first, LEONARDO DA VINCI, a vocational training programme 'intended to develop quality, innovation and the European dimension in vocational training systems and practices' (European Council, 1998, 430: 1–7). Increasing the employability of EU citizens through the development of language skills, multilingualism and multicultural communication is a central concern of this scheme. Secondly, the European Label has been established as an EU award to help stimulate interest in language learning. Co-ordinated by the European Commission, this EU benchmark is granted every year in each member state to those language learning initiatives that are deemed to be among the most innovative and outstanding. Thirdly, support for regional and minority languages. With almost 40 million regional/minority language-speaking EU citizens, the Commission has developed schemes to safeguard and promote their cultural and linguistic heritage. MERCATOR, for instance, an information and documentation network, aims at improving the exchange and circulation of material on minority languages and cultures within the EU member states. Finally, the European Commission has adopted a proposal to designate 2001 the European Year of Languages (EU Information Service, 1999, 204: 18). Organised by the European Union and the Council of Europe, this scheme is intended as a celebration of Europe's linguistic diversity. It will therefore comprise activities and promotional measures regarding language learning and related skills (a website, conferences, publications, exhibitions, etc.). At the time of the proposal, the Education and Culture Commissioner, Viviane Reding, indicated that the European Year of Languages would aim to give every European citizen the opportunity to learn at least two other languages apart from their own mother tongue (EU Information Service, 1999, 204: 18). This EU scheme would be aimed at the eleven official EU languages together with other sanctioned regional tongues such as Irish Gaelic and Catalan. The Commission is also to target 'lesser' minority languages within the EU member states through development of an additional programme: ARCHIPEL (EU Information Service, 1999, 204: 18). Its main objective is 'to reach all groups of citizens and to remind them of the advantages of learning languages not only because of enhanced professional possibilities, but also for understanding other cultures' (European Council, 1999, 378: 1–8).

In the best European tradition, this myriad of schemes to promote knowledge of EU languages is meant to add to EU citizens' personal and cultural fulfilment as well as providing them with important tools of communication. It is also intended to further transnational co-operation and EU integration. Above all, the sheer number of existing language-oriented programmes is geared towards the realisation of the European Babel ideal. Within an increasingly diverse Union, the latter endeavours to nurture, in a pluralist fashion, the mosaic of languages and cultures at the core of its very foundations. This illusion of linguistic equality however, becomes quickly shattered when the overwhelming influence English exerts in the Union's everyday life is taken into consideration. As Eurobarometer reminds us, 47 per cent of the EU population already speaks English (32 per cent speaks German, 28 per cent French, 18 per cent Italian and 15 per cent Spanish), while 89 per cent of all secondary pupils in the Union currently learn it as the first foreign language in education (32 per cent learn French, 18 per cent German, and 8 per cent Spanish) (EUROPA, 2000: 1–8). Although all EU member states' tongues enjoy a similar official status, English certainly remains the language most widely used, a true first among equals. It has long been spoken as a second language in Scandinavia and The Netherlands, while in southern and eastern Europe, it remains the most extensively utilised foreign language.[4] In addition to the powerful influence of English, there are a number of factors that further challenge the European Babel myth. In analysing them, the following sections will reveal a widening gap between the EU pluralistic ideology and the reality of multiculturalism in twenty-first century Europe.

LANGUAGE HIERARCHIES AND THE REALITY OF MULTICULTURALISM

The philosophy behind the EU's social construction is based on the idea of community. Europe's multilingual approach is meant to contribute to a better understanding and awareness of the various member states' cultural and linguistic heritage. The EU aims at being a community, and a community requires partnership and not domination, least of all linguistic domination. The concept of a dominant language does not, in theory, fit this European pluralist ideal. A predominant language may arguably suppress not only other languages, but it may also impede the development of certain peoples' cultures to a point of threatening their very existence. It is not through a leading language, but through the diversification of foreign language provision that European language policy seems to have been envisaged. Ironically, this seemingly equitable and inclusive European model is subjected to the same hierarchical rules that have elevated English to the top of the list of the world's languages. Within the EU indeed, various orders of preference have been traditionally established in the usage of supposedly co-equal tongues. The linguistic experience of Luxembourg provides a case in point. Here, the entire citizenry becomes trilingual, with Luxembourgish, German and French being learned both through schooling and the larger socio-economic environment (Beardsmore and Kohls, 1985: 1–15; Khoo et al., 1994: 5). Within this apparently pluralistic system however, oral communication seems to be carried out primarily in Luxembourgish, whereas for written communication German is by far the most widely deployed language (Beardsmore and Kohls, 1985: 5). As David Graddol has argued, 'languages are not equal in political or social status, particularly in multilingual contexts' (1997: 5). Languages are often hierarchically ordered according to the socio-economic position they occupy in the wider society. To the extent that such divisions are institutionalised, the classification of languages can be thought of as applying to countries as much as to a given repertoire of individual speakers.

There are three basic levels of use in which languages can be ranked (Graddol, 1997: 12–13). At the bottom end of the scale, there are tongues mainly used for interaction with family and close friends. They are usually confined to migrant communities and are the first tongues learned by children. In the EU, for example, vernacular varieties of indigenous languages include Albanian, Aragonese, Breton, Cornish, Croat, Franco-Provençal, Friulan, Karelian, Lallans, Macedonian, Manx, Polish, Romany, Samish, Serbian, Slovene, Turkish and Vlach. The second level of language use refers to tongues found in formal and public domains which have greater territorial reach. These officially recognised languages form the medium of primary and secondary education, newspapers, radio broadcasts and local commerce. Such are the cases of Alsatian, Asturian, Basque, Catalan, Corsican, Frisian, Gaelic, Galician, Ladin, Luxembourg-ish, Occitan, Sardinian and Welsh. The final level of the linguistic hier-archy is occupied by lawfully sanctioned languages with the widest territorial and cultural reach. Their scope encompasses all areas of a country's social, scientific and economic life, being used in government administration, national media, higher education and international com-munication. Within the EU, the official languages of its member states comprise this category, thus: Danish, Dutch, English, Finnish, French, German, Greek, Italian, Portuguese, Spanish and Swedish.

Against this background, the reality of multilingualism translates into assimilationist practices, with socio-economically stronger languages exerting a dominant influence over weaker minority ones. It appears that languages already play a decisive role in the degree of participation by the different EU member states in the Union's language education pro-grammes. Data from the Commission indicates that Britain is represented in two-thirds of all ERASMUS schemes (European Commission, 1990: 11). Furthermore, this linguistic imbalance results in a lack of reciprocity in students' exchanges. For instance, there are far more ERASMUS students going to Britain than British students going to a partner country, parti-cularly if it is not an English-speaking country. Similarly, in Franco-German educational exchanges, many German students travel to France, but few go in the other direction (European Commission, 1990: 11). In short, there is no such a thing as true equality among languages. On the contrary, when in contact, languages inevitably enter into hierarchical relationships. Here, the status, perceived usefulness and pertinence of one language in relation to others becomes of paramount importance. The Commission's own research confirms that in the overwhelming majority of EU member states the provision of modern foreign languages is dominated by the English language, followed by French and German. In contrast, the other languages of the EU are poorly represented. As the Commission put it: 'in state education, it has been noted that the foreign languages on offer are generally insufficient' (European Commission, 1990: 21). In the context of a linguistically diverse EU, the development of such classifications among differently valued languages have far-reaching consequences. This is particularly so when considering the impact that the global supremacy of a language like English may have on the use and maintenance of Europe's ethnic minority tongues (Graddol, 1997).[5]

LINGUISTIC NATIONALISM AMONG THE EU MEMBER STATES

Rosemary Khoo has pointed out that European integration is in no way comparable with developments in younger nations where linguistic diversity, be it through immigration or based on indigenous heterogeneity, can be overcome by consensus or the interventionist promotion of a common language (Khoo et al., 1994). Linguistic communities in Europe are for the most part closely tied in with feelings of regional or national identity, and few would ever envisage sacrificing their linguistic or cultural heritage on the altar of European unity (*Time*, winter 1998–99). Catalonia's bilingual policy, which caters for speakers of a minority language within an otherwise multilingual Spain, illustrates this trend. The historical process by which the Catalonian tongue has acquired a dominant position has been characterised by its political deployment as a nationalistic tool of self-determination (Artigal, 1995: 172). While fostering bilingualism in the national Spanish language, Catalonia's policy strategy is overwhelmingly aimed at nurturing its indigenous Catalonian tongue (Artigal, 1995: 169–81). Whether in Spain, Germany, Austria, Greece or Italy, the national policy discourses of EU member states inevitably endeavour to preserve their particular dominant native languages. As Bruno Chiaverini, Director of International Relations for the Rhone-Alps region of France, has put it: 'we function with the overall goals and constraints of national policies . . . we are nowhere near the point where we'd start putting regional ahead of national interests' (*Time*, winter 1998–99: 40–3). The implications for the construction of a lasting European Babel are far-reaching. Indeed, the realisation of Europe's pluralistic ideal in no way follows from European integration. An insight into the linguistic experiences of France and Britain illustrate this reality.

France's language policy strategy provides a clear example of an EU member state vigorously pursuing a nationalistic linguistic agenda. The country's public discourse is driven by an assimilationist ideology, which equates the French language with the embodiment of national identity. The status of French as 'the' language of the Republic has been overtly sanctioned since the sixteenth century, when the first language-planning law in France was introduced (Battye and Hintze, 1992). In 1539, Article 111 of the *Edicts of Villers-Cotterets* required the French tongue 'and not otherwise' to be used in oral presentations, in legal documents such as contracts and in judgments rendered in French courts (Ager, 1996: 40). Over 200 years later, the French Revolution did for this language what the Roman Empire had done for Latin: it transformed French into a symbol of national unity. In the same way as all Roman subjects had come to speak Latin across the Empire's different dominions, French citizens everywhere would speak the French language.

Up to the present day, the government of the Republic has deployed its official language as part of a continuing process of social acculturation and political control (Lodge, 1993). The country's school system is overtly geared towards enabling non-French speaking pupils to access French-dominated mainstream education (Ager, 1994: 35–52). Compensatory programmes for immigrant children, with French being taught as a second language, have existed since the early 1970s (Varro, 1992: 137–62). Their underlying assumption has been that the progression from foreigner into French citizen can only be accomplished through mastering the French language. Against this background, the linguistic heritage of coexisting ethnic minority groups has all but been neglected. In spite of the presence of over one million immigrants from the Maghreb countries in France by 1990, the use of minority languages remains marginalised (Katzner, 1992). In 1972, President Pompidou infamously remarked that 'there is no place for regional languages in a France which is destined to play a fundamental role in Europe' (Ager, 1996: 43). Twenty-three years after they were uttered, echoes of those words continue to reverberate. By 1995, the Republic was being accused of using its six-month presidency of the EU to defend the diversity of European languages in order to protect the French tongue (*Economist*, 14 January 1995: 334). More recently, the political controversy surrounding Lionel Jospin's Socialist-led coalition's concessions on Corsican autonomy has once more highlighted the depth of France's nationalistic linguistic sentiment (*New York Times*, 12 July 2000). The French Prime Minister's plans, which could see the Corsican language become an obligatory part of the school curriculum, have already led to the resignation of his interior minister, Jean-Pierre Chevènement. On stepping down, the minister attacked the government's proposals for posing 'a threat to the very definition of France' (*New York Times*, 30 August 2000). As he indicated, essential to the unity of the country is the preservation of a French-speaking nationhood.

Following France's example, Britain has developed a monolingual policy model, which similarly elevates the country's national language to a uniquely prominent position. The English language is the official language of the United Kingdom and mastery of the former becomes paramount in this English-speaking nation.[6] The terms of reference of the 1988 Report of the Commission of Inquiry into the Teaching of English, in the run up to the National Curriculum, epitomise the ideology behind Britain's language policy, thus: 'it must be a primary objective of the educational system to enable and encourage every child to use the English language to the fullest effect in speaking, writing, listening and reading' (DES, 1998, iii). The National Curriculum itself, with an overwhelmingly English-biased syllabus, is clearly aimed at an English-speaking school population. The topics taught in the classroom include three core subjects and a further seven foundation courses (DfEE, 1989). All but one of these subjects (the obvious exception being Modern Languages) are taught in English. The overall structure of the National Curriculum therefore makes it imperative for any student within Britain's educational system to acquire fluency in English. To this end, compensatory language education programmes have been in place since the mid-1960s (Baker and Eversley, 2000: 61–2; Home Office, 1990). They have sought to remedy what has been mostly perceived as a linguistic deficiency on the part of non English-speaking students, most of whom are immigrants (Baker and Eversley, 2000: 61–6; *Local Government Review*, 1989: 803–6). The newly created *Ethnic Minority Achievement Grant* is indeed specifically aimed 'to meet the particular needs of pupils for whom English is an additional language (EAL); and to raise standards of achievement for those minority ethnic groups who are particularly at risk of under-achieving' (DfEE, 1999: 1). Here, fluency in the latter is meant to provide non English-speaking pupils with equality of access to an English-dominated school curriculum. As the 1985 *Education for All* Report, hailed as a 'landmark in pluralism' (Verma, 1989), indicates: 'we believe that essential to equality of opportunity, to academic success and more broadly to participation on equal terms as a full member of society, is a good command of English and that first priority in language learning by all pupils must therefore be given to the learning of English' (DES, 1985: 671). As in the French case, language education policy in Britain seems to be based on the assumption that progressing from being a foreigner to a full-fledged British citizen can only be achieved through mastery of the English language.

In the face of such an overtly assimilationist policy discourse, teaching of ethnic minority tongues in Britain has become marginalised. The Commission for Racial Equality (CRE) has raised serious concerns about the status of ethnic minority languages within the country's educational system. In its 1992 Submission to the National Commission on Education the CRE argued that 'these languages are regarded as second class – compared with EU languages – and that there are few resources or incentives for their inclusion in mainstream National Curriculum teaching' (CRE, 1992: 9). The overall structure of the National Curriculum indeed guarantees that children may have access to a modern foreign language only at the secondary level of schooling. Estimates on language learning in Britain's primary schools illustrate the effects of the country's governing linguistic nationalism. Despite growing interest in early language tuition, by 1994 the Centre for Information on Language Teaching and Research (CILT) had calculated that only between 5 and 7 per cent of primary pupils in the UK were learning a modern language (*Guardian*, 31 March 1998: 6).

When, in March 1998, Tony Blair addressed the French National Assembly he made newspapers headlines (*Guardian*, 15 July 1998: 19). It was not so much the content of his speech that grabbed public attention, but the language in which it was delivered. The Prime Minister's lecture in fluent French highlighted the failure of the nation's language education strategy to produce successful Britons able to operate in modern languages other than English. The fact that such an occurrence made front pages reflects the scarcity of a multilingual British phenomenon. This marked linguistic deficiency can be said to be the result of 'educational failure, cultural provincialism, and the absence of a pragmatic utility for bilingualism' (Anderson and Boyer, 1970: 84). On the other hand, it can be attributed to a logical response to the willingness of the rest of the world to learn English. Whatever the reasons, the marked monolingualism among indigenous English-speaking British citizens masks a public discourse dominated by a misconceived assimilationist ideology.

The intensity of linguistic nationalism among the different EU member states varies greatly from country to country. It takes on different meanings according to the historic circumstances, demographic composition and socio-political idiosyncrasies of each European nation. This brand of self-determinism inevitably translates into domestic policy agendas that actively promote individual national languages at the expense of coexisting ethnic minority tongues. Ultimately, the reality of such an assimilationist discourse among EU member states does not augur well for the larger European multilingual ideal.

SCENARIOS FOR THE FUTURE: THE CHALLENGE OF ENLARGEMENT

During the course of this discussion a widening gap has clearly emerged between Europe's Babel ideal and the reality of multiculturalism within the EU. Against the background of a 'multicultural global village', supposedly co-equal EU languages have been shown to develop hierarchical relationships. Value differentials among these tongues have inevitably impinged upon the otherwise successful European education programmes. Europe's seemingly multilingual schemes have appeared heavily skewed towards socio-economically strong EU languages such as English, French and German; in turn serving as a vehicle to reinforce their already powerful position. On the other hand, the EU member states have translated their nationalistic public discourses into assimilationist linguistic agendas. Here, the maintenance and promotion of indigenous national languages have been vigorously pursued. Whether in the context of monolingual, bilingual or trilingual education policies, mastering of these dominant languages has become imperative. As a result, the learning and teaching of co-existing ethnic minority tongues has remained largely marginalised. While European integration has helped to promote the cultural diversity of the EU member states, it has also provided a platform for their individual linguistic nationalisms.

In the light of these trends, the EU's imminent enlargement certainly represents its greatest challenge in the foreseeable future. New member states will undoubtedly enrich the formidable cultural and linguistic wealth the EU already possesses. Their multilingual presence however will exacerbate the aforementioned existing problems as well as creating fresh ones. In particular, new member states will add a substantial burden to the Union's already overloaded communication system. What initially appears to be a mere logistic matter may force the EU to modify its pluralistic multilingual ideal in the long term. A look at the difficulties facing the Union's information machine illustrates this reality.

Publication of EU official documents; translation and interpreting of public proceedings; advertising and mass media communication; transnational commerce; exchange of ideas; promulgation of social and scientific research; and the transmission of printed and broadcast European news are some of the daily activities undertaken by the Union's information and communication services. Within this complex multilingual environment, all the EU official languages are meant to be equally represented. Because of the huge services required by the institutions of the EU over 2,000 translators are permanently employed (Hartmann, 1996: 2). As early as 1992, the implementation of such a pluralistic ideal was being perceived as cumbersome. A policy statement regarding the EU's language services at the time indicates concern about the implications of future additions to the Union:

> Enlargement will bring additional languages to the European Union, thus enriching its cultural diversity. But more languages will also complicate its work. In the Union of 12 members there are 9 official languages in normal use; in a Union of 20 members there could be as many as 15 languages; with 30 members there could be as many as 25 languages. For reasons of principle, legal acts and important documents should continue to be translated into the official languages of all member states. To ensure effective communication in meetings, pragmatic solutions will have to be found by each of the institutions. (European Commission, 1992)

The next phase of enlargement, to take place in the first decade of the twenty-first century, will be the largest in the history of the EU. Although it is expected to progress rather slowly at first, it could eventually bring the EU's membership up to twenty-seven or more states commanding over twenty official languages. In 1996, a year after Austria, Finland and Sweden joined the Union, the Translation Centre for the bodies of the EU reported a two-fold increase in its workload. The Centre noted that the number of pages translated had doubled compared with the previous year: in 1995, 20,204 pages were translated whereas by 1996, 40,899 pages had been processed (Translation Centre, 1997). With the projected EU enlargement, additional translating and interpreting staff could be required to cater for Hungarian, Polish, Czech, Estonian, Slovene, Bulgarian, Romanian, Slovak, Latvian, Lithuanian, Turkish and Maltese. The costs of such substantial language services will have to be added to the €686,000 (£417,000) annually spent by the EU on translation alone. Now, on the threshold of EU enlargement, this already overstretched communication system has started to crumble. Under the headlines 'Walkout by Interpreters Leaves Europe's Diplomats Tongue-tied' the *Guardian* reminds us of the progressive impracticability of a European Babel ideal (*Guardian*, 10 March 2000: 17). The interpreters' walkout early in 2000 seemed to have been rooted in an unrelated long-running dispute over EU tax rate entitlements. What followed their action however brought attention to the long-term implications of a saturated EU communication system. On the occasion of the interpreters walking out disaster was avoided only because the fifteen ambassadors affected by their dispute 'managed to get by in French and English' (ibid.). That only reinforced the fundamental flaw at the heart of Europe's multilingual project. As one diplomat put it: 'it's [the interpreters' absence] not actually bringing the wheels of the EU institutions to a grinding halt, but . . . it is highlighting the difficulty of the language issue, which is clearly only going to get worse' (ibid.).

It is precisely the deficiencies of the present European system that are giving way to the use of compensatory although limited remedies. Inside the multilingual web of the EU information machine, translators and interpreters have devised shortcuts which allow them to perform their increasingly unattainable tasks. When the totality of member states are present at the elaborate meetings of the various EU bodies, well over a hundred pairs of languages may require translation services. In such cases, it becomes impossible to find expert translators for all language pairs (simultaneous translations from and into a language), or to provide maximum coverage on all occasions. A relay system has therefore been developed by which English is used as an 'inter-lingua' or intermediary language. For instance, if there is not a Finish/Greek translator available, one person would translate a speech from Finnish into English, and another would translate the result from English into Greek (European Commission, 1992). Such practices confirm that despite the illusion of equality among the official EU languages, English remains the main working language within the Union. They also illustrate the widening gap between Europe's Babel ideal and the reality of multiculturalism within the EU.

There is little doubt that EU legislation and information will continue to be made available in the Union's official languages 'to ensure full understanding and wide application' (European Commission, 1995: 6; 1996: 40–8). As the EU's membership progressively swells though, effective long-term provision of these fundamental services will inevitably be jeopardised. The smooth running of such a large and complex collective calls indeed for a unified linguistic code to process the phenomenal volume of information it inevitably generates. While striving to realise a pluralistic multilingual Europe is a desirable endeavour, the Union must face up to the reality of implementing such an ideal. In the context of an increasingly larger, linguistically complex, and technologically advanced Europe, long-term policy solutions to these problems remain wanting.

VIABLE ALTERNATIVES TO A MODERN PARADOX

Standing at the threshold of a new era we are faced with a modern paradox, namely the globalisation of the English language in an increasingly multicultural and multilingual world. Within highly diverse, interdependent and technologically advanced societies, the English language has indeed become an essential tool of global communication (Crystal, 1997: 79). To be able to operate successfully in such a complex environment, European citizens of the twenty-first century will have to equip themselves with a combination of academic, technological and linguistic knowledge. The role played by the EU's language policy in shaping the future will greatly depend on its capacity to accommodate both ends of this contemporary paradox: on the one hand, the need to provide multilingual and multicultural education; and on the other hand the necessity of mastering the English language.

In the first instance, the EU must continue to foster the maintenance of its member states' rich cultural and linguistic heritage. Within the context of a 'multicultural global village', Europe's policies and programmes should indeed nurture multilingualism as a desirable educational goal. The cognitive, socio-cultural and educational advantages of proficiency in several languages greatly outweigh that of monolingual or even bilingual education. It is furthermore through in-depth understanding of a foreign language that the learner obtains a qualitatively different view of the world and a broadening of her or his own perspectives. Notwithstanding intellectual and spiritual enrichment, economic considerations also add weight to the case for multilingual education. As integration encourages greater co-operation among EU member states, there is an ever-growing need for higher levels of multilingual proficiency among its workforce. To give a startling example, the Volkswagen car manufacturer in Germany already expects its managers to be able to work in three different languages (*Guardian Higher*, 31 March 1998: ii–iii). The Union must certainly aim to produce a multilingual and highly qualified labour force able to compete successfully in both the Union's internal market as well as on the international stage.

Education and schooling play a significant role in establishing and maintaining Europe's multilingual agenda. In the wake of increased mobility among member states, schools across the Union are confronted with the task of integrating their pupils into a unified educational framework. The latter must be able to provide equality of opportunity as well as the optimum academic achievement of all pupils. At the same time, the school curriculum must respect and encourage the maintenance of these pupils' cultural and linguistic heritage. The challenge for the EU is to deliver education which is culturally and linguistically demanding, while also being effective. The provision of multilingual policies which make allowances for both the cultural and cognitive aspects of national as well as minority languages would offer an ideal solution to these conflicts. The socio-economic costs of implementing such policies within a climate of co-operation (which for historical reasons often does not exist), however, renders them unfeasible. The frequently voiced determination to protect minority languages must therefore be balanced against more pragmatic considerations, whereby encouragement would be given to reinforcing languages that are already widely known (European Commission, 1997a: 12). Many ethnic minority languages simply lack the advanced literature and specialised vocabulary necessary to become fully viable modern languages. Sylheti, for instance, only survives in oral form, having long lost its written tradition. Recognising this fact would not only amount to political incorrectness, it most certainly would cause offence to speakers of such tongues. The intrinsic cultural value of any ethnic minority language is indeed undeniable. The overwhelming demand for English, French and German among European students seems to indicate however, that economic advantage prevails over cultural considerations. Knowledge and maintenance of minority languages, nevertheless should remain an objective of the EU member states' educational agendas. They must indeed shape up their nationalistic domestic policies to allow pupils to become more culturally open and linguistically capable. The EU member states should ultimately aim at helping the next generation of European citizens to surpass the linguistic and educational achievements of their predecessors.

While the EU has striven to address the challenges posed by multilingual education, it has failed to adequately respond to the globalisation of the English language. Its two-pronged approach of ideologically advocating multilingualism, but in practice using English widely illustrates this reality. Whether in the academic, commercial, political, bureaucratic or social areas, English certainly dominates every aspect of the Union's life. Even at the core of Europe's multilingual information machine, English has become a dominant presence. Tom McArthur has gone as far as to refer to the 'Europeanness of English' (McArthur, 1996: 3–15). Regardless of its equal status with the other EU official languages, English enjoys a unique position both in Europe and in the world at large. Choosing to ignore this fact represents an educational disservice to the citizens of the Union. The challenge for the EU must be to capitalise on the potential English proficiency provides to all Europeans. Teaching of English should be actively encouraged as the first foreign language in education. Becoming fluent in

English must be at the core of the EU's language policy strategy. Multi-lingual education in Europe has therefore to be understood as the learning of English together with other languages. The EU should not aim at producing multilingual individuals per se, but English-speaking multilingual Europeans. Bilingualism with English is already fast becoming a fact of life for the citizens of Europe, as habitual use of English within the Union is found to be either essential or potentially necessary. Indeed, it would be reasonable to suggest that in order to partake in Europe, and thus to benefit politically, economically and socially, it is desirable to master the English language.

In matters pertaining to language education policy neither sentiment nor political correctness should be the ruling factor. Decisions about language policy within the EU, however, are normally made by politicians, not by linguists; and for political reasons rather than pedagogic considerations. As a result, pragmatism rarely prevails. Regardless of the difficulties it presents to the European pluralistic ideology, a rational approach to the supremacy of the English language must be sought. The responsibility to develop and implement effective policy responses lies with the EU collective as much as with its individual member states. Only courageous, imaginative and future-oriented initiatives will succeed in bridging the gap between the European multilingual ideal and the reality of multicultural-ism. On 1 January 1999 the EU took its boldest step towards integration when eleven member states scrapped centuries of history to adopt the euro as their common currency. As monetary union becomes a reality we may ask how long will linguistic uniformity take to materialise.

NOTES

1   It must be noted that Microsoft has translated its Windows 95 program into at least thirty different languages, including Slovenian and Catalan. While a combination of commercial and technical reasons may lie behind Microsoft's selective process, more research is needed into the criteria used to ascertain the worthiness of one language over another.
2   The volume of EU commerce aforementioned does not count commercial activity between the member states themselves.
3   For example, COMENIUS facilitates different types of school partnerships to nurture language learning; ERASMUS encourages the linguistic preparation of university students; and GRUNDTVIG promotes the learning of languages in adult education. See 'Languages' in *EUROPA* the official website of the European Commission at http://www.europa.eu.int/comm/education/languages/actions/commactions.html
4   The high level of bilingualism (with English) existing in Denmark, The Netherlands, Norway, and Sweden is the consequence of the successful long-term institutionalised learning of English by these countries' citizenry. This justifies the view, which is still controversial and sometimes troubling in these nations, that English is no longer really foreign, but a strong second language that is steadily becoming nativicised. The recent advent and popularity, espe-

cially among the young, of multichannel English-language satellite television only serves to consolidate and accelerate this process.

5 It is possible to conceptualise a world linguistic hierarchy, like that outlined for Europe, with English as the global lingua franca at its apex. The world's many national languages coexisting with English would occupy a middle layer, with ethnic linguistic tongues being situated at its base. As the English language appears to be colonising the lower levels of this linguistic pyramid, 'lesser' ethnic tongues are increasingly in danger of becoming extinct.

6 In the absence of a written British Constitution stating the officialdom of English, the de facto status of the latter has nevertheless been traditionally presumed in numerous educational acts, reports of parliamentary committees of inquiry and government literature.

REFERENCES

Ager, D. (1994) 'Immigration and Language Policy in France', *Journal of Intercultural Studies*, 15 (2): 35–52.

Ager, D. (1996) *Language Policy in Britain and France: The Processes of Policy*. London: Cassell.

Anderson, Theodore and Boyer, Mildred (eds) (1970) *Bilingual Learning in the United States*. Austin, TX: Southwest Educational Development Laboratory.

Artigal, J.M. (1995) 'Multiways Towards Multi-lingualism: The Catalan Immersion Programme Experience', *European Studies on Multi-lingualism*, 4: 161–81.

Baker, Philip and Eversley, John (eds) (2000) *Multilingual Capital*. London: Battlebridge Publications.

Battye, A. and Hintze, M.A. (eds) (1992) *The French Language Today*. London: Routledge.

Beardsmore, H. Baetens and Kohls, J. (1985) 'Designing Bilingual Education: Aspects of Immersion and European School Models', *Journal of Multilingual and Multicultural Development*, 6 (1): 1–15.

CRE (Commission for Racial Equality) (1992) *The CRE Submission to the National Commission on Education*. London: CRE.

Crystal, David (1995) *The Cambridge Encyclopaedia of the English Language*. Cambridge: Cambridge University Press.

Crystal, David (1997) *English as a Global Language*. Cambridge: Cambridge University Press.

DES (Department for Education and Sciences) (1985) *Education for All: The Report of the Committee of Inquiry into the Education of Children from Ethnic Minority Groups*. London: HMSO.

DES (1988) *Report of the Committee of Inquiry into the Teaching of English Language*. London: HMSO.

DfEE (Department for Education and Employment) (1989) *Education Reform Act 1988: Circular No. 5/89*. London: HMSO.

DfEE (1999) *Ethnic Minority Achievement Grant: Consultation Paper*. London: DfEE.

Edwards, J. (1995) *Multilingualism*. London: Penguin Books.

Encyclopaedia Britannica (1995) 14th edn. Chicago: Encyclopaedia Britannica Inc.

Eurobarometer, 17 July 2000: 1–8.

EU Information Service (1999) *2001: A Babel Odyssey*, European Information Service, 204: 18.

EUROPA (2000) 'Languages'. Official website of the European Commission (http://www.europa.eu).

European Commission (1990) *Mobility of Students in Europe: Linguistic and Socio-cultural Conditions*. Luxembourg: Office for Official Publications of the European Communities.

European Commission (1992) *Europe and the Challenge of Enlargement*. Brussels: European Commission.

European Commission (1995) The Multilingual Information Society. Brussels: European Commission.

European Commission (1996) 'Council Decision of 21 November 1996 on the Adoption of a Multi-annual Programme to Promote the Linguistic Diversity of the Community in the Information Society', *Official Journal of the European Communities*, 306: 40–8.

European Commission (1997a) 'Learning Modern Languages at School in the European Union', *Education Training Youth Studies*. Luxembourg: Office for Official Publications of the European Communities.

European Commission (1997b) 'Council Resolution of 16 December 1997 on the Early Teaching of European Union Languages', *Official Journal of the European Union*, 1: 2–3.

European Commission (1999) 'Council Resolution of 17 December 1999 on Into the New Millennium: Developing New Working Procedures for European Co-operation in the Field of Education and Training', *Official Journal of the European Union*, 8: 6–7.

European Council (1998) '2147th Council Meeting: Education', The European Council Press Release, 430: 1–7. Brussels: EC.

European Council (1999) '2224th Council Meeting: Education', The European Council Press Release, 378: 1–8. Brussels: EC.

Graddol, David (1997) *The Future of English?* London: The British Council.

Hartmann, R. (ed.) (1996) *English Language in Europe*. Oxford: Intellect.

Home Office (1990) *Section 11 of the Local Government Act 1966. Grant Administration: Policy Criteria*. London: HMSO.

Katzner, Kenneth (1992) *The Languages of the World*. London: Routledge.

Khoo, Rosemary, Kreher, Ursula and Wong, Ruth (eds) (1994) *Toward Global Multilingualism: European Models and Asian Realities*. Clevendon: Multi-lingual Matters Ltd.

Local Government Review (1989) 153 (41): 803–6.

Lodge, R.A. (1993) *French: From Dialect to Standard*. London: Routledge.

McArthur, Tom (1996) 'English in the World and Europe', in R. Hartmann (ed.) *English Language in Europe*. Oxford: Intellect.

Nugent, Neill (1999) *The Government and Politics of the European Union*, 4th edn. London: Macmillan.

Penguin Encyclopaedia of Popular Music (1990). London: Penguin.

Santer, Jaques (1996) Speech by the President of the European Commission at the Centre Européan de l'Alliance française, Brussels, 25 June.

Specter, Michael (1996) 'World, Wide, Web: Three English Words', *New York Times*, April.

Time Special Issue: Visions of Europe, winter 1998–99.

Translation Centre for the Bodies of the European Union (1997) *Report on the Activities 1996*. Luxembourg: Office for Official Publications of the European Communities.

Varro, G. (1992) 'Immigrants' Languages in the French School', *Language Problems and Language Planning*, 16 (2): 137–62.

Verma, Gajendra K. (ed.) (1989) *Education for All: A Landmark in Pluralism*. London: The Falmer Press.

Walsh, Mark (1998) 'Microsoft Set to Wreck Language of Vikings', *Guardian*, 1 July: 15.

Conclusion: Possible European Futures

Mary Farrell

The start of a new century and a new millennium presents an opportunity for looking back at the past and trying to anticipate possible futures. A critical review of where the European Union is going represents more than just sentimental reminiscing or idle speculation. For the EU has reached a critical juncture in its development, with a full agenda of activities and plans towards a widening and deepening of the integration process over the next few years. It is not simply because future integration will challenge the internal structures of the union and its external relations with the rest of the world in unprecedented ways that this review has become both urgent and vital. It is also because the world in which the Community was conceived and constructed has changed beyond recognition.

It is possible, when thinking about likely future scenarios, to become influenced by some of the more obvious developments underway and to ignore other factors, issues or ideas that fail to fit within prevailing ortho-doxies and operating paradigms. In this case, it can be easy to miss vital evidence and clues that offer a picture of future developments. Even seasoned observers were taken aback by the collapse of the former Soviet Union, and by the speed of developments that followed its demise. Simi-larly, despite their direct concern with the maintenance of stability in the international system, the experts in the World Bank and International Monetary Fund failed to predict the 1997 Asian financial crisis or its economic repercussions. And yet, if we are to avoid the excesses of 'futurology' we have to consider the evidence of what lies before us and base our predictions about the future, at least in part, on what we know of the present. This is largely the approach adopted in this volume.

One of the most striking aspects of this collective endeavour is the extent of the divergence – perceived by all of the contributors – between the current outcomes of integration and those they consider desirable. This also results in agreement that there is a gap between *probability* and *desirability* with respect to the future of the whole European project. There is also a lack of overall direction in the EU that may well present serious obstacles to ever closing this gap in the future, and may hinder the emergence of a truly cohesive and democratic political community.

UNITY AND DIVERSITY – WHERE WE STAND

As Alan Milward suggests, the weight of history is evident in the contemporary European Union. The evolving path towards deeper European integration among the member states has not reduced their ability to retain control over the process or their desire to protect their power. Member states exercise this control in the Council of Ministers and they will continue to do so in the aftermath of the institutional developments in the Treaty of Nice agreed in December 2000. The continued desire to protect national sovereignty shapes their attitudes towards any challenges or threats (perceived or real) against such traditional bastions of the nation-state as policies in the fields of welfare, defence and external relations. These areas and issues remain deeply embedded in the historical roots of each country.

Yet, as Milward also argues, while history has much to offer by way of explaining our contemporary world, it may be a limited guide to predicting the future of the European Union. For example, the new applicants will not face the favourable conditions that earlier entrants to the EC/EU were able to negotiate – conditions that would subsequently enter the formal arrangements of the European Union and its *acquis communautaire*. Britain was granted a transition period and later secured a rebate in the level of national contributions to the EU budget, opening the door to further progress in European integration in the 1980s; Spain received a significant share of the Structural Funds, and negotiated the Cohesion Fund, allowing the formal ratification of the Maastricht Treaty in 1992; and, more recently, both Britain and Denmark negotiated opt-outs to monetary union. These special economic deals will not be available to new members of the Community. And, therefore, the possibilities for the protection of their national sovereignty remain limited compared with those guaranteed to the existing member states.

The weight of history is also implicit in the relationship between the small and large states within the union. But, as Esko Antola argues, a key problem for the future is to identify how small states might develop a more influential position in the institutional structure and the politics of the Community. In the EU-15, ten states can be categorised as 'small', and enlargement will increase the number. But what kind of unity can emerge, and what type of community will result from a grouping that is dominated by the larger member states? The question raises both positive and normative concerns that reach to the core of any serious attempt to deepen European integration. Again, Antola presents a dilemma for the analyst seeking ways of democratising the European Union through a more favourable representation of all national interests. There are grounds for pessimism about this for the Nice agreement involved a clear shift in the weighting of votes in favour of the large states. In other areas too there are clear tendencies threatening the doctrine of equal participation for all states. The disproportionate representation of officials from the larger countries in the institutions, the proposals to curtail the rotating presidency of the European Union, and to limit the number of official languages (highlighted also in the chapter by Christina Julios) are areas of concern. However, there is some room for optimism if, as Antola hopes, the small states can practise 'niche diplomacy', focusing on particular issues, facilitating coalition-building, and becoming more proactive in their approach.

Most of the contributors recognise the strength and depth of the economic integration that has developed in the European Union. Milward stresses the importance of economic motives in the origins of the European Community, raising the possibility of a path dependency shaping its future. Boles and colleagues are concerned more with the contemporary phase of economic integration in their examination of the challenges facing the euro in the international monetary system, as a potential rival to the dollar as the principal international reserve currency. While they regard the introduction and adoption of the euro throughout the EU as a given, they locate instability at the wider level in the emerging struggle between the euro and the dollar.

Europe's monetary authorities have remained coy about their vision for the euro in the international system. In the time since the introduction of the euro in January 1999, the European Central Bank has tried to maintain a low-key approach, refusing to be drawn on anything other than its unwavering commitment to monetary stability *within* the European Union. Even if it has not always succeeded in limiting its public statements to matters of monetary stability, and announcing interest rate changes, it has not so far indicated any desire to set a course of action with the aim of toppling the supremacy of the dollar. Boles et al. consider what factors might push the euro in that direction without any such ECB initiatives. It is their contention that the EU cannot rely solely on its undoubted strength as an economic bloc to enable the euro to qualify as a currency for international use. Here we may use the evidence of history once more, but this time to conclude that what worked for the United States in the post-Second World War period (the growing economic strength that enabled dollar supremacy to emerge) cannot be relied on to do the same for the European Union in the twenty-first century. Their contention that the European Union must also have equity, bond, and capital markets of sufficient size to rival those of the United States is eminently reasonable, and all the more so when we recognise both the deeper integration of the global capital market and the much increased levels of mobility in the contemporary international financial system. Boles et al. acknowledge the important role played by the Federal Reserve Board of the United States in maintaining the position of the dollar. This raises the issue of how the ECB might emulate the efforts of its American counterpart. More fundamentally, the entire economic orthodoxy underlying the EU might be criticised both in relation to its influence in shaping the role and authority of the institutions and the policies associated with monetary union. Externally, similar criticism may be directed towards the international institutions that hold responsibility for ensuring the stability of trade and capital flows.

While the reform of the international monetary institutions is not the principal concern here, it is evident that the EU both affects and is affected by the international regime. Certainly, the regulatory framework for a global/international financial system must of necessity be established by a global/international organisation, with jurisdiction beyond the legal and regulatory boundaries of the European Union. Even if the European monetary authorities have no desire for a head-to-head confrontation with regulatory authorities elsewhere (and this is not proven), the very fact of international interdependence does impact upon the achievement of domestic stability goals. A second, and indeed related, point to consider from Boles et al. concerns the conclusion that the different regulatory approaches of the European Union and the United States – with the EU's preference for intervention, and the US for non-intervention and 'benign neglect' – might present a problem in international co-ordination. This would certainly affect the future development of the European economy, but it is not yet clear whether the EU will decide to take a more assertive position with regard to the nature and substance of international co-ordination, or even if there are substantive differences in the respective regulatory approaches of the two regions.

Not all of the contributors to this volume would accept the view that the European Union has a distinctive regulatory framework. On the contrary, many of them acknowledge, either explicitly or implicitly, a distinct bias in the direction of a neo-liberal community, where economic interests hold sway in both the political processes and the policy outcomes over wider social concerns. Monica Threlfall's contribution addresses this question directly. In particular, she analyses social integration, which she regards as an unintended outcome of economic integration. Social integration is distinguished from social policy, from regulation, and from social inclusion. It is an outcome of policies, but an unplanned one. By contrast, social policy is planned, the result of a set of decisions taken through the political processes of the European Union. Social integration has arisen almost by accident, as a by-product of other EU policies, and has emerged on a very incremental basis.

The liberalisation of trade, capital and labour movements was central to the Community envisioned in the Treaty of Rome. But what was not foreseen in the provision for the free movement of workers was the myriad of practical issues associated with the actual movement of workers across national boundaries. Many of these are only indirectly related to legal matters, and are more concerned with questions relating to family life, access to housing and health care, and to the enjoyment of the social practices of other member states. Threlfall regards the responses of individuals to these practical issues, and the difficulties they experienced within the context of cross-border movement, as providing the catalyst for social integration to evolve. Moreover, a practical need to respond to, or resolve, the contradictions that arose from the application of EU laws also provided a catalyst.

As Threlfall acknowledges, the provision on free movement was radical in allowing for the emergence of social integration, albeit on a still limited scale. The processes she outlines suggest some pointers towards a democratic, and socially inclusive European Union. However, we might also need a longer historical perspective to properly assess the substantive implications of free movement for a deepening of social integration. For social integration means an extension of individual rights and their protection against encroachment either by the perverse implementation of the policies of member states, or through the neo-liberal Community regulatory model which permits market forces to dominate employment relations, working conditions, and competitive business practices. Slowly, individuals are demanding such rights but it is too early to be sure how this process will affect the future of the EU. Nevertheless, once rights are acknowledged, it is also crucial to ensure that there are mechanisms to prevent their infringement. What this requires, as an absolute minimum, is the provision of more information regarding the rights and entitlements that result from the creation of a single economic space. Linked to this is a requirement for higher standards of transparency in the political processes at both national and supranational levels, to facilitate improved communication between the different levels, and to incorporate the interest groups representing social concerns more directly, and more equally, into the political processes of the European Union. The Brussels bureaucratic machinery is rightly regarded as being more porous than national bureaucracies, but this counts for very little when access is hindered by limitations such as financial resources, organisational capacity, or the generally more fragmented nature of European societal groups. Similar arguments apply in regard to the access to other European institutions – the European Parliament, the Economic and Social Committee, and the Committee of the Regions. But we should also apply these arguments, with perhaps even greater emphasis to the Council of Ministers and the European Council.

These proposals are important in two senses. On the one hand, the provision of information regarding rights and entitlements, and the associated improvement of transparency, pushes forward the processes of social integration. But there is a second consideration here, which may also be an unintended consequence of social integration. For this has been based upon pressure from below, from the articulation of demands by citizens, individuals and members of European society directed at the political authorities located at the national and at the supranational levels. It constitutes, essentially, active participation in European integration – even though this may not have been so perceived by the actors at the time. The expansion of social integration serves a very important objective in the context of the present discussion. For it creates through the active participation of citizens a sense of 'ownership' in the political processes of the European Union itself. Active participation by individuals, citizens and society, which allows for the development of this sense of 'ownership', can lead ultimately to a correction of the democratic deficit that has long featured in the operation of the European Union.

The question of democracy is addressed explicitly by Alex Warleigh, who offers a cogent summary of the position to date, when he states that 'After fifty years of European integration we have no United States of Europe, but rather an unwieldy product of the tension between the desire for national autonomy and the continued need for co-operation.' In effect, the member states have created a governance system that avoids serious conflict between them and at the same time offers the ability or capacity to provide more general welfare than would be available through the individual national efforts. He sets out the scenario of a future integration process that is based upon flexible integration, which seems to be the preferred approach of allowing a core group of states to move forward at a faster pace determined by their interests, needs or demands. While questioning the democratic nature of this approach, since it allows for the creation of inequalities between the states, Warleigh suggests that it can be harnessed to the notion of deliberative democracy in which policies, principles and ideas are negotiated and from which an EU value-set can emerge. This would then form the basis for an institutional design and policy outcomes. Crucial in all of this is citizen participation. But such an approach must identify active mechanisms to initiate and incorporate greater citizen participation and avoid a situation in which dominant or powerful interests shape the outcomes.

Madeleine Colvin's chapter on the EU approach to internal security shows how far we are from this situation at present. The picture that emerges from her analysis is of a Community that is willing to sacrifice individual human rights to the demands of internal security as defined by a narrow group within the member states. She takes issue, not with the development and strengthening of supranational police co-operation per se, but rather with the implementation of the procedures for co-operation, and the policies on information-gathering and storage that impinge upon individual rights. Integration in the matter of internal security seems to result too often in a sidelining of rights to privacy, to a fair trial, and to redress of injury resulting from the excessive zeal of supranational security systems. She advocates action at several levels. For one thing, it is essential to provide for a proper judicial and democratic oversight of EU bodies, such as Europol, whose activities may impinge directly on the criminal judicial system in any of the member states. Secondly, these security developments, and the related EU level system of criminal justice laws and procedures that have direct implications for the correct observance of human rights, are developing under the intergovernmental third pillar, without adequate judicial safeguards or acceptable standards of democratic scrutiny. The challenge, therefore, is to change all this and to guarantee the protection of human rights, irrespective of nationality. Colvin's call for greater attention to be paid to the impact on individuals as a result of new cross-border policing methods, judicial decisions and data systems in the context of creating an internal security community is also relevant to our concern with delineating desirable futures. It should be heeded with greater urgency in the face of rising immigration to the European Union and the increase of refugees and asylum seekers. The extreme reluctance of the European Union to open its borders to the free inward movement of people is strikingly at odds with its support for the unfettered movement of goods, capital and finance. In terms of the Community, and the constituent member states' stance on immigration, there is truly a 'fortress Europe'.

This 'fortress Europe' mentality is reflected in the EU cultural policy, as Enrique Banús demonstrates in his chapter. For he suggests that what passes for a 'European' cultural policy demonstrates the strength of nationalist sentiment that pervades the thinking of the member states and is, in reality, merely an add-on to national cultural policies. While the latter have served to build and reinforce a sense of national identity through their support for national cultural activities, the initiatives served up under the guise of a European cultural policy have not gone any way towards creating a 'European identity'. Part of the problem here lies with the European Comission's ongoing concern to stress cultural diversity in relation to the member states, and to emphasise the need to respect this diversity. This approach inevitably played into the hands of the nation-states, and effectively endorsed their efforts to protect the 'national heritage' and the 'national identity', enabling them to 'capture' European cultural policy to serve the same objectives.

Notwithstanding the difficulties inherent in identifying a European cultural identity, Banús presents a persuasive case to suggest that it is based around a notion of cultural citizenship. Like Milward, he calls upon history to support his contention that continual interchanges over many centuries across culture and literature have 'forged a patchwork map of Europe' with local, regional and European elements. His view of culture as a dynamic process, continually shaped and reshaped by many forces, highlights the missing elements in the EU's own understanding. But the real cost of a dominant nationalist interpretation of cultural identity is the diversity and tolerance that could be nurtured in a European community open to different cultural and ethnic traditions. On present trends, this lack of tolerance bodes ill for a future EU enlarged to accept new members with a wide variety of cultural traditions.

The chapter by Christina Julios leads towards a similar conclusion. Both she and Banús are acutely aware of a rich, cultural tradition across Europe, but it is one which both consider to have been ill used in the project to create European unity. The strategy of the EU language policy in promoting diversity is presented as positive. But the truth here, as Julios demonstrates, is that the reality fails to match the stirring rhetoric of the European authorities. Practical difficulties, from the global dominance of English to the linguistic nationalism of some member states (clothed in an assimilationist discourse) combined with logistical problems relating to translation (which are likely to assume even greater importance with future enlargement), have resulted in the abandonment of linguistic diversity in favour of the emergence of socio-economically strong languages. Instead of the preservation of diversity, and support for a multilingual ideal, the EU has adopted its own form of assimilation and has conceded to the global domination of English, which now emerges as the main working language of the EU. Julios asserts the overwhelming case for multilingualism, and the 'cognitive, socio-cultural, and educational advantages of proficiency in several languages'.

Diversity of a different nature lies behind the contributions on security presented in the chapters by Elżbieta Stadtmüller and Peter Gowan. Both of them see it as essential to consider European security issues in the broader world context, although there are differences in emphases with respect to the two positions. In the call for a multidimensional approach to defining security combined with a crucial review of the geographic boundaries of 'Europe', Stadtmüller sets out important markers for a future Europe. She acknowledges the evident reliance by the Europeans on a security guarantee system provided through the NATO/WEU framework. But she also notes that in the contemporary world, military force by international organisations may be useful in reducing conflict, but not in resolving it. Moreover, the use or threat of military force may in practice serve to exacerbate instability. And this is particularly likely where interventions by international military organisations are made in direct contravention of international law. Her proposals for democratising the enforcement of international law, and the adherence to the underlying norms and standards by pressure from below, rather than the 'imposition' of peace from the top is in harmony with aspirations for the creation of a democratic European Union. Equally, her view of security as both a goal and a medium leads her to consider economic development as a key ingredient in meeting the security concerns of states on the borders of Europe, where domestic instability is endemic. However, it seems almost impossible for such states to realise economic development through export-led growth, when the European Union pursues protectionist policies with regard to trade and other policy areas. Gowan takes a more critical role of the European Union's external relations. His chapter presents an indictment of the European Union as an international actor, documenting its failures of leadership in providing critical support in the wake of regional disintegration, while pursuing its own interests in its relation to the 'frontier belt' countries – Poland, the Czech Republic, Slovakia, Hungary and Slovenia.

Gowan suggests that the recent history of EU–US relations in the different regions of Eastern Europe may be characterised by the dominant role played by the United States, with the European Union taking a secondary role to its Atlantic 'partner'. But is the EU in a position to provide a viable alternative? Certainly, it was ill-prepared to take on the challenge of addressing the problems in the region since, from its inception, it has been inward looking, intolerant of diversity and, in the areas of defence and foreign policy, restricted by the constraints imposed by the member states. This is, however, a serious and regrettable defect in a political community that has (or might have) aspirations towards democracy, justice and a tolerance of diversity. Finally, an analysis of the forces unleashed by the disintegration of the region to the east of the European frontier must take account not only of the geo-strategic interests at play but also the local interests, aspirations, and rivalries among different ethnic groups in their search for autonomy and a legitimacy grounded in a preferred political system. Not to do so is to repeat the past mistakes of global powers, and to continue with foreign policies grounded in realist notions of the sovereign state. Moreover, by not recognising the legitimate aspirations of ethnic communities towards democratic and equal representation in a political system, western states (or 'powers') perpetuate the sources of instability identified by Stadtmüller.

TOWARDS A SYNTHESIS – AND BEYOND?

So, what picture emerges from the volume as a whole? In general, the EU is seen as a community where economic integration holds sway. It is a community where social integration has barely begun, and where democracy is more conspicuous by its absence than its active presence in the political processes. Politically, the community is shaped by its neo-liberal bias, from the overwhelming emphasis on economic policy and the marginalisation of other policy areas, through to the dominant role of economic interest groups. The introduction of the euro serves to reinforce this bias. Undoubtedly, the new money in the pockets of European society may serve to bring European integration closer to the citizens, but it is questionable whether it will serve the longer-term purpose of closer unity based on 'ownership' of the process. Certainly, this will be problematic in the short term if the replacement of national currencies with the euro coincides with observed inflationary pressures created by producers and retailers 'rounding up' prices – a development likely to alienate the citizens rather than anything else. Furthermore, the history of money suggests the importance of a socialisation process to ensure the acceptability of whatever object is offered as a medium of exchange. In other words, a money will gain in usage if people who want to engage in exchange are willing to accept it to facilitate such exchanges. This is separate from, and in addition to, the creation of the legal institutions that guarantee its legitimacy. From this, one can assume that for national governments to swear never-ending allegiance to fiscal rectitude may not be a sufficient condition to guarantee the socialisation and acceptability of the euro.

This leads to a more general conclusion that neo-liberalism is still too pervasive within the EU. The neo-liberal model upholds the virtues of the market, and favours those with the capacity (linked to financial and other resources) to compete in that market. Any individuals or groups that are not so fortunately endowed will face marginalisation. This means that social policy does little to prevent the exclusion of those who lack financial and other resources. The neo-liberal model therefore cultivates a 'fortress Europe' both internally and externally. Externally, we can observe it in a myriad of ways, from trade policy to immigration and refugee policy, and to the hierarchically structured set of relations that constitute EU development (including aid) policy. However, the inconsistency of neo-liberalism is most clearly reflected in the closed door stance adopted both individually and collectively towards those who seek to cross its frontiers. Yet there are sound economic arguments for extending the principle of free movement. Europe has an ageing population, and demographic changes have led to a rising dependency rate and a falling activity rate. The EU would benefit from the energy, motivation and productivity of people in the working age (tax-paying) groups. There are thus economic and ethical arguments for a more tolerant approach to immigration, and for a respect for diversity in all its forms. However, if we extrapolate from current trends, the most probable future holds out little prospect of a socially inclusive Europe.

This is not to suggest that the EU has no positive features. Even with all its defects, the Community has managed to bind the states of this once warring region into a network of alliances, institutions and decision-making frameworks, where the strength of co-operative bonds make the possibility of disintegration more remote, and non-cooperation more costly than co-operation. But for those who consider normative ideals to be worth aiming for, tinkering with the general system through piecemeal, flexible integration is not enough. The proposed Intergovernmental Conference, due to take place in 2004, seems already to be limited in its ambition and scope to just this kind of marginal adjustment at the edges. Yet it is our contention that the European Union can become far more inclusive both internally and externally.

To do so, it must offer a more distinctive option. Otherwise, people may begin to ask the question already posed by the liberal-leaning *Economist* magazine, 'What is the point of 'Europe', if 'Europe' is turning out to be another United States?' (*The Economist*, 2000). The approach of Romano Prodi, the President of the European Commission, in addressing the European Parliament in Strasbourg in February 2001, calling for a 'no holds barred' constitutional debate on the fundamental nature of the union, might appear more encouraging. However, the tone of the presentation suggested that there is much to be done in shaping the values of those at the top, as part of the overall design for a European community of democratic values. For in his query to the Parliament, he asked: 'Are we all clear that we want to build something that can aspire to be a world power? In other words, not just a trading bloc but a political entity' (*Financial Times*, 14 February 2001).

The question of democratic values is one of the first crucial issues to be addressed within the broader framework of enquiry as to the kind of European community we want in the new century. In 1972, the Reith lecture for the BBC given by Andrew Shonfield treated Europe as 'a journey to an unknown destination'. Since then any consideration of possible futures has been relegated to the margins of discussion. In proceeding on a piecemeal basis, and tinkering with the institutional structure as a response to the claims of a democratic deficit, the European integration process has avoided any great confrontation with entrenched interests. But while discussions on flexibility, on identifying ways of addressing the democratic deficit and institutional reform, and other debates over the functionality of the European Union are relevant and important, they avoid the central question that must be addressed at some point by the European Community. Otherwise there is the danger that a community will emerge by default, lacking the values that can underpin European unity.

Contemporary Europe does not have any unifying myths around which to build a community, in the way that nation-states are supposed to have emerged through history. However, this need not be a problem in creating a European community. For we live in an age where myths are no longer central, or even believable (Smith, 1992). Despite this, European society now faces many different myths, traditions and cultures in a slowly evolving multiculturalism on the one hand, and a spreading globalisation of the capitalist-dominated value system on the other. The lack of confidence in political processes and in the political institutions of modern democracy, reflected in the growing degree of voter apathy throughout Western democracies is mirrored at the supranational level. This might be overcome if the necessary political strategies to be pursued at the local, national and supranational level can be identified.

European unity remains a goal to be pursued. While unity within the conceptual framework of the founders of the European Community back in the 1950s may have been secured, there remains much more scope for a union that is based upon values of democracy, social inclusion and human rights. A direct engagement by political and social interests within and across national boundaries with the future of the European community, in terms of debating the final destination, is vital if a more meaningful form of unity is to be established. In the past, the absence of a clearly defined goal may have been advantageous. However, it seems increasingly untenable with the current pace and scope of integration, and the processes of globalisation which also create their own interdependence. Now is the time, however, for Europe to pose the question 'where are we headed?' and to launch a debate to consider the possible futures. In this context, it is encouraging that the Forward Studies Unit of the European Commision has made a start by envisaging future scenarios, with the publication of a report in 1998 (European Commission, 1998). This sets out five possible scenarios, based around an imaginative review of trends and prospects, and bearing such evocative titles as 'The Hundred Flowers', 'Creative Societies', and 'Turbulent Neighbourhoods'. While the substantive nature of these scenarios may not be convincing, they contribute to the crucial task of thinking actively about the future.

This concluding chapter has deliberately eschewed the consideration of various scenarios. It is more important to highlight the need for a constructive debate throughout Europe concerning the direction in which the European community might develop. Proposed outlines of a desirable future have been sketched out. But changes must depend upon political judgements and political processes based upon the conviction that the future is not predetermined.

REFERENCES

The Economist (2000) 'What is Europe?', 12 February: 13.

European Commission (1998) *Scenarios Europe 2010 – Five Possible Futures for Europe*, Forward Studies Unit Working Paper, Brussels.

Moravcsik, A. (1998) *The Choice for Europe: Social Purpose and State Power from Messina to Maastricht*. New York: Cornell University Press.

Smith, A.D. (1992) 'National Identity and the Idea of European Unity', *International Affairs*, 68 (1): 55–76.

Index